THE VOICE OF

COLLEGE

the Freshmen Experience

THE VOICE OF

COLLEGE

the Freshmen Experience

Dr. Michael Severin
Kipp Van Dyke

Illustrated by Nicolas Kline

www.thevoiceofcollege.com
2009

DEDICATION

We dedicate this book to every high school senior student and college freshman who has ever been on the struggle bus, experienced an awkward moment or shared a scare, as they discovered and grew and became the *Voices* of College.

ACKNOWLEDGEMENTS

We'd like to thank all of those people who helped us during our own college experiences. We continue to be blessed by our family, friends, and mentors who have been with us since our first thoughts of college and are still there for us. Without these people and their influences in our lives, this book would not have been possible.

We hope reading this book will help prepare you to be successful and enjoy your college experience. College is truly a remarkable time in the lives of students and families. We wish you the best wherever you are in your own journey.

ABOUT THE AUTHORS

College Expert **Dr. Michael Severin** has helped hundreds of freshmen students over the past eight years. He has extensive leadership involvement within the residence halls including three years as a Resident Assistant, two years as an Academic Resource Coordinator, one year as a Community Advisor, and one year as a Resident Manager. He first helped incoming college students as a summer freshmen orientation leader. Michael served as a Supplemental Instructor for popular freshmen courses and co-taught a university introduction course for freshmen Honor students.

Michael earned a Bachelor of Science degree in Zoology from Iowa State University (ISU) in 2005. He was involved in the Honors program and graduated in the top 2% of students in the College of Agriculture. He was then accepted into a professional program after three years of undergraduate study and earned his Doctorate of Veterinary Medicine (DVM) in 2006. He was involved in entrepreneurship studies and graduated in the top 10% of his class. Michael is a resident in small animal cardiology and a masters student in physiology. Michael lives with his wife, Lindsay, in Ames, Iowa.

College expert **Kipp Van Dyke** has made helping college students his career choice. His extensive work in the residence halls includes two years as a Resident Assistant, one year as a Community Advisor, two years as an Assistant Complex Director in an all freshman building, and five years as a Residence Life Coordinator in a 600-bed residence hall. He has worked extensively with the orientation program while a college student serving as an orientation leader and also advising this group as an undergraduate student. While in graduate school at Minnesota State University, Mankato, Kipp was the first graduate student to win the Vic Swenson Student Friendly Award. The following year he was named the "Advisor of the Year" in his first year as a young professional at Kansas State University. He has also been nominated for both a regional and national "Outstanding New Professional" award through two different professional organizations.

Kipp earned a Bachelor of Science degree in Child and Family services from Iowa State University in 2002. He was involved in two honor societies at his college and also served as a Substance Abuse Peer Educator for the campus. Kipp went on to graduate school, earning his Master of Science degree in Community Counseling from Minnesota State, Mankato in 2004. He taught a university course in Career and Life Planning for freshman. He and his wife Breanna are the proud parents of Olivia Belle.

Amateur artist **Nicolas Kline** graduated with a Bachelor of Science in Management Information Systems from Kansas State University in Manhattan, KS. Nicolas served college students for several years as a resident assistant while living in the residence halls.

Nicolas has enjoyed art as a hobby throughout his life, but started digitally drawing in college. During his early college days, web blogging started building in popularity and Nicolas decided to join the trend, but preferred to blog using pictures instead of words. He enjoys drawing pictures that reflect real-life situations that he's seen or been a part of. With a devout Christian faith, he also enjoys converting biblical scriptures into drawings in attempt to present them from a new perspective. Nicolas resides in Overland Park, KS, with his wife Julie and he works as a Software Engineer for Cerner Corporation in Kansas City.

PREFACE

Why this book was written:

As recognized college leaders, we were contacted to provide quotes for a college advice book. After a market analysis of current books on college life, we discovered a void of organized and realistic books for freshmen college students even though they all proclaim they have the "real" insights to college. Thus, we embarked on our own endeavor instead to provide an organized handbook for college freshmen that was more meaningful, insightful and in-touch with the college scene of today. We have used our unique sense of humor to make this book fun and easy to read.

We met one summer on the college campus of Iowa State University working together as freshmen orientation leaders. Our job responsibilities included talking and interacting with thousands of incoming first year students and their families, answering questions and relating our own college experience. Through our extensive leadership as residence hall staff members (see About the Authors) we have worked with hundreds of first year students in meaningful ways as they have transitioned through first year issues and struggles. Our leadership positions provided constant interaction with college students and we have witnessed the characteristics of struggling students to student leaders. We have been involved with college campuses longer than any typical college experience. As professional and graduate students ourselves, we have discovered the keys to being successful college students.

After nearly two years since its beginning, we would like to share with you *The Voice of College: the Freshmen Experience.*

What this book has to offer:

The Voice of College: the Freshmen Experience is written for high school seniors and college freshmen students. The book is arranged in a chronological order of everything you will encounter your first year, starting with summer orientation to leaving campus in the spring. The book is organized into three main units, Summer, Fall and Spring, with the Fall Unit further divided into major parts including College Life, Choices, Academics and College Memories.

Through insights, stories and advice the book provides helpful, useful and practical information. It provides up-to-date, in-touch and real answers which is information a first year student needs and wants. The book is a collection of our knowledge and thoughts on the college experience and was written using our own college experiences. We wrote this book in a way that is not condescending or falsely chic. For example we won't insult your intelligence by relating everything "in terms of pizza and beer"; other authors on college life who insist on stereotyping the "typical college student" have lost the meaning and understanding of what it really means to be a college freshman. We keep it simple and to the point by leaving out the philosophy and theory of higher education and irrelevant research statistics. The book is streamlined to not be overly wordy and easy to read using numerous symbols, story boxes, and lists. Unique humor and creativity makes the book fun to read. We recognized we could not speak on the specifics of all colleges and universities; however the majority of information applies to the majority of freshmen students. You can use the information and logic presented to make your own decisions and draw your own conclusions.

How to use this book:

1. When you first pick up the book, flip through it:
   - Enjoy the humorous college stories, the awkward moment lists, the personality line ups, shared scares, struggle bus issues, and top 10 lists of insights and advice.
   - Read your favorite chapters, including popular college topics such as sex and dating life, college parties and alcohol, residence hall life and roommates, college academics and coursework, and finances.
2. The summer before college read the entire book cover to cover
   - The book is arranged in a chronological order of everything you will encounter your first year, starting with summer orientation to leaving campus in the spring.
3. Refer back to specific time frames as you experience your freshmen year.
   - The specific advice will be more practical, the insights will make more sense and the humor will take on more meaning.

Reoccurring themes:

Various symbols are used throughout the book to highlight important ideas, concepts and insights. These symbols represent themes reoccurring throughout the book. To decode the following symbols, see the Symbol Legend: Shared Scares, Struggle Bus, Magic Carpet, Word on the Street, Liquid Gold and Awkward Moments.

Through observations of college students year after year, numerous patterns and principles were detected. These themes led to the creation of *The 3 C's of College: Connections, Confidence and Comedy*, a 90-minute presentation for high school seniors and college freshmen that brings the ideas and humor of this book alive. To learn more about our keynote presentations and availability, go to www.thevoiceofcollege.com.

Chapter Highlights:

These selected chapter synopses listed below demonstrate what sets this college freshmen book apart from all others:

- *Sex and Dating Life*
  focus is on relationships, emotions, perspectives, scenarios and less on specifics of STDs and contraceptives

- *College Parties and Alcohol*
  the focus is on decision making/choices, and perspectives

- *Residence Hall Life and Roommates*
  real insider information/advice from people who have lived in and slept in residence halls for the better part of a decade, both as students and as staff members

- *College Academics and Coursework*
  taken from serious successful professional college students with powerful, realistic tips on succeeding within the academic side of college

- *Finances*
  money management, how to be college-thrifty...

We hope you find our book helpful and humorous as you discover your own college experience. We appreciate any questions or suggestions you have for *The Voice of College*.

The College Experts,
Michael Severin
Kipp Van Dyke
collegeexperts@thevoiceofcollege.com

THE VOICE OF COLLEGE:
the Freshmen Experience

TABLE OF CONTENTS

Summer

Fall

College Life

College Memories

Spring

SYMBOL LEGEND

For ease of reading, various symbols are used in the margins throughout the book to highlight important ideas, concepts and insights. Use this legend to decode the symbols:

Shared Scares
Shared Scares are common concerns all college students share and fear. You may have felt you were alone in your thoughts and questions, but will discover others have the same anxieties.

Struggle Bus
Struggle Bus entails common hardships and tough times faced by most college students at some point. Get away from the dark cloud over your head and hop on the struggle bus!

Magic Carpet
The Magic Carpet rolls out insights, advice and tips that will give you the competitive edge over your peers. It will help you navigate college and fly you directly to the final results.

Liquid Gold
Information so useful and powerful to know, it's as good as having liquid gold.

Awkward Moments
Awkward Moments will help remind you college is a fun time and to a take a breather from stresses in your life. Everyone at some point will experience an awkward moment so just smile and laugh at the situation.

Word on the Street
The Word on the Street is the information you need to know, that you may not find anywhere else.

CHAPTER 1
INTRODUCTION
THE COLLEGE EXPERIENCE

"College is about 3 things: homework, fun, and sleep...but you can only choose 2."

College is an important and exciting chapter in your life. You start with an open canvas. You are about to set on a course of events and decisions that will alter the outcome of the rest of your life. The decisions you make now will shape core foundations in the rest of your professional and personal life. Your education choice will ultimately lead to your career, which can lead you to a life of stimulating learning and rewarding opportunities. The people you meet will become your colleagues, friends, and possibly your future partner you'll retire with someday. You will learn more about yourself, see how others perceive you, find out what you are truly made of and transform into an adult.

There is no *one* college experience. Your college experience is completely individual to you. There's no set number of parties to attend, no set number of people to meet, no set number of textbook pages to read. Your college experience will be totally unique to you: the chance encounters of people who become important in your life, the random events and situations that alter your path, and the decisions you make that open some doors and close others. What works for one person doesn't mean it will work for another. It's what you make of it: this is *your* college experience.

Freshmen of today are:

- Informed and aware of current events
- Technology savvy
- Accepting of diversity
- Community-service orientated
- Comfortable and confident with their body image
- Conscious of fashions and trends
- Coming into college with some college credit from high school
- Looking for value in their education as prices increase
- Health-conscious; wellness decisions based on exercise, diet, sleep and alcohol and tobacco usage
- Have balance in their lives, making time for family, friends, hobbies and fun
- Bringing more leadership experience
- Looking to fit in with their peer group

Common threads of freshmen:

- Friendly and interested in genuine relationships
- Large ideals and dreams for the future
- Looking for those "college moments"
- Energetic
- Homesick
- Scared and unsure about the future
- Worried about money
- Transitioning from high school drama to college life
- Looking for their niche
- Very knowledgeable of university facts and traditions

The vision you have for college and yourself today may change completely by the time you graduate. You may discover you have new interests or skills that led you to a different field of study, withdrawal at an opportune time to start your own company, or continue your education through graduate-research or professional school. Financial, medical, family, or world events may also change your college path. Thus, your college experience may not go "according to plan." In its imperfection, you are preparing yourself for life itself, as in life, you will be forced to make hard choices and decisions as unforeseen events or opportunities present themselves. Believe in yourself and advance forward with confidence.

Only you have the power to realize your potential. You can create your own future: there is nothing you can't do. How you live your life is up to you. Discover who you are, what you're about and what you are trying to achieve by asking these questions about your core beliefs:

- What do you want your life to be like in the future and how are you achieving this goal?
- How do you fit into this world? What is your role in life?
- What do you want out of life?
- Are you living life the way *you* want to live?

Top 5 Cliché 'Going to College Advice':

1. *College coursework is so much harder than high school.*

College is a continuum from high school; you are ready for this next step. There may be a few surprises along the way as you adjust, but it is within your reach to succeed and thrive your first semester. In the *Fall* unit, the *Academics* section will empower you with tips and strategies to help you learn the ropes. Most of the time your high school experience will reflect your college experience. If you worked hard in high school, studied outside of class and took challenging classes, you will most likely continue to do so in college; however if you did the bare minimum to get by, maximized your free periods and didn't crack a book, you will probably do so in college as well. There are, of course, exceptions to this generalization and college is a great time to have a "fresh" academic start.

2. *You can pretend to be anyone you want to be.*

You are who you are. Your core personality, values, and interests will probably not change dramatically over the summer before you enter college. However, you are starting college with a clean slate. Your new college friends will only know what you share with them and the moments you create together; you are able to leave behind any embarrassing events or "casts" of yourself from high school. In this way, you have the chance to start fresh; but be honest with others and yourself. You will find a group of friends who will accept you for who you are and not for someone you are pretending to be.

3. College will be the best four years of your life.

There is sometimes disappointment following the hype in planning milestones. Without a doubt, college will bring with it many great moments and friends as well as new-found and welcomed freedoms; but it will also bring new responsibilities and hardships. Enjoy the current moment you are in. In the end, you will have discovered more about yourself as you experience new people and thoughts.

4. College is where you will meet your future husband or wife.

Maybe you will meet that perfect person. Maybe you won't. Just be yourself, hang out with lots of different people and follow your heart. There is no requirement to have a ring on your finger as you get your diploma your senior year.

5. You have to have an academic major going into college.

Many students coming to college are unsure of what they want to study. It's ok to go to school with several options and take some classes to figure out what seems right. In fact, many peoples' careers after college have little to do with their actual coursework, but they are successful because of the experiences they chose to participate in during college.

10 College Keystones:

- **Be Goal-Oriented**

  Visualize what you want to accomplish during your college years. Set yourself up for success by *planning* your resume: what skills, internship experience, leadership involvement and community service will make you a highly marketable candidate for your future employer? You have the next four years to build that impressive resume.

- **Be Knowledgeable**

Know what's going on around you: around campus, in your community and world events. Learn how to use the resources available to you, such as the bus system or the university library. Be familiar with the terms and conditions of your residence and your university's handbook. Keep constant surveillance of upcoming events, involvement opportunities and award applications.

- **Be Open-Minded**

Be open to new experiences, ideas and lifestyles. Seek out new opportunities. View college as a place for personal growth. You will come across things that are unfamiliar to you. Don't automatically assume those new experiences are wrong or weird; it's just different from what you know growing up in your hometown.

- **Be in Charge of Your Life**

There are often "gray zones" in life where a clear choice is not always apparent. You won't necessarily have all the information or answers you would like to have when you will need to make those decisions. Seek others for support and advice, but ultimately, it's your life. You know yourself best. *You* are the sole person responsible to make the final decisions concerning your future.

- **Be OK With Failure**

During these formative years, there will be moments when you will be faced with hard choices and decisions and will want to give up. There will be times when you will want to cry. Learn from your past, and then pick yourself up and bounce back stronger. Be ok with taking risks. Turn your failures into motivation for success. Fail in order to succeed.

- **Be Connected**

Practice your skills in networking. One event, person, decision or connection today can lead to a whole series of events later in your life. Incidental people and trivial events can later become very

important to you.   Don't light bridges on fire.   Maintain
relationships.   Stay involved.   Look for opportunities.   Make
connections.

- **Be Friendly**

  Know the people around you beyond just their first names. Take a
  genuine interest in their lives and ask questions.   You will be
  amazed as to what you discover underneath the surface.   Others
  like to be around those who are happy and positive. Don't hate life.
  Laugh and smile often.

- **Be Curious**

  Learn for the sake of learning. Build life skills and habits now that
  will carry with you. Find out who you are and how others perceive
  you. Learn more about your religion, get involved with politics and
  learn more about your profession. Become well-rounded.

- **Be Adventurous**

  Opportunities will arise, which may at first seem crazy, but will be
  opportunities that may never present themselves again.   If the
  skydiving club is presenting a chance to try skydiving and you've
  always wanted to try, seize the opportunity. If a group of friends
  you meet at school are using their Spring Break to go rebuild homes
  in a poverty stricken area of the country or world, check it out. If
  you can take a Spanish class in Spain, don't be afraid to try it.

- **Be Excited**

  There are many people in this world who do not have the
  opportunity to go to college. This is a great opportunity and
  shouldn't be taken for granted. Be excited for this time in your life
  to study what you want to study, hang out with those who have
  similar interests, and experience life among some very intelligent
  and creative people.

Final Thoughts

You will grow and mature exponentially your first year of college without even realizing it. Life is always changing and changing you with it. Every experience, negative or positive, has culminated to make the person you are today.

Reflect on why you chose to attend college: the "next step"? to learn? for a career? to earn a future higher income? to meet your future spouse?

Points to Ponder

- Your college experience is what it is.
- Get involved and get connected.
- Plan success by not allowing the opportunity for failure.
- Keep a positive attitude.
- Set goals. Know what's around you. Seek out new experiences. Take responsibility for your decisions. Network. Love life. Take risks. Engage your learning. Live the adventure.
- Set up check points that will make it impossible for you not to reach your end goals.
- You're going to make mistakes. Lots of them, including some really big ones. Just keep moving forward.
- Try harder.
- Commit and dedicate yourself entirely to what you do.
- Don't get pregnant.
- Get excited!

CHAPTER 2

ORIENTATION
COLLEGE: DAY ONE

"What the hell kind of major is that?"

College is an investment of your time, your money and your life. The effort you put in now at the beginning of your college career will benefit and help you later as you network and make connections, learn core knowledge, and utilize available resources. At orientation you'll meet key people who will help you and could affect and change your college path. Try to remember peoples' names, faces, and positions. You will also meet students who will be in your graduating class. These are your new peers and new friends. This is Day One of College.

What is the purpose of orientation?

The purpose of orientation is to familiarize and acquaint yourself with the university. College orientation is generally held during the summer or right before fall classes begin. Use this chapter as a general outline to help guide you in the orientation process as you will have:
- People to meet
- Questions to ask
- Things to see
- Tasks to complete

Orientation is only a small fraction of the time you will invest in college, but it will help you make a strong start. Have fun at orientation, and begin making connections with your new school and new classmates.

What can I expect at orientation?

Orientation is a day designed and focused on you. Take advantage of any options and maximize opportunities (take the tours, go to the sessions, ask questions, buy a college shirt at the bookstore, etc). You will find a very welcoming environment and people will be friendly and helpful. You can expect to experience information overload (lots of general information for many people's different situations). Just relax, be open and pick up on as much as you can for now.

It is important to fully participate in orientation because you are laying the groundwork for your first semester of college. Orientation will give you pointers and hints to help you succeed and avoid frustrations in the fall. Don't assume you already know everything just because you had a friend or family member who attended the college. Don't fall into the "I'm too cool for that" attitude. Go to the sessions, stay overnight in the residence halls and eat at the dining hall (if possible) and ask plenty of questions. Things may change from year to year and orientation is the time you can learn about what you are paying for.

Top 5 good reasons to choose a school:

1. Reputation for your program of study
2. Financial considerations
3. Student activities and opportunities
4. Distance from home
5. School pride

Since college is a big investment, you want to be sure you are getting the most for your money. Usually it is a combination of all of the above which need to be considered to make a wise college decision.

Top 5 bad reasons to choose a school:

1. Boyfriend or girlfriend is attending
2. The basketball team had a great year
3. Reputation as a party school
4. Your best friend was accepted
5. The school colors are your favorite colors

You are going to school to get an education. This should be your top consideration when thinking about a school. While some of the above may change the experience, ultimately look at a school which best fits your needs.

Check-In and Welcome

Come prepared! Check to see what they told you to bring such as a calculator or #2 pencils for placement testing (usually in math or English skills). Bring any communications from the college such as housing or financial aid information. You will also want to bring:

- your photo identification (such as your driver's license or other government issued ID)
- vaccine history and past medical history
  Keep a copy of these records when you go to college, too.
- medical insurance card
- social security number
  If you don't know your social security number you should memorize it now. Having this number memorized will come in handy.
- high school transcript including any advanced placement (AP) classes
- college transcript (if you completed any coursework at a community college)
- map of the campus
- notepad and pen

Check the weather forecast before you leave to make sure you are prepared in case it rains or it is extremely hot or cool. You should wear comfortable clothes and shoes because there will be a lot of walking involved throughout the day. It is also a good idea to bring some water and snacks.

Students and parents may be separated for different sessions. It's a good idea to have a plan of how to meet up later when you are in unfamiliar environment. One easy way to communicate is through cell phones; or have a preplanned location and time to meet such as "meet at the car at noon for lunch".

College ID

You will probably have your picture taken for your college identification card. Be sure to look nice for this photo because you will use this card for the next four years of college. Your college ID card might be used in any of the following functions: meal pass, library card, bus pass, laundry card, admittance to campus services (recreation facility, sporting events, etc.), ATM bank card, test verification, student discounts, and many others. As you can see your college ID card is very important and you will want to protect it and keep it with you at all times.

Be sure to bring your current valid driver's license and check to see if other documentation is required.

College Email

You will probably register for your college email address. If your email isn't automatically assigned, choose your username appropriately because you will use your email to communicate with professors and use it on your resume when you graduate. Choose something simple and easy such as the first letter of your first name combined with your last name to use as a username or your initials. Beth Leigh Green would choose *bgreen@collegename.edu* or *blg@collegename.edu*. While it may be tempting to be *hockeyguy@collegename.edu*, it won't be professional when you're trying to land an internship in a competitive market.

Agenda

Here is an overview of the general items you can expect to be covered at orientation. Beyond this basic overview, there may be additional options for special circumstances such as music or choir auditions, athletic or cheerleader try-outs, ROTC (Reserve Officers Training Corps) for those interested in the military, minority student services, Greek housing and recruitment, non-traditional students, etc. Many times these types of activities may require special arrangements prior to arriving to campus, so be sure to plan early.

The purpose of orientation is to answer your questions and prepare you for the fall semester, so don't be afraid to ask questions. If you are shy and don't want to ask questions in large group sessions, there is usually time afterwards to approach the speaker or college representatives about your question in a more private setting. During large group sessions, consider if your question is an individual need that is best saved for after the session or a group question that would benefit everyone. Also ask yourself if you really have a question or are you just trying to "tell your story" in a question format. Your question might have already been thought of so you can also check your orientation information under the "FAQ" or frequently asked questions section. You'll want to ask your question during the appropriate session so familiarize yourself with the day's agenda. For example, it is not appropriate to ask about residence hall room sizes at the financial aid session. It is important to realize the answer you receive may just be the opinion or experience of one individual, so be sure to get other people's perspectives before drawing your own conclusion.

Academics

Universities (example: Harvard, Iowa State) are subdivided into "colleges" (example: College of Liberal Arts and Sciences, College of Engineering). These colleges are further subdivided into various departments that house specific majors (example: meteorology, economics).

Choosing your Major

When you are deciding on your major you will want to explore your options and be flexible. Your university will have a course catalog that will list all the majors offered as well as the classes required for that major. Look at all the options for different majors and read the descriptions of the classes that are required. Choose your major based on your interests and strengths. Seek input from your parents, advisors, orientation sessions, and classes. You may even consider signing up for an extra class to explore another major you are considering.

Consider the career and job options you want as you decide your major. What are the job prospects for that job? Can you see yourself working in this job as a long term career? **Are the jobs offered compatible with your expectations on income level, time commitment, additional training or education, etc?**

You don't need to choose your major right away and it's ok to be undecided. In this case you can enroll in general college studies and take prerequisites or required university courses that everyone has to take as you explore and decide on a major. This way you won't "fall behind" because you will have already taken the required classes that every student will need to complete regardless of their major. It will help if you know what broad area you are most likely to choose (such as science or art) because then you can enroll as undecided in that college.

It is not uncommon for college students to change their major at least once, if not more.

You may be assigned or may meet an academic advisor. Your advisor can help you choose classes to keep you on the right track. An advisor is like your high school counselor except your advisor is assigned based on the academic department your major falls under and so he or she will have more familiarity with your program of study.

Class Registration: creating your class schedule

At orientation you might register for classes and create your fall class schedule. Be sure to take into consideration any classes you already have credit for from transfer credits and bring the appropriate documentation. Your schedule will appear different from what you are used to in a high school schedule. Your courses might not be back to back and you might have a couple hours between classes to study or catch a meal. You might have classes late in the evening or you might not even have classes every day. As a freshman, you might not always get the most ideal class times since scheduling is typically completed based on seniority. However, keep in mind most seniors aren't enrolling in freshmen classes. Be patient in this planning process and don't be disappointed if you don't get all the classes you were hoping. You'll have at least seven other semesters to fit them in. See Chapter 21 on classes to learn more about college versus high school credits.

Consider taking an "introduction to college course" to learn about campus resources and college study skills.

Finances

The cost of attending college is probably the first major investment you have made so far in your life. Education is one of the best investments you can make for yourself. College finances are important and the decisions you make now will impact your future discretionary income later. You will need to learn about these three main considerations:

- Know your costs and any unexpected or hidden extra costs
- Know your sources of income

- Know your options for payment

See Chapter 14 College Finances and Budgets. Be sure to ask your questions during the Financial Aid session or make an appointment for individual needs.

Home Banking versus College Banking

While you are visiting campus you will also want to find out about your banking options. Is your home bank present? Can you access your account? How close to campus is the bank? Your money needs to be accessible to you for everyday costs and emergencies. You may consider switching to a more convenient bank or having both a "home bank" and a "college bank".

Housing and Dining

Living and eating on campus is a convenient and great way to connect to the university and meet new people. Visualize what it will be like to live at college on a day-to-day basis.

Residence Halls ("Dorms")

The Department of Residence will host an information session and a tour of their facilities. Check-out what your living situation will look like. You might not be able to see your exact room but you will probably see a standard room that will be very similar to yours. You will want to find out the dimensions of your room and what is already included in your room. Check to see if there is an option of spending a night in a residence hall room during orientation. See Chapter 7: Campus Housing.

Also ask about the mattress size to ensure the sheets you are bringing will fit as some residence halls provide extra long mattresses.

If you are not planning on living in the residence halls check to see if there are off-campus or Greek housing sessions and tours. This is a good time to finalize move-in dates and times.

Dining Services

If possible, have a meal in the dining hall during orientation. You will want to ask about meal plans and ask about any of your special dietary concerns. See Chapter 10: Campus Food.

It can be intimidating at first to meet new people but it is a skill you must develop for college. You will have multiple opportunities throughout the day to meet new people---don't be afraid to branch out and introduce yourself. Make it your goal to talk to at least ten people you don't know who are also going through orientation. By the end of the day you'll have several people you already know on campus and maybe a couple of them are in some of your classes.

Start recording important campus phone numbers to know and keep this list in your wallet or purse. Your list may include the phone numbers for the following: emergencies, police, RA on duty, Hall Desk, Residence Hall Maintenance, etc.

Tours

Whether you take an official or unofficial tour you'll want to get a feel of the campus and community that will become your new home.

Always stay towards the front near the tour guide when on a guided tour so you can hear the information better; also as you walk in-between places you can ask the tour guide specific questions. Pay attention to what they say during a tour; your tour guide is pointing out information to you for a reason even if you don't understand why or when it will become important.

Campus tour

Get a feel of what campus life will be like. Check out some of the buildings you will be having class in if you already have your class schedule. Look at typical classrooms.

Where are the other buildings on campus such as the library, student union, bookstore, and fitness center?

Community tour

Explore your new community.

Where is the mall? Where is your bank? Where are good restaurants? Where can you go to church? Where will you get your haircut? Where is the hospital? What are some activities to do off-campus? Where can you take your car for repairs? Where can you find bus stations or airport access?

Before you leave!

Area businesses are aware of orientation and will often offer incoming first year students and their families orientation specials or discounts that you will want to check out before you leave. Other things you may want to investigate before you leave:
- Season tickets for athletic events
- Campus bookstore for fall books or clothing
- Parking passes
- New Student Day Programs (social mixer for incoming freshmen with more in-depth orientation)
- Souvenir for the little brother or sister who wasn't able to come to orientation

Swing by the student health center and take care of any paperwork they might require to be on file such as insurance information. When you do become sick or injured you'll appreciate the fact that you took that extra time during orientation to already have this taken care of.

Grab an extra copy of a local phone book if you can for parents to keep at home. This can come in handy if you need them to help you locate or take care of a particular service, such as car problems. Also they will have the numbers of local businesses on hand when they want to have something like flowers or other gifts delivered to you as a surprise. Another idea is to subscribe to a local newspaper the summer before you move to get a feel for the community, its businesses and events.

School Records

FERPA stands for the Family Educational Rights and Privacy Act. It is a federal law that protects the privacy of your education records and your right to review these records. If you would like a third party, such your parents, to have access to your confidential university information, such as your grade report, you will need to complete a Student Information Release Authorization form. Also, you will want to check where your university will send your grade report during interim breaks; they may send it to your "permanent address" (as opposed to your college address) which in most cases will be your parents' address. On a related note concerning privacy, you may ask the university what it considers public student information (such as your name, address, email and phone number appearing in a student directory). If you want to limit public disclosure of this information, orientation is a good place to inquire about the process to withhold your information before it is published.

Top questions asked during orientation:

- Do I need to bring a computer? Does the campus have wireless connections?
- Should I bring a car? Should I bring my bike?
- Where can I park on campus?
- Can I go see my residence hall room?
- Can we eat at the dining hall?
- How does the meal plan work?
- What is there to do for fun? What do students do on the weekends for fun?
- Are the classes hard?
- How big are the classes?
- How long does it take to walk from one class to another?
- What classes are required by the university and for my major? What are popular courses among freshmen?
- How much money should I budget to spend each week?
- What clubs or organizations can I join?
- How do I manage my time?
- Where is the bathroom?
- Is this a Coke® or Pepsi® campus?
- Is that a valuable session to attend?
- Do I have to take the placement testing for my classes?
- How is safety on campus?
- Do the residence halls have a curfew?
- What is the ratio of guys to girls on campus? How do I meet new people?
- Do people go home on the weekends?
- How do I find out where my classes are located?
- What do I do if I am having trouble in a class?
- Where can I get a job?
- How do I pay for college?

 After 30 seconds into a speakers lecture, shake your head and motion your hand back and forth in front of your neck to indicate as though the speaker just said something offending and to move onto the next topic.

- About two minutes into the speaker's lecture, motion the "wrap it up" hand gesture.
- During orientation or other new student day programs where you are bound to run into a motivational speaker, pick up on their key words and again and again start clapping, causing others to clap along with you: LEADERSHIP, yeah! Clap clap clap   OUR FUTURE! Clap clap clap LUNCHTIME! Clap clap clap
- In a small group situation use the word "too" in your questions to the tour guide or speaker. If they mention something about California, you can ask, "So you are from California too?" The word too helps imply that you are relating, whether that fact about you is true or not is not important.
- When you are tired of telling the millionth person at orientation your major, try these options:
    o Well I kind of want to be an English major but I really don't like to read..... and I don't like to write either....... and I definitely don't want to teach....... research, I want to go into English research. Cutting edge.
    o Double major: undecided in the humanities and undecided in engineering
    o "College"
    o Tell people your real major. And then tell them, though, if that doesn't work out your "back-up" plan is medical school.
- In *every* Q & A session, your top three questions always: Is there any lead-based paint in the residence halls? Which buildings on campus have been identified as containing asbestos? How many students on campus are infected with a sexually transmitted disease (STD)? Never seem satisfied with the answer given and follow-up with "are you sure?"

Since we brought it up, leasers must disclose the presence of any lead based paint and/or lead based paint hazards in the dwelling if the building was built prior to 1978.

Final Thoughts

As you can see, there is a lot to accomplish during orientation. Plan ahead. Make a list of what you need to bring; outline your schedule so you don't miss any opportunities; jot down questions as you think of them. All of your questions probably won't be answered, but that's ok. You have started the process of gathering resources and making connections that will help you later. Oh and everyone's parents are going to do something embarrassing, so don't worry about it.

Points to Ponder

- Come prepared and act professionally. Remember this is the start of college and you are laying important ground work.
- Soak it all in. Attend as many sessions and tours as you can to get a feel of your new home.
- Don't be afraid to ask all your questions; remember the struggle bus is packed today.
- Make it your goal to connect with ten other incoming students and exchange email addresses.
- Ask about how mail should be addressed to you and where you can pick up your mail and packages.
- Visit the college during the school year and ask a student if you can see their room so you can see how an actual room is set up.
- Memorize your new zip code (and your address and phone number if you know it already.

CHAPTER 3
PREMOVE
THE CHECK-LIST

"MOM!!! I need a couch!!"

You're at the end of the summer and moving to college is just a matter of days away. You're probably both excited and nervous at this point. Now is the time to start thinking of what you will need to complete to prepare and get ready for going to college.

Housing

Be educated about your housing and the style of your room. Be able to answer the following questions:

- What is already provided with my room?
- What are the dimensions of the room?
- Are there any specific rules or restrictions of what you're not allowed to bring?

If you don't know the answers to these questions, try:

- Reviewing information you received at orientation
- Visiting the housing's website
- Calling the housing department
- Reading any other information you received through the college by mail

In general your room will be provided with the following:

- Bed and mattress

- Desk and desk chair
- Closet or wardrobe
- Dresser

It may also come with:
- Waste basket
- Phone
- Carpet
- Window drapes
- Towel bar
- Shelving or storage space

Roommate

It's a good idea to contact your roommate if you know their phone number or email address. This conversation is important because this will be the person you will be living with for the next year. Don't make any assumptions about your future roommate! Find out about their background---where do they live? What do they plan to major in? Have they ever shared a room before? These questions can give you many insights. You will also want to find out:
- What do they plan to bring?
- Who will bring the: phone, carpet, marker board, bed lofts, futon, TV, microwave, refrigerator, etc?
- When do they plan to move in?
- How do they think the room should be set up?

Many students coming into college have had a room to themselves at home. Sharing a space with someone else can be an adjustment, so it's important to be open about expectations from the start. Put all your own personal stuff aside and look at this as a great opportunity to learn from a new person. Keep a positive attitude. Go into this relationship knowing it is a unique opportunity to learn about living close to someone else with its' triumphs and hardships. See Chapter 8: Roommates for more tips and hints.

The Packing List

This list will help you to start to think of the general things you may need when you move away from home. It is not meant to be a complete list. When you are packing you will have to take into consideration: your housing situation, your roommate, space limitations, your budget and your own preferences.

Legend Key:

- **Items appearing in bold** are commonly forgotten items.
- *Items appearing in italics* are college-specific items that you might not already have at home.
- (Items appearing in parentheses) are more suggestions that may not pertain to everyone.

CLOTHES:

- Fall Clothes
    - You'll want to pack comfortable everyday types of clothes. You will want to pack enough clothes to get you through to the beginning of the next season or until your next trip home.
- Shoes
    - Every-day, casual, workout, sandals/flip-flops, dress, boots
- Socks and Underwear
    - 2-3 week supply
- Workout clothes
- Professional dress clothes
    - You'll want to bring 1-2 nice outfits for such things as: award ceremonies, banquets, career fairs, formal dances, athletic, music or club functions, church, or just for fun to go out with your friends.
- Jackets
- Gloves/Hat if applicable
- **Clothes hangers**

BEDDING/TOWELS:

- Pillow
- Bed sheets, comforter, *egg crate foam mattress topper*
    - Some residence halls use extra long mattresses, so you'll want to be sure you know the mattresses' dimensions before you buy or pack your sheets.

	Fitted Sheet	Flat Sheet
Twin Mattress	39 inches X 75 inches	66 inches X 96 inches
Twin Extra Long Mattress	39 inches X 80 inches	66 inches X 102 inches

- Shower towel, washcloth, hand-towel
  - o Consider having two sets of towels in case you need to do laundry or to have another set on hand if you have a visiting guest.
- Fleece blanket, throw-blanket

LAUNDRY:

- **Laundry bag or basket**
  - o Depending on the size of the room, pick which will be most efficient. Baskets can be helpful later to carry stuff home or when moving, but bags take up much less space.
- Detergent, dryer sheets

(iron and ironing board)

See Chapter 9: Laundry

PERSONAL HYGIENE/TOILETRIES:

- Shampoo, soap
- *Shower sandals*
  - o You'll want to keep your bare feet from touching the bathroom floor, because public community showers can be breeding grounds for contagious feet infections. See Chapter 18: Health and Safety.
- *Shower caddy*
  - o Unlike home, you won't leave your shampoo and soap in the shower and will need to carry it with you each time you shower. It is much easier to carry your shampoo, conditioner, soap, washcloth, and loofah, if you have something to put them all in like a shower caddy or bucket.
- Toothbrush, toothpaste, cup
- Deodorant, perfume/cologne
- Razors, shaving cream
- Comb, hair spray/gel
- Eye Care
- Toiletry bag

(medications, vitamins, make-up, female hygiene products)

Think of other things that you will need to live on your own and be self-sufficient. Some "family supply" items you might take for granted at home include: Kleenex®, toilet paper, Q-tips®, hand lotion, nail clippers, tweezers, hair clippers, etc.

Also consider:

- **First Aid supplies** such as: cough or headache medicine, bandages, etc. See Chapter 18: Health and Safety for a more extensive list.
- **Cleaning supplies** such as: glass or all-purpose cleaner, paper towels, trash bags etc.

To save a little extra money, use plastic grocery bags as garbage bags.

SCHOOL SUPPLIES:

- Backpack
- Paper
  - o Notepads, loose-leaf paper, computer paper
- Pens, pencils
- Folders, binders
- Note cards, sticky notes
- Stapler, calculator
- Paper shredder
- Stamps, envelopes
  - o Bring a list of your family and friends' addresses.

Use your home and personal experience as you decide what school supplies to bring. It will also depend on your major (that is: a design major will need more art supplies while a science major may need a more advanced calculator). Your course instructors will let you know what you will need for the semester so you might want to wait until after your first week of classes to purchase supplies.

DOCUMENTS:

- College Information:
    - o Residence Hall/apartment information: address, room number, telephone number, roommate name and home phone number, etc
    - o Class schedule, campus map, phone numbers, information from orientation and resource lists, etc
- Bank information (account number)
- Medical history, vaccine history
- Insurance cards
- Social security card/number

You will also want to consider where in your room you will safely store these documents, as well as your money or other valuables.

ROOM:

Most of these items are not necessary but can be nice to have in your room, however, these large ticket/bulky items are difficult to move and can get ruined. Encourage your roommate to bring these things.

- *Loft*
    - o A loft is a wooden structure that elevates your bed off of the floor and thus provides additional floor space underneath your bed (for example, you might then move your desk underneath your lofted bed). The loft may already be provided with the room, may be available in pre-purchased kits, available to rent or you may build your own loft. If you construct your own loft, you will need to know the bed frame dimensions and be sure to ask about any restrictions.

 When you use a loft, you have essentially lifted your bed six or seven feet off of the ground and if you fall out of your bed you can cause severe bodily injuries including head concussions; **for you own safety, make sure your loft has a guard rail and leave the guard rail in place.** Also remember that you are sleeping very close to the ceiling and it is easy to bump your head.

- *Carpet*
    - Your room may not be provided with carpet leaving you with cold feet. You can bring a large area rug or use a company that cuts carpet squares specific for college rooms.
- Furniture
    - *Futons:* Futons are low to the ground couches that pull out and convert to a bed. The mattress is the most expensive part of the futon but a good investment for a comfortable night sleep. See discussion below about issues related to bringing large furniture items with you to college.
    - Something to sit on, whether it is a papasan chair or a bean bag.
- Fan
    - This could be the most important thing you bring if your room is not air-conditioned.
- Lights
    - Your room may be dim-lit having just one central fluorescent light.
- Waste Basket
    - Check with the Residence Halls Department to see if this is already provided.
- *Dishes/Microwave/Mini-Fridge*
    - See below

DÉCOR:

Your room will be pretty bland when you move in and you will want to personalize it to give it more of a home feeling. You don't have to spend a lot of money on room decorations if you are creative—simple things can add a lot to your room. Be aware of what image or message you are projecting to others from the things you choose to display in your room. You want people to feel comfortable in your room. What will your Resident Assistant think if your entire wall idolizes beer? What will your guests think about your personality if all they see is pictures of naked women or men on your walls?

- Photos
  - o Displaying photos of your family, friends and pets will spark memories of your home life. It is also a way to share some of your past with your new college friends.
- Posters
  - o A lot of college students will buy posters for their rooms. Posters can be expensive especially if you consider that you generally don't keep them long term and they tear easily from the tape when you take them down at the end of the year.
- Plants
  - o A plant is something you might want to consider getting later. It can add a lot to your room but it can also add another responsibility to your busy schedule and you will need to take care of it over school breaks.

ENTERTAINMENT:
- Television/DVD player/VCR/**Coax Cable/Power Strip**/TV Stand
  - o Consider the size of the TV you are bringing and where you will place the TV.
- Sports
  - o If you have a sports passion or play a unique sport, you'll want to bring it along. Otherwise the hall desk or campus fitness center will generally let you check out the sports equipment you need.
- Movies and Video Games
  - o "Movie nights" are popular among college students and are a casual fun way to bond with your friends. Remember though every item you bring takes up space in your room so just bring some of your favorite movies to share. You won't need to bring your entire movie collection, because your neighbors and friends will also be bringing movies.
- Books
  - o Bring some fun and light reading for when you want to escape your textbooks. Be selective though because you will have lots of other material to read for your classes.
- Music/CDs/Stereo/Radio/MP3 Player
  - o You'll definitely want some of your favorite music to enjoy. You won't need extensive stereo or large speakers.

Don't be "the nosebleed." Playing music excessively loud in a small space is a quick way to make enemies, not friends.

- o MP3 player: Many people choose to have their digital audio player to keep their music for the walk to class, studying or for the drive home.

TRANSPORTATION:

See Chapter 13: Transportation for information on bringing a car, bike, rollerblades, etc.

MISCELLANEOUS:

- The Voice of College: the Freshmen Experience
- Cell-phone and charger/Phone and phone cord/Answering Machine/ Clock/Alarm clock/Wrist-watch
  - o A wrist-watch is a good investment if you don't already have one. Unlike high school there are no bells to alert you to the start of class---you don't want to be late to your classes!
- Camera
- Full length mirror
- *Marker Board*
  - o A dry erase board is a handy thing for your friends to leave you messages on your door when you aren't home. Markers have a tendency to go missing so you'll want to attach the marker to the board and bring extra markers.
- Batteries
- Flashlight
- **Adhesive substance**
  - o 3M® makes strong adhesives that you can use to attach items to your wall that won't leave marks or holes.
- **Extension cords/Power strip/Coax (TV) Cable**
- **Duct Tape**
- *Door-stop*
- *Good quality water bottle*
  - o It is easy to forget to stay well hydrated at college if your own source of water is a drinking fountain. Carry a reusable plastic water bottle with you to class.
- Wallet/Purse
  - o It's a good idea to always have your college ID card with you because you will need it to use most campus services. If you don't

want to always carry your wallet or purse, consider buying a card holder that will fit in your back pocket.

Keep a spare key to your car in your back pocket along with your cards in case you lock yourself out of your car. Since your parents probably don't live near you while you are in college this simple foresight will save you from future frustration.

- Umbrella
  - Bring 2 umbrellas and keep one with you in your backpack. If you have an extra umbrella to offer on a rainy day, you can usually make an instant friend.
- Computer/*Ethernet Cord*/*Wireless Card*/*Laptop Lock* and Printer
  - See Chapter 12: Computers and Technology

What NOT to bring

You will need to review the specific terms and conditions of your housing contract, but the following is a list of items that is commonly not needed or not allowed in university housing:

- Weapons
  - Including paintball guns, BB-guns, long knives or anything that could be mistaken for a weapon including water-guns.
- Drugs, alcohol or alcohol containers
  - State and federal laws on alcohol still apply on college campuses, which means if you just graduated high school you still have about three years until your 21st birthday. Most residence halls will not allow you to keep alcohol containers such as empty kegs or empty wine bottles in your room. See Chapter 15: Alcohol.
- Candles
  - Candles are prohibited due to the extreme danger an unattended open flame presents to the residence hall community. There have been several reports in the news of a candle starting a residence hall building fire causing smoke, property damage and even human fatalities. Just leave the candle at home.
- Halogen lamps
  - These reach high temperatures and are a fire hazard.
- Pets
  - Animals are not allowed in residence halls due to sanitation and health considerations as well as the fact that other people may be allergic to the animal. Some pets may be allowed, such as fish,

but you should seriously think about the time and costs involved. Any living creature will require that you take care of it every day even over school breaks. You can probably also imagine what kind of smell your room will have with keeping an animal enclosed in a small room.

  o If you *really* feel the need to have a pet, consider a pet rock. They aren't too hard to catch in any parking lot or outdoor area. The added bonus, they are great pets for a busy college schedule. They don't need food or water, just a spot on your desk to sit.

- Room improvement projects (paint, window-curtains, etc)
  o You will most likely only be in your new room or apartment for less than a year. When you check out it is expected the room will be in exactly the same condition as when you moved in (less normal wear and tear) and you will be charged if there are damages, stains or holes or if they have to repaint the walls.

- Furniture
  o Check to see what is already provided with your place. If you are living in the residence halls you **won't** need to bring your bed from home. Keep in mind the size restriction of your living space, which is probably on the smaller size to begin with *and* you will most likely be sharing this space with another person.

- Appliances
  o A microwave or mini-refrigerator may already be provided with your room or in a common kitchenette area. There may also be a program at your school to rent these items. On the other hand, you might find that you don't even need these things. Anything that generates heat or has an open flame that could be a fire hazard is generally not allowed including: grills, toasters, electric sandwich makers, space heaters, etc. Leave the air conditioner at home.

- Full kitchen supplies or bulk supply of groceries
  o Most residence halls are not conducive to cooking because it is either assumed or required that you will have a meal plan for the dining center, so don't buy the case of 48 cans of soup. You also won't need a lot of dishes, silverware or pots and pans.

Buy now or later?

You might want to wait to buy some things until you actually know if you will need it. If you are waiting to buy a larger item such as a futon or loft until you arrive on campus you should consider:

1. How will you get this bulky item home when you move out in the spring? Will you need to rent a storage unit? Will it be worth paying for monthly storage?

2. If you will need the item right away you may consider buying it ahead of time because it is not uncommon for campus town stores to run out of popular items and you may have to wait a couple weeks for the next order.

Final Thoughts

You will probably forget something at home but don't sweat it, that's what care packages, visiting parents or trips home are all about. If you don't have a stereo or TV you don't need to run out and buy one. You can fill in any gaps over the next couple years by asking for these items as birthday or holiday gifts. But you will want to budget some money for unknown incidental expenses that you can't foresee during the first couple weeks.

Points to Ponder

- You will probably have a roommate and it is a good idea to coordinate beforehand what each of you will be bringing.
- The more you bring, the more you have to move and the more crowded your room will be.
- 100 college freshmen were polled by the authors and found:
    - **Things people forgot**: Pictures, junk food, hair straightener, door stop, rug, slippers, shelves, picture frames, decorations, DVDs, posters, extension cords, dishes/silverware, printer paper, air freshener, white board, alarm clock, batteries, soap, workout tape, snowboard, my comfy chair, power strip, hangers, rollerblades, basic t-shirts, toothbrush
    - **Things people brought but don't need**: Lamp, blanket, too many shoes and laundry baskets, huge safe, iron, markers, too many towels and boxes, extra make up, sweaters so soon, cooking utensils, so many big tub containers

CHAPTER 4
LEAVING HOME
GOODBYE OLD ROOM

"I'm outta here!"

The time has arrived. Thirteen years of K-12 schooling has ended and it's time to prepare to leave the familiarities of home for your new college life. This major transition in your life is filled with many emotions, opportunities, and relationship changes. This chapter will help navigate some of these areas and, hopefully, leave you ready to make a smooth transition to your new home.

The End of High School

The last few weeks of high school can be a mix of emotions. The ever cliché "light at the end of the tunnel" has been reached and graduation is near. There are usually a number of "Senior Sendoff" type parties and socials, yearbooks are feverishly signed, everyone asks what lies ahead and photos are snapped every few minutes to capture all of these closing memories. The above mentioned are important in making a successful transition. It's important to celebrate the accomplishments and friendships which have been made. But, it's also important to get excited about the future which is happening soon.

There is no official or exact closure to high school. Some would say the last day of school, others the final awards ceremony, graduation for others, the graduation party, and even the random summer hang out sessions could signify "the end." All of these are correct, depending on the person. And for some, there may be no official closure. So, say your "goodbyes," but know that you'll probably keep running into your friends and classmates until the day you roll out of your driveway for college and unless you're going to school in another country, you'll most likely see them one of the first weekends you come home from school and at the latest Thanksgiving break.

You attend a senior party and will often hear things such as "I miss you already" or "We'll probably never see each other again". The reality of the situation is it's always an awkward, "Oh Hey!, How's it going" the next day when you run into your friend at the local grocery store.

Don't leave us!

There are so many opportunities for students leaving high school. Sometimes there is a pocket of classmates or friends who do not have the opportunity to leave for college or choose a school really close to home. They may try to persuade you to stay closer to home and may make you feel bad for "leaving the gang." Remember, picking a college requires many different decisions, and it's important they are *your* decisions. The familiar is comfortable, but the opportunities available are so vast. You can always come back to your hometown, but the older you become, the harder it will be to leave.

Bye-Bye?

The summer before you leave will be full of "goodbyes." This is a great opportunity to thank those around you who have helped you be successful and supported you as you grew and matured. Be sure to take the time to visit extended family members if you will not be seeing them as much. It's also important to help explain to younger siblings what is happening. All they have known is having you around and they may not grasp exactly what is happening. Show them pictures of where you are moving, give them your address, and maybe give them a small personal item they can remember you by.

A very practical way to spend time with your family prior to leaving is going shopping for some of the essential items you'll be moving.

Kipp Story Box

My mother and I took some trips to the store to buy bed sheets, personal care items and other dorm room essentials prior to my move to school. This was a great time to get excited together and to share conversations about what the upcoming year would look like.

It's important to remember these goodbyes are not for good. Family and friends will still see you when you come home on weekends and can stay in contact with email or letters. Remember this as some of your classmates are acting as if you are going to college on the moon and insist on hanging out *every* night the summer before you leave.

Boyfriends and Girlfriends:

A part of many high school students' experiences includes having a boyfriend or girlfriend. The seriousness of these relationships vary for each person. For some, it was a date or two in high school, maybe a school dance or prom. For others, several years together as a couple with talks of spending the rest of your lives together. What does this mean as you get ready to leave for college? Definitely a time to think about decisions for both involved.

Each situation is different, but consider the following: If you've been dating someone for a long time, realize college does not mean the end of the relationship. It may take more work if distance is involved, but if the relationship is meant to be, this is a stage that is manageable. But as this book will illustrate, there are many great opportunities which come from the college experience, and it is important to try to take in as many as possible.

It's important that both people in the relationship openly share their thoughts, emotions, and expectations of how the relationship will work or not work. Many times couples choose to take a break when one goes off to college, because they are moving to a different stage of life. But, there are also many couples who are able to work through this stage and later end up married. Most importantly, make wise decisions that are well thought out. See Chapter 16: Relationships: Dating and Break-Ups.

Many freshmen miss out on a lot of social opportunities, because they are going home to spend time with their boyfriend or girlfriend. What happens a lot? They break up and the freshman in college is left saying, "I feel like I missed out on SO much at school."

Pets

Sometime around the age of seven or eight, you may have convinced your parents in allowing you to keep a puppy or kitten. You proudly gave *your pet* a name and spent countless hours playing with it. The pet quickly won a place in your family's heart and home with quirky behaviors, energetic playfulness and unconditional love. Now fast-forward over a decade later and you are preparing to leave home for college. Just like leaving your friends and family can be difficult, your pet will also be missed as you depart for school. There is no doubt that the unconditional companionship a pet offers will be missed.

Unfortunately, pets' life spans are never as long as we would like, and pets of this age group begin to experience major health issues that can affect their quality of life. When you are away from college, your parents and family may need to make a decision to humanely euthanize the pet to end his or her suffering. Distance from home, college obligations or the seriousness of the pet's problems may not allow you to spend extra time with the pet or even be present for the euthanasia. As your pet has been there for you with unconditional love during tough times, you may feel you are letting your pet down or a sense of abandonment by not being there for them in their final moments of need. Hopelessness, frustration and sadness are normal feelings experienced by college students in this situation. Talk with your parents before you leave about how decisions will be handled concerning the health of your pet. Show extra kindness to your family pet and take pictures with you to college.

Mixed Emotions

Sadness, excitement, anxiety, anger, confusion, fear, and EXCITEMENT!

Yes, these are all very normal emotions and feelings to have as you prepare to leave home. Whether home has been wonderful or stressful, it's been familiar and the unknown of what's to come can cause a variety of emotions. And remember, it's ok for parents and other family members to have these same emotions as well. Chat with your friends and you'll find they are also going through a lot of different emotions. It's important to share what you are feeling with those around you. Seek the advice from older siblings or friends who have gone through the process of leaving home.

Visiting Back Home

Parents and children often have different ideas about how often you will come home from school and what that will look like. It is important to talk about this. Distance from school and transportation can be a contributing factor that helps determine this.

One fun thing to consider is visiting the home of a new friend you meet at school. This is a great way to learn more about your new friends and see different parts of your state or country. Be sure to talk to your parents to see if it would be ok to have friends from school visit prior to showing up in your driveway.

Remember, you can't transition to college if you are never there. Sticking around your college or university on the weekends is a great way to socialize, get caught up on homework, and experience the many extra-curricular activities a college campus has to offer. Yes, high school homecoming football games will compete with these things as well, but your college will have a homecoming game as well. Sometimes the weekends are spent just relaxing and getting caught up in your residence hall room.

My room's a what?

A home office is something a lot of homes may not have...until someone moves off to school. Many families choose to reconfigure their homes when space opens up. Be sure to have conversations about what will happen with your bedroom. Sometimes a younger sibling will lay claim to the room because it is bigger than their current room. Other times, your parents may choose to redecorate and put in a home office or other specialty room. And sometimes the room is left exactly as it was prior to moving out. Be sure to talk about this as your family begins this transition.

Final Thoughts

The summer before you leave for college is one of the most exciting you'll ever have. It's important to have closure at home as you prepare for your new home.

Points to Ponder
- Saying goodbye is sad, but you'll see your friends and family again.
- Don't forget to spend some quality time with extended family, grandparents, younger siblings and pets before you leave.

CHAPTER 5

MOVE-IN DAY
I'M HERE!

"I'm dehydrated."

You're moving to college! The end of the summer has finally come: you've left your summer job, you're all packed and you are ready to move to college. Move-in day marks the transition to the beginning of your college-life.

What to Expect

The Scenario: Hundreds, if not thousands, of students moving into a small area in a limited amount of time. You will be just one of many doing the same things, experiencing the same emotions, standing in the same lines and with the same embarrassing parents.

It will be a long, crazy and busy day. The key to avoid frustrations and an emotional breakdown is to be patient and to go with the flow. Allow extra time in your schedule without a set agenda or deadlines. Delays happen: no close parking, long lines, slow or broken elevators, and congested hallways full of people and boxes. Take a step back and take things in stride. Traveling, checking-in, moving and unpacking is a whole day event. It's a long process: you're moving to college!

Final Checklist

- Check your packing list again (see Chapter 3: Pre-Move)
  - Make one last sweep through the house
- Review and bring any mailings from the college
  - Do you have directions and maps to where you need to go?

- o   Where are you supposed to park? Did you receive a parking pass?
- o   Where is the check-in location? What times can you check-in?
- o   Do you have your housing information?
- Bring a cooler of drinks and snacks. A bottle of cold water tastes very refreshing during move-in.
- Check the weather forecast for the place you are going.
- Pack a small bag of things you will want for the first night in case you don't get everything unpacked right away such as a change of clothes, essential bathroom supplies, and alarm clock.
- Carry a pen with you; it'll come in handy more than once.
- A familiar family treat, such as homemade cookies, may help ease some of the first days of being away from home.

Moving supplies:
- Boxes/containers
- Packing pads/blankets
- Straps/tie-downs/rope
- Tools (tape, hammer, power drill/screwdrivers, measuring tape, Allen wrench)
  - o   You don't need to bring the whole family toolbox. Think ahead of what you'll need to be selective of what to bring.
- Cleaning supplies (cleaner/disinfectant, paper towels, garbage bags)
  - o   It's a good idea to clean your room before you move in. It is much easier to clean before your room becomes cluttered with boxes.
- Door-stops
- Dolly or cart

 You will probably have to go through several doors to get to your room. It makes it a lot easier to move in large items such as a futon if you don't have to worry about keeping doors open.

 You will save yourself time as you combine multiple loads into one. You will be exhausted from moving all day, but your back and feet will be less sore when you use a cart.

Costs of Moving:
- Fuel
- Truck Rental
- Boxes, packing supplies
- Highway tolls, parking
- Food on the go
- Damage during transport

Loading the Car:
- Load last the things you will need right away so they come out first:
  - Tools and cleaning supplies
  - Carpet
  - Heat sensitive or valuable items
  - Bed sheets and pillow
- Keep the check-in information and maps up-front with you in a handy location.
- If you are bringing a cooler for water and snacks, pack it where you can easily access it.
- If your car is completely full now, you will have difficulties moving out in the spring. The simple truth is that you will accumulate more stuff by the time you move out.

It may seem like a great idea to hook up the horse trailer or rent the largest moving truck to move, but consider parking may be limited and congested on move-in day. A very large truck or trailer can become more hassle than help. Remember, many times you can purchase some items when you arrive or grab them if you visit home later in the semester.

 Are others from your hometown also going to the same school? Consider moving together or sharing one moving truck for everyone's large items.

Who's coming with and who's left behind:

Bring:
- Parents
- Brother/Sister
- Boyfriend or Girlfriend
- Family friend who is going to same college

- Your buddy who likes to move boxes

Don't bring:
- Grandma and Grandpa
  - o Invite them up the following week to see how you set up your room. Grandparents are good at bringing gifts or cookies and it will be nice to receive a little reminder of home life after your first week.
- Your 6-year old sibling
  - o They can easily get lost in the craziness of the day. Invite them up with your grandparents. It is important to include them too, so they can understand and adjust to the transition as well.
- The family pet
  - o Other students may be allergic to your pet and most residence halls have a policy against pets, even if just "visiting".

Check-In

The very first thing you need to do when you arrive on campus (right after finding the bathroom) is to check-in. Check-in can last anywhere from ten to 60 minutes or more, depending on the lines. The university regards you as an adult and the check-in is a student orientated process. You will be issued keys for your room, mailbox and/or building, and you will need to sign various forms and complete paperwork such as emergency data information. You will also receive information which might include your contract, rules & policies handbook, room information and/or a welcome letter that outlines upcoming events and where to locate things.

When you check-in ask about parking.
- Where is the best place to park while you move in?
- Where can your family park after the car is unloaded?
- Where can you park your car if you are keeping a car on campus?

Look around and be aware—don't wait in the wrong line!

Remove any tag or mark that identifies your key with your room number. This way, if you lose your key and it is found by someone else, they won't know what room the key unlocks. If you do lose your key, check with the hall desk or your RA for a replacement key. If you are unable to locate your lost key within a reasonable time frame, request to have the locks on your door changed and issued new keys. The expense of this may be passed along to you, but your peace of mind and safety is worth the investment.

Research your options regarding moving in dates and times. There may be an option to move in early if you are willing to pay an extra fee. This may be worthwhile to avoid the big move-in rush or to save your parents from having to take off work. The time of day can also affect your move-in experience. Morning and early afternoon seem to be the busiest times because everyone wants to get there as soon as possible to allow for as much time for moving and setting up. Instead of fighting parking and crowds, consider arriving in the late afternoon or evening--without all the congestion you won't waste time in long lines or trying to move around other people.

Important People to Know:
- Front Desk (Hall Desk) Worker
  - Person who is the primary person involved with the check in process and assigning you your key. This person is a good person to ask about where to park, where to eat, etc.
- Professional or Graduate Staff member
  - Person who manages the building or complex. This person is a good person to answer complex or situational questions or to make room changes.
- Resident Assistant (Community Advisor)
  - Person who supervises your floor or house community. This person is an excellent resource for many academic and social issues. He or she will probably seek you out within the first 48 hours to make sure everything is going well for you but don't be afraid to introduce yourself first.

- Custodian, Maintenance employee
    o Person who cleans and repairs facilities. This person is a good person to contact about fixing something in your room, borrowing a vacuum cleaner or borrowing a cleaning supply you forgot to bring.

Things to Consider:

- Moving is hard work; dress appropriately (exercise clothes IN; flip-flops OUT).
- Save boxes and send empty containers home. Boxes are scarce in the spring when you move out.
- Keep a shopping list of things you now realize you need or forgot.
- Don't plan to buy stuff in town because stores in college towns quickly run out of popular items. If you are waiting to buy larger items for your room, such as a futon, make sure you have a plan of how you plan to bring it home in the spring.
- Be helpful and offer to give a hand to other people moving in. It can be as simple as holding the door open for them. The other people moving in are your neighbors and this is a good way to start making friends.
- Be sure to note and report to your RA or hall desk any damages you find in your room when you move in. By having the damages documented now you avoid being blamed and charged for them at the end of the year.
- Look out for any upcoming social activities such as freshmen welcome activities, floor meetings or informal get-togethers.
- Get away from the craziness of moving in. Enjoy some time with your family before they leave. Walk around campus and have dinner together.

Unpacking:

- Don't make *any* assumptions about the room set-up without involving your roommate.
- Arrange your room in a way that is conducive to studying and sleeping. Also consider privacy factors for you and your roommate.
- Think about what you choose to display in your room. It will give an overall impression of who you are and what you value. Other people will read into this and make assumptions about you.
- Realize you don't need to have everything unpacked in one day.
- Be knowledgeable about the terms and conditions of your residence hall contract. What are the policies and rules on nails and adhesives?
- Your room set-up doesn't have to be perfect. You're probably going to rearrange your room several times throughout the year.
- Have a large trash bag on hand. You're going to generate a lot of trash the first few days.
- Lock your door and don't leave things unattended.

Saying Goodbye

Move-in day is emotional for both parents and students. As already mentioned, move-in day can be stressful, long, and draining. It's also the culmination of two very different points of view. You are eager to be on your own and "leave the nest" and for your parents, they are longing to hold on and pull you closer. This can be like oil and water, and with the added stressors present, this huge step for you can be tainted with fighting and disagreements.

It's important to have conversations prior to leaving home about saying goodbye. As an incoming student, there are so many exciting things happening as you move to school and this "official" goodbye sometimes is hard to make happen.

Most likely, new friends will be made while waiting in line to get your keys or while sharing a moment on an elevator. These new friends may ask you to go out for pizza or go to the bookstore together. These moments are equally as important to your transition as a having a good "goodbye" time with your family.

Remind your parents it's a great accomplishment to go to college and you are ready and excited for it to start. Tell them it is not hard to stay in contact with email, cell phones and visits.

Final Thoughts

The day is winding down and you have the sudden realization this is your first night of college. It's been a stressful day and you are physically and emotionally drained. Your parents are gone and your roommate arrives tomorrow. You're now alone in your new room, unpacked boxes all around you, nothing is plugged in, your alarm clock is blinking the wrong time and everything around you is unfamiliar. You are excited to meet people but you are finding out the first night is not the one big party you imagined it to be. You realize now that college isn't a constant 24/7 party. Don't worry, you are doing fine, you aren't missing anything. Enjoy the moment for what it is. You've just made the move to college. You are tired and decide to go to bed. You miss home already.

Points to Ponder

- This is it, you're now at college!
- Be prepared for an exhausting day both physically and mentally.
- The less you bring, the less you have to move in.
- Make sure your loft ladder is securely attached; never use an unattached ladder on non-carpeted floor or it will slip out from underneath you as your climb on it.
- A lanyard may be helpful to keep track of your keys. You may also be issued a card that serves as an electronic key to the outside of your building.
- Pause and take the 15 minutes needed to thoroughly fill out the room condition card; detail any damage to the room or furniture so that you aren't charged for damages during check out during the end of the year.
- Ease your parents' anxiety by sending them an "I'm doing great" email or card right away.
- Courtesy is contagious.

Freshmen Moments
THE FIRST DAY OF COLLEGE:

Welcome to college!! How's it going so far? What do you think? Is this how you envisioned college to be?

The first thing you may have noticed is there are people *everywhere*: as you walk to class, as you eat your lunch, and even in your bathroom. You can't even retreat to your own room for privacy because you are still trying to figure out this stranger in your room that keeps calling you "roomie". It's ok if you didn't know *anyone* before arriving on campus; in fact, not knowing anyone is sometimes better because it forces you to get out and make new connections instead of leaning on the 'security blanket' of high school friends who are at your college. People are *ridiculously* friendly. But you're loving it; meeting new people is one of the exciting things about college. Another thing is for sure: your feet are killing you from all this walking around campus! There are just so many places to go and things you need to do whether it is to drop off this form, pick up that book or meet some new friends. That's ok though, it will help fend off the Freshmen 15. In fact, do a simple exercise right now: weigh yourself and record it in a safe place. Then look at that weight again on graduation day, you might be surprised or find it interesting at the very least. Let's not talk about graduation day just yet though, since this is your first day! Did you get lost and walk into the wrong classroom today? No worries, no one will even remember by tomorrow. You can just chalk it up as a "freshmen moment". Even walking out of a building from a different entrance can be confusing. Good luck with the rest of the week. Don't forget to call your mom tonight; she misses you, she's been worried about you and would be very excited to hear from you. You would think that after over a decade of "the first day of school" you would be a pro at this by now, but alas you still had trouble falling asleep last night as you were laying there thinking about classes. Now you are tired—what time is college bedtime again?

CHAPTER SIX
INTRODUCTION
OPPORTUNITIES AND CHOICES

"Climb a tree, get a degree?
Outdoor Recreation sounds like the major for me!"

You've decided which college you are going to, got admitted and are feeling pretty good, right? Guess what? You're just getting started with many decisions yet to come! College is just the start of the rest of your life full of a series of choices, decisions to make and abundant opportunities. Up to this point, you were not an adult and many of the opportunities and decisions that were made were based on where you lived and with whom you lived (parents, parents, parents). You're now on your own to make some pretty important decisions.

As cliché as it may sound, going to college is going to provide you so many opportunities. Some of these may be insignificant (which type of shampoo you are now going to use), while others will be a bit more significant (your future career). There will be times you'll consult with friends and family as you make decisions. Other times, you'll have to make a quick decision. These opportunities and choices will culminate as you continue through college, and you'll soon realize you're developing problem solving skills and, hopefully, having an enjoyable and educational time doing so.

Changes, Changes, Changes

Your life is going to change more than you may have thought. Up to this point in your life, most things have been laid out for you. Your parents lived in a certain community and sent you to a certain school. That school probably had one option for lunch each day and when you got home, the food on the table was already in place. Most of the classes you took at your school were predetermined and the amount of extra activities was also somewhat limited. The toothpaste in the medicine cabinet was probably whatever your mom picked up at the store this week. Your expenses were probably limited to putting some gas in your car, weekend fun, and other smaller items.

You've now entered a world of many choices. The following chapters will help guide you through making wise decisions when these opportunities arrive. In fact, the classes and homework become the easy part for many college students, while all the other choices and consequences of the choices become the stressful part of the college life. Begin thinking of how you and your family make both insignificant and significant choices. Have you been pleased with how things have gone or would you have done things differently. Before you get too deep into college really think about these changes and how you'll handle them.

I Want To Be a _____ When I Grow Up

One of the first decisions you'll make is what you'll major in. There are many great options available at your school for you to choose and you may have even picked your specific college based on their options. Be sure to critically think through why you want to major in something. Are you thinking about the large paychecks which could come with certain degrees? Are you thinking something easy so you'll have more time to play intramural sports with your friends while in college? Will the major help you get into a certain graduate program? Make the decision based on what's best for YOU, not what your new friends you met at the dining hall want.

Be sure you don't rush this decision. If you have a few things you've been thinking about majoring in, explore these options a bit before you commit. Resist the temptation to do what your friend is doing because you want to take classes with them. Think about future job markets and your goals and dreams and how they all interact. Remember, you can always get a minor in an area that interests you but doesn't seem like a good career path. See Chapter 20 for more information on majors.

So Much to Do, So Little Time

While college may or may not be the best four (or five plus) years of your life, it for sure is a time in your life where the opportunities are abundant and unique. The atmosphere on a college campus provides opportunities to learn outside the classroom, try new things, and experience things you may never get to experience again. And at the end of your college journey, hopefully you're not saying, "I wish I would have."

These are the fun choices you are going to get to make. Maybe you've always wanted to learn ballroom dancing and you see a flyer for the ballroom dancing club? Should you go or not go? That's totally up to you! Your academic program may offer a study abroad program. When else in your life will you be able to travel to another country, experience their culture while learning and earn college credit? Maybe you witness a protest on campus which challenges your beliefs? You could try out to be your college's mascot. Again there are so many opportunities. Your job is to figure out what best fits your personality, goals, schedule and interests. If you maximize this time in college, your college experience may become some of the best years of your life, and you'll have lifelong memories.

Consequences

From a very early age, we are drilled with the idea that with every decision we make, there are consequences. Simple concept, yet still true as you continue through college. If you choose to stay up late with your friends playing video games, you'll be tired the next day and maybe less motivated to go to class. If you choose to go to a floor dinner in your residence hall, you may meet new friends. If everyone on the floor buys a new TV and you follow their lead, you'll have less money for other things. You get the idea of how consequences work. Some are more serious than others. If you choose to copy some answers from the person sitting next to you during an exam, you may instantly fail that test. If you choose to drink underage and the party is shut down by the police, you may be arrested.

Be sure to consider the positive and negative consequence of decisions you make while in college. Some consequences are short term and others longer term. Being sleepy the day after a fun night with friends is sometimes a welcomed consequence. Deciding to be a dance major to meet women may have long term consequences if you can't get a job and paid a lot of money for that degree. Always think through decisions and don't be afraid to seek advice and wisdom from trusted people in your life.

Final Thoughts

Be excited! You have so many great opportunities, and you get to direct which way your life is headed. Learn from those around you and ask lots of questions. Go beyond your comfort zone. Try tofu in the dining center if you haven't before or try an intramural sport you've never played. The opportunities are endless.

Enjoy learning how you make decisions. And remember, many of the decisions you get to make won't have a "right answer," so decide on what's best for you and move on. If you make a make a decision you are not happy with or it has consequences you weren't ready for, you can usually bounce back.

Points to Ponder
- Every decision you make will have some type of consequence
- How will you get outside of your comfort zone in college?
- What are you nervous about as you think about your transition?
- Who do you know that always seems to make wise decisions? How can you be more like them?
- Variety is good in your life.
- You are not the only one going through this.
- If you make a mistake, learn from it and move on.

CHAPTER 7

CAMPUS HOUSING
DORM-LIFE

"The harsh realities of dorm life: high-speed internet, cable TV, three meals a day."

Your new home away from home: the place you will live, sleep, eat, learn and meet with friends. College housing provides an unmatched social connection and will probably be the only time in your life where you live among so many people your age. Strong bonds are formed with the people who live near you, as you share the triumphs and set-backs of your formative first-year of college. This can lead to a unique phenomenon where the people you live with, through random housing assignments your first year, will become your future college roommates and still be your close friends when you are a graduating senior and beyond.

Definitions

On-campus vs. Off-campus:
Living "on-campus" means living in a facility owned or associated with the university which may include residence halls ("dorms") or Greek housing (fraternities-male housing, or sororities-female housing); Living "off-campus" means living in a facility not associated with the university, usually privately owned apartment complexes or houses.

Room vs. Board:
Room refers to the cost of the rent and utilities for your living space while board refers to the cost of the meal plan for dining services.

Standard Room vs. Suite Room:

A standard room is a single room usually shared with a roommate, typically with a community bathroom located on the floor; a suite is a room with its own bathroom or shared between two rooms.

Resident Assistant (RA) vs. Hall Director:

A Resident Assistant is an upperclassmen student hired to serve as a resource for you and lives on your floor; A Hall Director is a professional staff member who supervises the RA's and manages the residence hall building

Residence hall assignment priority is usually assigned on a first-come, first-serve basis. To reserve a spot, you are typically required to complete a housing application that includes a nonrefundable deposit. You are usually required to have been accepted by the university before you can apply for housing. Many schools also include a questionnaire to assist roommate matching (questions may include smoking, studying and sleeping habits). It is important to be truthful on your housing questionnaire to help prevent conflicts as a result of mismatched roommates.

You may have the option to request which housing building you would like to live in. It is important to research the benefits of each residence hall on campus and rank these benefits according to your own personal preference and priorities. "Hidden" benefits of a particular building may include: proximity to your classes, proximity to the fitness center, the number of first-year students who live on your floor or the number of students with the same major as you, etc.

What are the benefits of living in campus housing?

If you looked at residence halls from an outside perspective, you would be amazed at first that people even choose to live there. Imagine you moved to a new town and a realtor showed you a place that consisted of just a room, with no kitchen, living space or bathroom. And in this 12' X 18' room, you were expected to share it with someone you have never met (see Chapter 8: Roommates). Your bathroom and shower was located down the hallway, which is shared with 40 other strangers. You must pay for five months of rent all at once when you move-in, and the room rental rate is quite expensive when you consider your roommate is also paying the same rate for the room. This is the description of a typical residence hall. However the benefits of campus housing are unmatched:

- Community

    The people living around you share common space such as the bathroom, laundry room and dining center. A sense of comradery develops as you identify with your new home and form friendships.

    Take pride in your community and help keep it clean. Don't be a nosebleed and steal everyone's marker board markers or wipe off half of their messages causing it to be unreadable. Don't leave food in the drinking fountain. Take pride in where you live!

- Social Connections

    There are a variety of ways to get to know the people around you and to become an involved member of your living community. There may be opportunities for residence hall student government positions, intramural sport teams, study groups, social activities or even just joining a group for meals. The residence halls are the social hubs of most colleges.

- Academic Resources

    People living around you may be taking the same classes or have the same major as you. It is easy to form study groups, ask homework questions borrow textbooks, and walk to class together.

- Services

    The residence halls provides many services, such as cooking your meals, cleaning the facilities, and providing maintenance repairs for your room, to help save you time so that you can focus on being a student. They employ staff members to help you resolve conflicts or seek additional help for social or academic assistance. The hall desk may provide equipment rentals (which are often free) including power tools, sports gear or movies.

- Location

    Living on-campus among hundreds of your peers is part of the "college experience" that provides unique opportunities and lasting friendships and memories. You will also appreciate the proximity of your classes during unfavorable weather.

- Fixed Utility Costs

    No matter how much you crank the heat in the winter or if you leave your computer on 24/7, your utility use charges will not increase since it is already part of the room costs. But, it is always a good idea to conserve energy to help the environment and to keep costs lower for everyone.

- Free immunity

    Residence halls are the perfect breeding grounds for infectious diseases to spread with hundreds of students living in a small space, breathing the same air and sharing everything from door handles, to common dining hall silverware, to community bathrooms. All of this germ exposure will build your immune system day by day. So next time you are grossed out by the drinking fountain or condition of the bathroom, reframe your mindset to think what a great opportunity to become a stronger, healthier person—free immunity for everybody!

Top 10 Reasons People Move Out:

1. Roommate conflict

   It can be an uncomfortable and awkward situation if you do not get along with your roommate. Sharing the same common space with a person you do not trust or get along with makes it hard to avoid conflict.

2. Privacy

   You are constantly surrounded by people and you may feel you have no personal space to retreat to. Your roommate is always conscious of what you are doing in the room or if you are not home. There is only one door to your room and you can't avoid seeing people on your floor.

3. Noise

   With many people living in a small area, combined with thin walls, noise can be a very frustrating issue. Noise can affect your studying and sleeping habits.

4. Food

   Other people are choosing what you eat for each meal. You may miss certain favorite foods or want other foods during a particular meal. You may feel it would be cheaper to buy and cook your own food.

5. Rules and Resident Assistants

   You may not agree with certain policies or feel resentment for being documented for a judicial violation. You may feel you are being "policed" and have to watch your every step.

6. Stigma

   Some people feel it is not socially acceptable to still live in campus housing or the dorms as an upperclassman.

7. Didn't feel included or connected to the community

   You may not like the people you live around and were left excluded from activities and cliques.

8. Cost

   You may find a better deal off campus that provides you more space for less money.

9. Bathrooms

    Lack of bathroom privacy or cleanliness cause some people to move-out.

10. Different experiences

    Some people find other opportunities they want to experience such as Greek-life or living in an apartment.

Top 6 Reasons People Move Back To Residence Life after Living Off-campus:

1. Loneliness

    Off-campus living may lack the residence hall sense of community and people feel they are missing social opportunities. Most students off-campus don't even know their neighbors. They often eat alone and hang out with just their roommates.

2. Hunger

    People who move off-campus often underestimate the time required for preparing their meals including shopping, cooking and cleaning. As a result nutrition is often sacrificed for quick meals or more money is spent by dining out more often (see Chapter 10: Campus Food).

3. Un-enforced rules

    Students may find landlords are reluctant to enforce polices, such as noise, so as not to lose their renters. If there are roommate conflicts there are no resident assistants to help mediate.

4. Distance from campus

    You will have to drive, bike or walk an extra distance to arrive on campus. The benefits of living on campus near your classes are more appreciated during inclement weather. Living off-campus also means you have to allow for more time to get to your classes and have to wake up that much earlier in the morning.

5. Landlords

    Some landlords can be slow to repair problems with your apartment and most do not offer help in mediating social conflicts. Also, you may have to sign a one-year lease even if you do not plan to live there during the summer; if this is the case, then it is your responsibility to either find a sub-leaser (usually offered at a discounted rental rate at a loss to you) for those summer months or to pay the rent while you are not living there.

6. Cash-Flow problems

    Some students are not able to budget well and run out of money before bills are paid each month. This can be especially true during either cold or hot weather when energy costs can spike as more gas or electricity is used to heat or cool your apartment. Many students will forgo many of the luxuries they took for granted while living in the residence halls such as cable TV and internet to save costs.

A Closer Look at Residence Halls

Your Room

Arrange your room to maximize space (see Chapter 3: Premove to see what is included in a typical dorm room). Keep privacy as well as studying and sleeping preferences in mind.

Your RA may have welcomed you to the residence halls by placing a decoration on your door with your name. Most students will place a marker board on their door for their friends to leave messages and some will choose to place photos of themselves on the door. Think carefully about what you post on your door. Other people will pass by your door every day and will make assumptions about you based on what you post on your door. Don't post schedules of where you are and when you aren't home. Think about other pictures, new paper articles, comic strips, etc you are posting and what message you are sending. Keep in mind RAs, parents, visiting high school seniors and even children are likely to see your door postings as well.

You can usually tell if someone is home by watching the light coming through their peephole. If the light switches back and forth from light to dark they are probably looking at you. If you don't want people to know you are home, hang a towel behind your peephole or cover it with something else to block the light.

Also, be aware that some people may try to "reverse" your peephole—allowing them to see *into* your room from the outside hallway. Hanging a towel over your peephole helps decrease this potential invasion of privacy.

A word on lofts

When you think about it for the next year or more you will be sleeping in the air, probably less than a couple feet from the ceiling. Follow your common sense to prevent injuries from your loft:

- If you are inebriated consider sleeping on the floor, futon or couch for the night to avoid the risk of falling out of your loft.
- Don't forget how close you are to the ceiling to prevent hitting your head.
- Make sure you put it together properly.
- Leave guard rails attached to prevent rolling out of your loft.

- Also make sure the ladder is securely attached before using it; never use an unattached ladder on a non-carpeted floor.
- Set up your loft so that you could quickly climb down in case of an emergency and that your loft is not blocking your exit.

Co-ed Housing Myths
There are many misconceptions to the definition of "co-ed" housing. Some falsely believe this means their roommate could be someone of the opposite sex or that the community bathroom and showers will be shared by both men and women. Co-ed housing can mean a variety of things but neither of the aforementioned examples is correct. Co-ed housing typically means you share common spaces with the opposite sex and that both males and females live on your floor. However, bathroom facilities are kept separate and your roommate will be of the same sex.

Lock your door.

Always, *always* lock your door. Make sure you and your roommate agree that if no one is home, the door should be locked. You should also lock it at night as well when you are asleep. And here's why:

1. Theft

    College dorm rooms are full of high-value targets including cash, laptops, DVDs, CDs, MP3 players, expensive textbooks, etc, all conveniently located in a small space. The best way to remedy this is to keep your door locked...plain and simple.

2. Room damage

    Intoxicated people returning home late on a weekend night might mistake your room for the bathroom. It has happened plenty of times and there are few things worse than waking up in the middle of the night as the sound of urine or vomit is hitting all of your stuff.

Mike Story Box

A fellow RA at my college received a strange duty phone call early in the morning. A resident's boyfriend had been visiting and became intoxicated. He was too drunk to get back to his girlfriend's room after using the restroom and instead crashed in the next available unlocked room. When the residents of the room woke up the next morning, they found a completely naked guy passed out and curled up on their floor.

3. Sexual Assault
       Although rare, it does happen on college campuses. As simple as locking your door at night could prevent this devastating nightmare.

Generally, door to door solicitation is not allowed in residence halls due to safety considerations. **Know that you do not always have to answer your door.** Be cautious of any solicitors who would like to talk more inside your room or who need money on the spot, including checks. A classical example of a solicitation scam are solicitors who are selling magazine subscriptions and either swindle you out of money for a false magazine subscription that is never delivered or attempts to sexually assault you by inviting themselves inside your room for a closer look at the magazine lists they are offering. Unfortunately, the no solicitation rules also may mean no Halloween trick-or-treaters and no Girl Scout Cookies.

Make it a routine to check your mailbox on a daily basis to stay abreast on important mailings and to help keep your mailbox clear as your mailbox space will be limited. After dinner is a convenient time to check your mailbox. In college, you can even occasionally receive mail on Sundays if someone is working the desk and non-postal ("campus mail"), university notifications or club flyers are distributed. Remember to discuss with your roommate beforehand how they would like their mail to be handled (see Chapter 8: Roommates).

Hall Desk

The hall desk serves as a service desk and is a great resource for many of your questions. The hall desk often serves as the mail center where you will receive your mail as well as packages and special deliveries such as flowers. The hall desk may provide other services such as checking-out power tools, sports equipment or movies.

To reduce the amount of junk mail and/or credit card applications you receive, contact the mailing company directly and ask them to permanently remove you from their advertising list or search the internet for various sources that will help remove your information from multiple sources.

Dining Center

In addition to the main dining center where you will eat most of your meals (see Chapter 10: Campus Food), there may be other food venues or convenience-stores run by dining services for after meal snacking.

When you order a pizza they may not deliver it directly to your door. Your residence hall may have a designated spot, such as the hall desk, for meeting delivery food drivers.

Community Bathrooms

If you do not live in a suite-style room (see above), you will most likely use a community bathroom located on your floor. Typically the bathroom will contain three to five bathroom stalls, three to five showers and five or more sinks and is cleaned daily by professional custodians. A public bathroom is a public bathroom. That is: you don't need to come back to the residence hall bathroom if you are on campus during the day.

 Designate a pair of sandals or flip-flops when showering to keep your feet off the floor. Besides people urinating in the shower, find out other reasons why in the Chapter 18: Health and Safety.

 Figure out the best time in your schedule to shower to avoid long-lines and to avoid running out of hot water. There will be a "morning-rush" for shower use. Another factor to consider is to plan your showers shortly after the bathroom is cleaned for the day.

Community bathrooms will challenge your comfort level, from walking down the hallway in just your towel or robe, having to listen to other people urinate, using not so private showers and trying to find just the right position to set your toiletry bag on the sink counter without it touching any rogue hairs or makeup. The mutual experience of these less than optimal conditions can lead to a common bond among your floor mates while you brush your teeth as you discuss the unexplained smell always associated with turning on shower #2.

Common Floor Spaces

Your residence may have a large meeting room where you will gather for "floor meetings" to discuss upcoming events or residence issues. There may be rooms designated for quiet or group study space. There may also be a kitchenette, which consists of a stove/oven and sink. The kitchenette is used for cooking the occasional meal or baking homemade treats such as cookies. There may also be some "green space" for you to play and catch Frisbees or football as well as basketball courts, tennis courts, etc.

You may not have realized it but your only source of water may be the drinking fountain. Be sure to make a conscious effort to stay hydrated by carrying a water bottle with you.

Laundry Room

This typically consists of one central facility with multiple washers and dryers, making "laundry day" quite efficient as you can run several loads of wash at once.   For more advice on laundry at college see Chapter 9: Laundry.

Parking

Parking is usually limited or nonexistent in the area where you live due the value of land space on college campuses.   Close parking is usually reserved for university faculty, residence hall staff, student government or students with off-campus jobs.   See Chapter 13: Transportation, for more information on cars and parking.

Trash

You are usually responsible for removing your own room trash.   There will either be a trash chute or collection area on your floor or a dumpster outside the building.

Protect your identity by using a paper shredder for any papers that include your personal information—this is especially important in college as you may receive many documents with important numbers on them including your student identification number, your social security number, your loan or bank information or unsolicited credit card applications.

Use grocery bags or bags as garbage bags to save money.

Computer Lab

The computer lab may consist of five to 20 computers, usually with a mix of Window and Mac computers. You may have to supply your own paper for the printers. Computer labs are not as popular as they once were as many students now have their own personal laptop. However computer labs are great for group project work.

Maintenance Center

Most residence halls will have their own maintenance center that helps fix and repair your facilities. Their functions range from changing door locks and replacing air-conditioning filters to replacing missing peep-holes or burnt-out lights. If you need something fixed in your room, there should be a process for you (online submission form, number to call, report problem to RA, etc) to request a work order to have it repaired.

Elevator

If your building is big enough, there may be an elevator. There are many unwritten rules to using the elevator. For instance, in a ten story building, be prepared to get many angry looks if you hit the "2" button as you get on. While elevator pranks may seem fun, remember these are very costly pieces of equipment and if they are damaged, you probably don't want to foot the bill. This includes trying to cram as many people in as possible.

College Curfew?
Generally, there is not a designated college curfew or college bedtime. The cause of this misconception is because the exterior doors to the outside of your residence hall building may be locked after a specified time each night. You can still enter your building after this time; you just need to remember to bring your keys or other access device (such as an 'electronic key card') with you.

Fire Drills

As you acquaint yourself with your new room and building, find out where the nearest fire exits are and the location of fire extinguishers. Do you know what you should do if there is a tornado, hurricane, earthquake or terrorist attack? There will most likely be a scheduled fire drill planned shortly after you arrive in the fall. Every year college students are killed in fires: take every fire alarm seriously. Whenever you hear the fire alarm, exit the building as fast as you can, even if you just finished showering or it's 3:00 in the morning. Don't try to carry any of your stuff out with you although you usually will have time to slip on shoes and grab a coat, if needed, as you are exiting. Close your door behind you to help prevent smoke damage and fire spread. Move away from the building when you exit to stay safe and to allow emergency personnel access to the problem. If you are not hurt, consider leaving the area for a while to study or socialize with friends and come back later after the alarm has been reset instead of having to stand outside for long periods of time.

Working in the Halls

Having a quarter or part-time job while in college can help reduce your final loan debt or give you extra discretionary income (see Chapter 14: Finances). Finding a job on campus is beneficial because:

- Employers understand you are a student first and adapt your work-schedule around your class schedule.
- You are close enough to your job that you can walk there, saving you both time and money.
- Most of your coworkers will be other students, and it's another way to connect with other people.

On-campus part-time residence hall jobs to consider include:

- Hall desk worker
  - Responsibilities may include: sorting student mail, checking out equipment or keys and other administrative duties
- Dining Services
  - Responsibilities may include: serving food, re-supplying dishware, cleaning tables and washing dishes

- Janitorial Services
    - Responsibilities may include: collecting bathroom trash, vacuuming hallways and cleaning windows
- Maintenance
    - Responsibilities may include: general facility repairs, regularly scheduled filter and battery replacements, emergency facility crisis response (ex: flooding water)
- Student Security
    - Responsibilities may include: locking doors, documenting policy violations and responding to calls
- Resident Assistant:
    - See below

Resident Assistants

Residents Assistants or Community Advisors are upperclassmen who have been hired by the Department of Residence to serve as a representative and liaison between the department and students as a live-in staff member. At first you may be afraid of your RA because you have been told of their role as an enforcer of policies, but you will soon discover your RA is beneficial for networking and meeting other students, helpful for connecting you with academic or social resources and can help mediate conflicts and solve problems. RAs are "in the know" of upcoming events, and building issues. They gather bits and pieces of information from everyone and can see overall patterns or complete stories. It is important to get to know your RA; they will be interested in getting to know you as well.

RAs are:

- Advisors
- Resources
- Advocates
- Role-Models
- Friends
- Activity Planners
- Students, too!

Other Responsibilities of the RA usually include:

- RA training
- Conducting Check-ins and check-outs
- Keeping in touch with all residents
- Working at the hall desk
- Staff meetings and floor meetings
- Regularly reporting to the hall director

- "On-call" duty overnights
- Programming initiatives
- Opening and closing of the hall responsibilities

Personality Line-Up: RA personalities

- the cop RA
    The RA who polices you like a hawk. Oh no, is that an illegal toaster in your room?
- the hider RA
    The RA who is too busy and involved in other campus organizations, you never see him or her. The floor rules in chaos.
- the RA-RA
    The RA who seems to be on a different wavelength and "doesn't get it". They want to apply RA theories to the floor and have no realistic ideas and don't relate well to the residents.
- the Barney RA
    The "let's all be friends" push-over RA that will let you get away with murder on the floor in order to avoid confrontation and keep everyone on their friend list.
- the good RA
    The all around good RA who does their job well, is there when you need them and is respected.
- the milker RA
    This RA is there for one reason only, the money. Often a "burnt-out" RA who is around for one more year before cashing out.

Do you want to be an RA?

There are many benefits to the RA position beyond the monetary compensation, which typically includes free room and board and a semester stipend. As a RA, you will meet a lot of people you probably wouldn't have otherwise met. RAs on staff together usually form close friendships and offer each other support; RAs are typically campus leaders and well connected and influential individuals. You will learn and practice important skills that will carry over and be beneficial in your future workplace such as conflict-resolution, problem-solving and networking. Your RA experiences will build your resume. Many future employers will see this experience and value your responsibility and leadership. Being an RA carries immediate trust and people you just met will confide their secrets to you. You can understand and get to know people on a deeper level. And there can be other little perks: like moving in early, having your own room and planning activities.

There is usually no-set personality or "mold" that the Department of Residence is looking for (they take all types), but typically they value people with diversity experience, academic strength and people who want to learn and grow personally and professionally from the position. They generally don't prefer applicants that just want the money or those that won't have time for the position. Be confident in yourself and ask your RA how to apply.

Mike Story Box

As a RA, you can also influence many decisions about upcoming activities and how house or hall money is spent. Multiple fundraisers for the local animal shelter were organized under my direction as a RA which I influenced as a pre-vet major. My community service work through these fundraisers later helped me earn scholarships during veterinary school.

Professional Staff

Usually your building or complex will have a full-time professional in charge, namely a hall director or complex director (and many times a graduate student as well). These people have extensive training in many different areas and are there to oversee the operations of the hall. They have chosen a profession that helps college students succeed, so don't be afraid to get to know them. Ask your RA about the professional staff in your area and stop and meet them. They can assist if there are issues on your floor, if you are having roommate issues or if you need some advice.

Residence Hall Policies

Residence hall polices can be found in the Terms and Conditions of your housing contract. This document is usually available online or obtained by calling your housing department and asking for a copy. Residence hall policies exist mainly for safety reasons. The policies are also intended to help maintain peace and harmony among many students, typically of the ages 18-22, who are living, eating and breathing in a small space. The policies serve as a starting point to help mediate conflict between students.

Each policy has a purpose to it. For example, let's assume you have the option to live in a "dry" building (alcohol-free) or a "wet" building (alcohol is allowed). Your first reaction may be to choose the "wet" building, but you should consider how a "dry" building may benefit you:

1. By living in an alcohol-free building, you live in an environment that is free from negative alcohol-related behavior and nuisances. The community bathroom will stay cleaner on the weekends from less inappropriate urination and vomiting. Your sleep and study schedules will be interrupted less frequently due to noise from loud parties or from inebriated people shouting in the hallways. Your living space will be safer with less random acts of vandalism.

2. If you are a college freshman, you are most likely under the legal age to purchase, possess or consume alcohol and thus living in a "dry" building would have no effect on your current liberties and will help prevent any situational university 'misunderstanding' that effects your judicial standing.

Respect and Tolerance

There will be many different types of people living in relatively small community. Some of these people will look, act or think differently than you and that's alright. In fact, it's a great opportunity to learn about how others live their lives. What's not a good idea is to be harassing *any* individuals. Remember, everyone has a right to feel safe and be comfortable in their living environment. Doing or saying discriminatory things against another person is a quick way to face some serious consequences while in college (and may be your ticket out the door).

Noise

When you are part of a residence hall community, you have to realize that your actions can affect multiple people since everyone lives so close together. Being excessively loud is a prime example. Noise not only affects people who are trying to study, but also people who are sleeping or taking a nap, have a headache or don't feel well, or talking on the phone or watching a movie, etc. And so, if you are playing your music really loudly it won't take long for you to become unpopular. Students often cite "loudness" as a reason for leaving the residence halls; and usually it is only a handful of people that are actually being loud. Here is some advice to keep the peace with your neighbors:

- Follow quiet hours.
- Play your music at appropriate times (Wednesday evening people are studying; Saturday evening people are socializing).
- When you do play your music, don't play it for hours on end.
- Keep your door shut when you are being loud. As much as you would like to think the other people around you enjoy the same music, they don't.
- Follow 24 hour courtesy hours. If someone asks you to turn down your music, don't be a jerk about it, and just turn it down. You don't know when you might need the same courtesy. Also, keep in mind there are two sides to quiet hours: late at night and early in the morning.

- Don't assume that just because it is a weekend night, that no one needs it quiet. Some weekends, athletes have to get up early to leave for a game, band members might have to practice early in the morning, most graduate testing is at 8 AM on Saturdays, some clubs meet early on the weekends to leave for a trip, etc.
- If you do have a neighbor that is constantly loud, *you* need to take the initiative to ask them to turn it down. Don't assume a RA can hear it too or is around to confront it. You probably don't want to cause unnecessary conflict with your neighbors, but it is better to confront it early in the semester than to let it grow into a bigger problem.
- If someone does keep coming to you about noise, get the hint! Talk with them and figure out a schedule that works for both of you for quiet time and not so quiet time.

Don't be the nosebleed who forgets to turn off their alarm-clock before leaving for the weekend. If your alarm clock goes off all day, your RA may have to enter your room when you aren't there to turn it off. Do you really want a RA in your room when you're not around?

Policy highlights

Candles
Candles are usually prohibited due to the extreme danger an unattended open flame presents to the residence hall community. There are multiple reports in the news of candles starting building fires causing smoke and property damage and even human fatalities.

Alcohol
Alcohol and related-behavior, such as noise, vandalism and vomiting can affect the residence hall community at-large. Alcohol can also cause many social, financial and academic problems. If you are under the age of 21 and you choose to drink alcohol, be prepared for any consequences for your decision, which may include fines, alcohol-education classes, or university probation or notation on your permanent record. See Chapter 15: Alcohol for more information.

You can be caught for drinking even *after* your party. For example, you throw away the empty beer cans with your pizza boxes: the same pizza boxes that have your name, room number and phone number.

Hall sports

Most residence halls prohibit playing sports in the hallways such as kicking a ball or throwing a Frisbee indoors. This is mainly for safety reasons, if someone were to walk onto the floor or leave a room when a ball is flying through the air and it could hit them; the ball can also cause damage to walls or bulletin boards. Bouncing a basketball indoors is extremely annoying to anyone below you or anyone who is studying.

Guests

You are responsible for your visiting guests and their behaviors. If your guest violates a policy, you are equally responsible for the consequences.

Be a good host when your friend from high school or buddy from another college comes to visit you: give them your attention, show them around campus, plan some fun activities, and include them with your friends. You'll also want to check to be sure it's ok with your roommate, find out where they can park their car and provide them clean towels and bed (futon) sheets. Also find out how you can purchase extra meal passes to your dining hall.

The Judicial Process

So what happens when you are caught violating a residence hall or university policy? Usually it is brought to the attention of a RA, who will document the alleged violation and your behaviors, either through an email or incident report, which will be sent to the hall director. The hall director will then contact you to set up a time to meet with you to discuss the incident during a judicial hearing. At this time the hall director will determine what role you had in violating a policy and will impose sanctions depending on the severity of the violation which can include: a verbal reprimand, a warning letter, fines, education assignments or classes, or residence hall probation or expulsion. Some schools also turn this process over to the students who live in the area by using a judicial board of student leaders.

If you are confronted by a residence hall staff member, such as a RA, for a policy violation, it is in your best interests to be honest and cooperative (that is, don't try to run away). Cooperation on your part may help you later during your judicial hearing and consequent sanctions. Be polite to the RA confronting you. It is their job to enforce policies. Most RAs would rather spend their time on community building and social activities than on confronting and documenting policy violations.

Top Four Reasons People Are Caught Violating a Policy

- Your *behavior* is affecting the community (ex: loud music) or an individual (ex: roommate harassment).
- You failed to read the terms and conditions of your residence hall contract or the university student handbook and do not fully understand the expectations.
- Violating the policy (ex: illegally drinking alcohol in your room) has become so habitual that you have lost concern of being caught because you have gotten away with it for so many times before.
- Bad timing. (ex: the exact moment you are trying to sneak alcohol into your room is the same moment the RA walking by on duty-rounds turns the corner and sees you).

At most universities, staff members do not have the right to invade your personal space, unless a life-threatening emergency or court-ordered warrant mandated it. However, they can *ask* to come into your room or they can *ask* you to open your backpack or refrigerator.

College Pranks

Your parents or others may tell you of college pranks they pulled "back in the day". All good college pranks have five elements:

1. No rules are broken. There are two documents you need to find: your university student handbook and the residence hall's terms and conditions. Knowledge of loopholes is the keystone: make sure you know the rules inside and out so you know exactly what will get you in trouble and what won't.
2. No individual person or groups of people are the victims of your prank. Your prank needs to be appropriate so that anyone can have a good laugh. Targeting a specific campus group is in bad-taste, especially if it is racist or sexist and will not be tolerated by your university; targeting an individual person is mean-spirited and cruel.
3. No one is harmed and no property is damaged. If you make a mess, you take responsibility to clean it up after the prank is completed.
4. No one is inconvenienced by your prank.
5. The prank is original, unique and has a surprise element to it. No one else on your campus has ever played the prank before.

Some examples of bad pranks vs. good pranks:

Bad pranks:
1. Pulling the fire alarm or discharging a fire extinguisher. This is a bad prank because not only will you get into serious trouble with the law and your university, but all of your friends will be upset with you because they had to evacuate their rooms.
2. "Pennying" someone's door. This is a bad prank because the person is not able to leave their room to use the bathroom, attend class or to exit quickly if there is an emergency until the door is fixed. It also damages the door/door jam which is considered vandalism and you may be responsible for costs needed to fix it.

 To "penny" someone's door means to jam pennies or other coins into the very small space found between the door and the door frame when the door is closed. When "pennied-in", it is almost impossible to open the door.

 If you are "pennied-in", try pushing the door up and to the side if there is a small space underneath your door for your hands to grab a hold of the door from the bottom; this will often cause the pennies' positions to shift and fall out, enabling you to open your door. If this is not successful, call your RA or maintenance center so that they can dissemble the door from the outside in order for you to exit your room.

3. Having pop-cans or popcorn fall into someone's room when they open the door. This is a bad prank because it has been done so many times before and it requires a lot of clean-up.

Good pranks:
1. Recruit your friends to help build a snowman inside the first shower stall in the community bathroom right before other students are waking up for the day. As your floor-mates are about to take their morning shower, they will be quite surprised and confused to see a snowman looking back at them when they draw the shower curtain back. This is a good prank, because everyone can find it humorous, it works on more than one person

without targeting any specific person and it is easy to clean up (give the snowman a hot shower and watch as it melts down the drain).

2. Load your mini-dorm fridge with one of every possible drink you can think of. Use vending machines to purchase individual cans or bottles. Then, invite your friends over for a movie night and offer them a drink. When they ask what you have to offer, most will expect two or three choices, but you can name off the 40 or 50 drinks you have stored in your mini dorm fridge. This is a good prank because your friends will not be expecting it and it is easy to accomplish.

3. Outline several body forms in chalk outside your residence hall entrance doors to create the appearance of a crime scene. Make it complete with a few small circles for the bullet shell case outlines. This is a good prank because the chalk is easily washed away and no one is actually hurt.

At the hall desk, ask if you can put nails in the wall to hang pictures? They will say no. Then ask, "But, what if I remove the nails before I check out?" The answer will still remain no. Finally ask to check out a hammer.

- Give a guided tour of your room: bedroom (your lofted bed), study den (your desk with a computer on it), your kitchen (consists of a mini-fridge and maybe a microwave), your TV room (futon across from your TV), your hallway entrance (consists of about 12 inches as you first enter your room), your planetarium (glow in the dark stars on ceiling), your aquarium (beta fish in a small bowl on your desk), etc.

- Be proud of the fact you live in the residence halls. Tell people about the 1,000 room mansion you live in, the full-time chefs that prepare you three meals a day, the team of custodians that clean your bathroom every single day, the full fire suppression system in place complete with sprinklers, the security and guard system including automatic locks and 24/7 on-call assistance, etc.

- Keep fish in your room where the fish's names changes to whoever is visiting you at the moment----people find it an odd coincidence the fish have the same name as them but they also feel kind of special too. This will create an awkward situation when the person later visits with friend and the fish's name has changed.

- Tell your friends to thank their mom for sending you a care package. When they act surprised, ask "oh, she didn't send you one too?" Then shrug your shoulders and look confused and mumble, "the cookies were delicious."

- When the fire alarm sounds, "Alright! Now we get to use the fire emergency exit only door!!!"

- Pushing the elevator button for level three when they really want four--in large groups people just follow each other off, then quickly close the doors.

- Be right there at the elevator doors to rush in when they open. Push the people trying to exit if necessary.

- After a long weekend when the all of the floor bathroom sinks are really gross and dirty, clean one up really well and place an "out of order sign" on it.

- Tuck in your roommate at night.

- Have a "wet t-shirt" contest. Literally, wet t-shirts on hangers.

Final Thoughts

This is your community. Take pride. Speak up. You should be able to solve your own confrontations. Use your RA to help you develop conflict-resolution skills or to help mediate if the other person is not being reasonable.

No one is going to tell you to clean your room or make your bed. On the other hand, no one is going to clean your room or make your bed except you. Get in the habit to take at least an hour or so a week to spruce up your room: take out the trash, organize your stuff, run the vacuum, dust, etc. Don't be the messy kid no one wants to hang out with.

Points to Ponder

- As a general rule of thumb, if your door is out of sight, lock it. Always, always lock your door.
- If you do not receive your first choice in housing, remember a room is a room and the experience you have is what you make of it.
- Make the most of your first eight weeks of living in the residence halls; get out and meet as many new people as you can.
- Know your RA.
- Your residence hall room is your new home. You will spend the majority of your time here, whether it is sleeping, eating or studying.
- There is more to meeting people than just leaving your door open. Be proactive, and reach out to the people who live around you. Be friendly, and invite others to join you for meals.
- Help conserve energy by not leaving electronics or lights in your room run endlessly.
- Tucking in all four corners of your lofted bed is one of the first challenges you will encounter in college. Unfortunately the problem reoccurs every time you wash your bed sheets and never seems to become easier.
- Send junk mail right back to companies who provide a postage-paid envelope.
- Finding a vacuum cleaner that works is like finding a four-leaf clover.
- If your smoke detector starts "chirping", the battery needs to be replaced.
- When using the kitchenette to cook a frozen pizza, save the box and tear the top off to use it as a plate. This will save on the number of dishes you have to wash.
- A little fan mounted on your loft can serve as "white noise" to block out background sounds.
- Go to the floor meetings to stay up to date with floor issues and upcoming events. Go to the floor meetings to socialize so you aren't labeled as the "loner" no one knows. Get involved.

CHAPTER 8

ROOMMATES
WHAT ARE YOU DOING IN MY ROOM?

"I'm feeling an 'undercurrent of discontent' developing here."

Living in the residence halls is a unique experience--a prime example is sharing a small room with someone you might not even know. If you had siblings you may have shared a room before and that experience will come in handy. If not and you have never shared a room before, or perhaps you have had your room to yourself since high school, here are some pointers to keep in mind when sharing a room:

1. Compromise.
    Common things you may need to compromise on are room temperature settings, shower times, phone use, guests and TV times.
2. Be considerate.
    Clean up the bathroom sink area after you make a mess. If you are having an extended phone conversation, talk out in the hallway to give both you and your roommate privacy.
3. Be flexible.
    You come back to your room after class for some quiet study time and find your roommate practicing their guitar. Let your roommate know that you have a test you would like to study for, but you can come back in an hour (by being flexible and eating dinner or taking a shower a little sooner) so they can have time to finish playing.
4. Be understanding.
    A roommate is visibly upset but does not want to talk about it. Be understanding by not pressuring for details and allowing them some privacy.

5. Be friendly.

> This can be as simple as acknowledging and greeting your roommate when they come into the room. When your roommate is excited about something, listen and be excited and happy for them.

6. Be respectful.

> You need to stay up late tonight to study for a test, and your roommate goes to bed. Be respectful by turning off the main room light and switching to a smaller light at your desk.

7. Be giving.

> If your roommate is having a bad day, grab them a study snack on your way home. If your roommate runs out of laundry detergent midway through his weekend laundry detail, lend them a cup or yours.

8. Be fun.

> You may have planned to use the entire weekend to study for your upcoming tests, but if your roommate asks you to go play football or run to the mall. Take a break and seize these opportunities to spend time with your roommate having fun.

9. Communicate.

> If you have a big week of tests coming up, let your roommate know so they can adjust accordingly. Let them know what's going on in your life, and let them know you'd like to know what's happening in their life.

10. Be honest.

> If you'd be uncomfortable with them having up a poster of someone in a swimsuit, let them know. If you think there are areas you and your roommate's relationship could be improved, tell them.

You and your roommate should have an open discussion to lay out "house rules" before your first conflict even arises (see "Roommate Contracts" below). This is best completed within the first couple of nights.

Your roommate is also mutually interested in building a positive relationship with you. Your roommate will want to get along with you and help maintain harmony. Keep in mind that your roommate is an individual who has their own "quirks" and behaviors, with their own needs and wants. They may have different expectations of your relationship, or their background may lead to different values of what is acceptable or important.

Living with a roommate is not a horrible experience you need to dread. Your roommate can lead to many positive things such as:
- Introduction to their friends and a way to meet more people
- Late night chats and an "outsider" perspective on issues within your circle of friends
- A brotherly or sisterly bond with another person going through many of the same struggles and successes you are going through
- Learning different ways to do things you may have been doing for 18 years
- Academic help or support if they have taken a class already or are strong in a subject area
- A friendship which can last a lifetime

Should I live with my best friend from high school?
There are an equal number of stories of best friends who are roommates and either loved every minute of it or who never talked to each other again. In general, it is a good idea not to room with your best friend. Living together with someone can change the dimensions of your friendship. If you truly want to be by your best friend, consider if they could live on the same floor as you. Being too close, (spending 24/7, eating all meals together, having the same circle of friends), can become a source of conflict. Often this is the "easy" route at first because you are rooming with someone familiar; however you do not branch out and meet other people and you don't struggle through some of those issues of compromising and working things out with someone new.
If you do choose to room with someone you already know, communication of room expectations is probably more important as you may have assumptions of how things will be because this person is already a friend. Talk about the dynamics of living with a good friend and if it's not going great, it is ok to stop being roommates to save your friendship.

Move-in day may be the first time you are meeting your roommate. But hopefully you have had the chance to already talk with him or her (see Chapter 3: Premove). Here is a review of the questions to ask:
- What is their name, major and hometown?
- What are their hobbies?
- What are they bringing with them? In particular, what large items are they bringing?
- How do they think the room should be set up?

 Don't make *any* assumptions about room set-up without talking to your roommate first. You both have an equal say in the room. Don't set yourself up for future conflict before your roommate even arrives by immediately claiming the best area (ex: putting your desk under the window) or things (ex: choosing the top dresser drawers or best towel bar) in the room. Remember everything in the room should be divided equally (ex: don't take ¾ of the closet space). Don't be the nosebleed by hogging all of the best space.

Roommate Bill of Rights

These are the basic guidelines of all roommate relationships. When these inherent rights are broken, roommate conflict will result.

- You have a right to a fair share of the space, and feeling "at-home".
- You have the right to have free access to your place.
- You have the right to an academic atmosphere that is conducive to studying.
- You have the right to a quiet environment that is conducive to sleeping.
- You have the right to a clean place.
- You have the right to feel safe in your space, free from verbal threats or physical harm.
- You have the right to initiate open discussions of concerns or suggestions and have equal weight in the decision-making process.
- You have the right to disagree.
- You have the right to expect respect for your personal belongings and your privacy, including your roommate not participating in pranks or gossip.
- You have the right to say "no" if your roommate wants to have a guest spend the night.

Roommate Conflict

Everyone is going to have roommate conflicts, big and small. Expect it. You are sharing a limited space with someone unrelated to you throughout your first year of college. View college as a functional community to learn and practice life skills. Your annoying roommate today will only become your annoying coworker of tomorrow.

Sources of Roommate Conflict

- Noise
- Sleeping Habits
- Guests
- Privacy
- Using other's personal belongings
- Sharing food
- Cleanliness standards
- Room Setup
- Value differences
- Alcohol behaviors
- Locking the door
- Phone Messages

The key to a successful roommate relationship is not how many conflicts arise, but *how* those conflicts are addressed. Your first two instincts in order to avoid confrontation and prevent awkwardness may be to either 1. ignore the problem and hope it goes away, or 2. seek "silent revenge" by doing the same thing back to your roommate. For example, your roommate stops washing dishes, so you stop washing dishes too without saying anything ("silent revenge" or passive aggressiveness) until every dish in the room is dirty and there is a huge stack of dishes by the sink that no one is willing to clean. Neither one of these methods will work. Usually, ignoring the problem or using "silent revenge" will only escalate the problem and ensure it will explode on a later date. This future day is almost always at a time of immense stress such as midterms or the end of the semester during finals week as you prepare to go home.

An example is used to illustrate this pattern using a common scenario:

Shannon and Megan did not know each other before coming to college and becoming roommates, but they found they have many similar interests and hit it off right away. They are both really excited about being at college and the freedoms of being away from home. Megan has a boyfriend from high school and he wants to visit during the second weekend of the semester. Shannon does not want her roommate to be mad at her and doesn't want her roommate to think she is "uncool" and so agrees to him sleeping over. The weekend goes well and they all have fun together. A couple more weeks go by and the boyfriend is back for the weekend. Megan did not ask Shannon if this was ok. She assumed it would be ok since Megan agreed before and everyone had a good time. Shannon was a little shocked to see the boyfriend in the room without Megan when she got back from class that Friday, but she did not say anything to Megan. The frequency of the boyfriend visits only increased and he jokingly added his name to the door as the "third roommate" because he was there so often. Shannon found she had to change her clothes in the community bathroom to get privacy from the boyfriend. She often felt alienated from her own room because Shannon and her boyfriend always wanted some "alone time". The boyfriend was not very clean and would leave his stuff all over the room. He watched TV a lot, and Shannon would have to find somewhere else quiet to study. Shannon soon felt uncomfortable and that she no longer had an equal share in the room as she was outnumbered. She did not know how to confront Megan, because besides the issues caused by the boyfriend on the weekend, they got along really well. Shannon decided to ignore it, secretly hoping they would break up, and spent more and more time at the library. By the end of the semester, Shannon is stressed out by finals and tired of not being able to use the room. Shannon explodes one afternoon after finding the boyfriend ate her last muffin and yells at Megan. Shannon begins crying and wants to move out tonight, even though she has a Calculus final in the morning. Megan doesn't understand why Shannon is so upset and promises her she will buy her a dozen new muffins in the morning.

Confronting Conflict:

The thought of addressing conflict can build up in your mind to the point that you are fearful and dreadful. However, keep these points in mind:

- Talk directly to the person who is the source of the problem and allow them the opportunity to listen, discuss and modify their actions. Most of the time they don't even know they are doing something that bothers you.
- Realize you are not "attacking" the *person* (Jim, you're a good guy…), but have identified a *behavior* (…but I would appreciate it if you wouldn't play your music at 2 AM because I have class in the morning) that you would like to stop.
- Talk to your roommate when it is convenient for both of you, when you can have a private conversation and when no distractions are present. It doesn't have to be a "formal sit-down" talk, but don't pass it off as a joke.
- Talk to your roommate in a timely fashion. Confront within 48 hours of the problem; otherwise if you did not address the issue during this time, then it probably wasn't that important and move on. ← "48 Hour Rule"
- Be willing to take feedback from your roommate. Listen to what they are saying. Don't become defensive; they are trying to tell you something.
- Put your pride aside. If your roommate confronts you with concerns, listen to what they have to say and be willing to work on it, even if you feel they are wrong. They may be helping you be a better person in the long run.
- The "bad day" syndrome: Some days in college are rough and on those days, little things your roommate may have done could really upset you.

Be sure to be fair in confronting conflict and remember: roommates have bad days as well.

Take strides. See this as an opportunity to practice your people skills and test how you handle conflict. And yes, there will be some situations where the best thing to do is to just move out of the room. Your Resident Assistant or Hall Director will be able to help you with this process (see Chapter 7: Campus Housing). You will still need to talk with your roommate and you *both* may be required to move-out of the room.

Awkward Message Boards (to leave for your roommate or randomly for people on your floor):
Congrats! Have you told your parents? When is the baby shower?
- What part of the word "flush" don't you understand?
- Who was that girl leaving at 3 AM last night?
- What's the cat food and litter pan for? Did we get a cat?
- Get your crap out of my room!
- Your manager from the strip club called, you don't have to come in tonight.
- Student health called, the STD report came back negative.

Roommate Contract:

Your Resident Assistant may provide you with a Roommate Contract during the first week of school. If not, you can take the ideas from this chapter to create your own, or at least talk to your roommate about the ideas expressed in this chapter. The contract is completed between you and your roommate together. The main purpose of the contract is to act as a discussion facilitator and to address potential concerns before they become problems. Be honest how you truly feel when discussing these topics. Take the discussion of the contract seriously or its purpose will be defeated. Don't be afraid to speak up and express your thoughts. You need to have a frank and open talk with your roommate about the following:
- Sleeping Habits
  Find out if your roommate is a "night owl" or a "morning bird". Ask them what time they plan to go to bed, wake up in the morning and what time they have class.
  o After what time will it be quiet for sleeping? After what time will we turn off the main light for sleeping? At what time in the

morning can we make noise (ex: blow-drying your hair)? At what time in the morning can I turn on the lights? Will weekdays be treated different from weekends?

- Noise

    Noise is one of the most frustrating and common problems between roommates.

    o When can we agree on set times every day that will be quiet for studying? When are appropriate times to watch TV, listen to music, play video games, talk on the phone or have friends over? Will weekdays be treated different from weekends?

- Guests

    You are responsible for your guests and your guests should be held accountable to the "house rules". Consider your own privacy issues and feeling alienated from your own room if you allow over-night guests.

    o Are opposite-sex guests allowed to spend the night? How many days advanced notice should be given when guests will be staying over? How many nights can a guest stay? How many guests can sleep over? Where will the guests be sleeping? Are guests allowed to be in the room when neither roommate is home? Can guests use the roommate's stuff or eat their food? Can guests sit on your bed or use your chair? Are we violating a policy by having a guest?

- Privacy

    Is your roommate allowed to read your mail or documents left on your desk? Can your roommate open computer files on your computer? Can your roommate ask you about things they heard while you were talking on the phone? Can your roommate listen to your phone messages? Do you want your roommate to tell people where you are if they stop by or call and you aren't home? If you or your roommate want "alone time" with a significant other, how will you communicate this without making the other person feel forced from the room?

- Using other's personal belongings

    Common sources of conflict include: sharing clothes; sharing food; computer usage; and refrigerator usage.

    o What items are common items to be shared by both (ex: futon, TV, marker board, etc)? What items are off-limits (ex: laundry soap, dishes, books, etc)?

- Sharing food

    o Are we going to share certain food (such as condiments) but other food will be off-limits or will all food be shared? Who will buy the food? How will the cost be divided?

- Buying supplies
  - o Who will buy bathroom supplies such as toilet paper, hand soap and tissue paper if in a suite? Who will buy cleaning supplies such as window cleaner, trash bags and paper towels? Who will decide what items need to be purchased and when? Who will buy office supplies such as dry erase markers or computer paper? How will the cost be divided?
- Cleaning chores and cleanliness standards
  - o What needs to be cleaned on a regular basis? Who will clean it and when? How will cleaning tasks be divided? What happens if someone doesn't complete their cleaning task or cleans below standards?
- Room Setup
  - o How will the room be arranged? When and how can the room be re-arranged? What pictures, posters, or quotes can be placed on the walls and door? How will dressers, closet space, floor space, etc, be divided?
- Value differences
  - o You are focused on studying and your roommate is focused on partying. Talk about this dynamic and though your values may differ, this doesn't mean you can't be roommates. In fact, it could be a great opportunity to learn about other peoples' values.
- Alcohol behaviors
  - o Will alcohol be kept in the room? Who will pay for the alcohol? Will parties be hosted in the room? Who will pay for anything broken as a result of intoxication? Who will clean up for any messes including vomit or urine as a result of intoxication? Is this behavior against policy?
- Illegal
  - o Is there anything illegal in the room? What will you do if you find something illegal in the room (example: drugs, weapons, other contraband)?
- Pets
  - o Will pets be allowed in the room? Who will be the primary person responsible for cleaning the pet's area or any messes? Who will be the primary person responsible for feeding the pet? Who is allowed to interact and play with the pet? Who will pay for the expenses associated with keeping the pet?
- Locking the door
  You should always lock the door when no one is home. The door should be locked at night when you are asleep. (see Chapter 7: Campus Living)
  - o When will the door be locked? Can friends or family borrow or be given keys to the room?
  - o Consider:

- A roommate leaving in the morning for a class while the other roommate is still sleeping should lock the door behind them.
- If you take a shower, you should carry your room key with you. This way, if your roommate needs to leave while you are still showering, they can leave without leaving the room unlocked and you can still enter after your shower. You don't want to be standing out in the hallway in just your towel or bathrobe after your roommate unintentionally locked you out if they didn't know you were in the shower.

- Temperature
  - At what temperature will we keep the room? Will we adjust the room temperature at night? When can the temperature be changed? Will we leave the windows open?

 Leaving your window slightly cracked will help circulate air exchange and prevent stale air and any unpleasant smells from developing in your room. Be cautious of leaving your window open during cold weather, however, as water pipes may freeze and crack, leading to water flooding your room.

- Mail

  Picking up the mail or losing mail can become a source of roommate conflict. Your roommate's mail and your mail will most likely be delivered in the same mailbox—discuss with your roommate beforehand how he or she (and you) would like your mail to be handled (i.e. leave any mail behind in the mailbox that isn't addressed to you for them to check and pick up later or to bring all the mail back to the room and have a designated area to leave mail for each other).

- Phone Charges and Phone Messages

  Today, most students have their own cell phone for calls and messages. However, if there is a common land line phone, you will want to divide the service cost and long distance costs fairly. Also, you need to establish a way to leave each other messages so they are readily noticeable and do not get lost. Writing messages down and leaving them in a consistent spot is the best way to ensure the message is communicated.

  Be helpful by including:
  - Date and time of phone call
  - Who called and their number

- Why they are calling
- Find out if the roommate should call them back and when would be a good time to call back

  o How will phone charges be divided? How will phone messages be handled? What information may be shared over the phone when taking a message?

Courtesy calls will usually ask for you by name; when they do, act very excited and say, "yes this he/she. Oh my gosh! Did I win something!? Tell me what I won!!" This is then the reoccurring theme you must drive for the rest of the phone call. Surely, you ask, you must have won something. Or immediately try to sell them something; in fact you are so glad they called because you have a great offer for them.

- When someone calls for your roommate, yell for them like you would at home, even though in any typical dorm room they are no more than ten feet away. "ROOMMATE, PHONE!"
- Ask the other person on the phone if they are using a secure line.
- Call people collect. Always. Even for local calls.
- Always answer the phone, no matter what time of day, like you just woke up: "ello? ....what time is it?"
- Add an automated hold function to your phone services so that you can advertise to your friends. Put them on hold often.
- Answer your phone by asking if you are there. That is, when your phone rings, pick it up and say, "Hi, is *your name* there?"----this confuses people.

Final Thoughts

It may surprise you how easy it is to talk to your roommate about something that is bothering you. They too want to keep the peace, and will listen to your concerns. By opening the discussion you may find they have some concerns that you can fix as well. If you don't let your roommate know something is bothering you, they won't have a chance to correct it.

Consider renter's insurance for fire, flood, theft and vandalism damage to your personal belongings. Check to see if your parents' homeowners insurance covers your dorm room. In most cases, your personal belongings are not covered by the university or Department of Residence insurance policy.

Points to Ponder

- Don't ignore problems and hope they will go away; they won't.
- The issue between Shannon and Megan had nothing to do with the muffins.
- There are few things that rank higher on the scale of awkwardness than walking in on your roommate having sex or being in the room while they are having sex.
- Don't seek "silent revenge"; your roommate will never pick up on the hint.
- You have a roommate; of course you're going to have embarrassing moments.
- If you need to hide something valuable, wrap it in tinfoil, place in Tupperware and label it as "asparagus" and put it in the freezer compartment of your dorm fridge. *No one* is ever tempted or gets the urge to eat frozen asparagus as a snack.
- Carry your room key with you to the shower and you won't end up in the hallway in your towel, locked out.

CHAPTER 9
LAUNDRY
CLEAN CLOTHES AND YOU

"Where's my other sock!?"

In case you didn't wash your own clothes at home or skipped that home economics class, this chapter will provide you with some tips that will help you avoid some common laundry mistakes. The easiest way to learn how to do laundry is to have someone show you. Wash some loads of laundry before you leave for college so that your parents can give you some advice and instructions. If you left home with no laundry experience, ask one of your neighbors or someone in the laundry room to help you.

When you are washing laundry the two main things you want to avoid is shrinking and discoloring your clothes. Be sure to read the instructions of any bleach or detergent you use. You will also want to read the "care label" instruction tag on your clothes. This will tell you any special considerations you may have to take for delicate fabrics.

When in doubt, it is better to wash things on "cold", not add bleach and allow it to air dry.

With most college laundry rooms there will be several washers and dryers. That's one of the greatest parts of college life---you'll be able to run several laundry loads simultaneously and won't have to spend all day washing your clothes.

Laundry Tips:

- Avoid peak laundry times such as the weekends. The worst time to do your laundry is in the evening and on Sundays. The best time to do your laundry is really early or really late in the day when most people are asleep or weekday afternoons when people are at class.

- Sort your clothes into whites and colors. Some color dyes "bleed out" when washed and can stain light colored clothes. In general you'll want to wash whites with hot water and colors with cold water.

- Check and empty pockets as you sort clothes or you could end up with wet dollar bills, lost phone numbers or ink stained clothes.

- **Be sure you have enough money for the washers and dryers before you start.** You will want to check to see how the machine accepts money; some machines are coin operated while others are linked to a student account through your college ID card.

- Be sure to activate the machine you plan on using to make sure it works before you dump detergent all over your clothes only to find out that machine is out of order.

- Don't overload the washer machine. In the end it won't save you any money if you are shoving your clothes and packing them so tight that the machine can't thoroughly and properly clean them.

- You will want to consider washing these things separately: towels, shoes, rugs, new clothes or really dirty clothes.

- **Always, always watch your laundry.** Unlike your laundry room at home this is a public space. Unattended laundry can have bad things happen to it including theft. Bring some homework to read while you wait or bring along a laundry friend to talk with. It's also a great time to catch up on phone calls.

- Remove your laundry from the washer and dryer as soon as you are done. Other people will be waiting to use the same machines and you may find your clothes in a heap on the dirty floor if you aren't on time.

- If you must move someone else's laundry to use a machine, treat it how you would want your clothes to be treated.

- Be respectful: clean up any detergent spills, don't throw dryer sheets on the floor, clean out the lint tray.

- Shake your clothes out before placing them in the dryer. This will reduce the amount of drying time that you will need.

- Having your parents buy you the economy family-sized laundry detergent soap when you arrive to college may seem like a good idea until you realize you will have to carry that extra 20 pounds of liquid soap, down the hallway or even down stairs, every time you do laundry since the laundry room will most likely not be located right next to your room.

- Be sure to double check the dryer when you are unloading for any hiding socks.

- Hang and fold your clothes right away after drying to avoid wrinkles.

- There is usually an 800-number posted for the company who maintains the laundry machines. Don't hesitate to call this number if a machine ate your money or if a machine is broken.

During an extended weekend or break, people will often go home and take their laundry with them to have their parents wash their clothes for free. This is where you come in and slip an open condom wrapper into the jean's pocket of your roommate's or friend's dirty laundry. It will be sure to stir up a conversation at home.

Final Thoughts

Laundry is a relatively simple process: sort, wash and dry. You'll be a laundry pro in no time. It is easier to keep up with your laundry weekly or biweekly than to wait for one giant "marathon" laundry session. Don't make assumptions or you might ruin your clothes one load at a time. If you are not sure about something: read the detergent label; read the clothes tag; call home or even better, take your clothes home.

Points to Ponder
- Always watch your laundry.
- Make sure the washing machine is working before you pour soap all over your clothes.
- Avoid Sunday Laundry Days.
- College laundry rooms are efficient because you have access to multiple washers and dryers to complete several loads worth of laundry in just a couple hours.
- When in doubt, use cold water.

CHAPTER 10

DINING SERVICES AND CAMPUS FOOD
"WE BE EATING GOOD TONIGHT!"

"I try to eat healthy on Tuesdays"

Campus dining centers often receive an unfair and undeserving bad reputation. Parents often reminisce about their college dining hall of decades ago of lukewarm food, limited options and bad service. The campus dining experience has completely changed since the college era of your parents. You can expect a better variety of tasty and fresh food choices to satisfy even the pickiest of eaters. Many campuses offer unlimited servings in self-serve buffets, so you don't have to worry about leaving hungry. If you have special dietary needs, a dietitian is usually available to help you set up an individual meal plan. It is also very convenient and time saving for your busy schedule. Meal time is a huge social connection as you will eat most of your meals with your friends and have a chance to make new friends.

How do meal plans work?

Each college will have different meal plan options. Some campus will have a block number of meals for the week or the semester, or a plan based on points or dining "cash". Commonly your meal plan will be linked to your college ID card which you will need to enter the dining facility. You will want to consider each meal plan option offered and determine which one fits you best. Carefully look at the prices because there might only be a slight difference in cost between eating ten meals per week versus doubling it at 20 meals per week. It is important to maximize your plan by knowing your eating habits—will you really wake up every morning for breakfast? Do you usually eat out a couple times a week such as on the weekends? Take these things into consideration when you select a meal plan. Many people don't realize they pay double for a meal when they eat out or eat in their room and let their pre-paid meal at dining services go unused.

Questions to ask about your meal plan:
1. What time is the dining hall open? Does that conflict with your class schedule and if so, what are other options offered, such as a bagged/sacked "travel meal" to take with you to class?
2. Can you use your meal plan or points at other residence hall dining centers, the student union, campus catering or the campus convenience store?
3. What happens to the meals or points you don't use at the end of the week or end of the semester?
4. Where can you find nutritional information and the day's menu?

What are the benefits of dining services?

Without dining services, you would need to find time to shop for groceries, prepare your meals, and clean up afterwards. The convenience of dining services allows you more time for studying or hanging out with your friends. Although cooking on your own might appear to be less expensive and more appealing than "eating at the dorms" you should consider:
- time spent going to the store, preplanning and preparing meals
- time spent on cleaning and washing dishes
- the challenge of cooking for one person with spoilage of fresh foods such as fruits and vegetables
- bulk packaging of food that would require either food wastage or repeated nights of left-over meals
- investment in cooking utensils and dishes
- learning to cook your own meals

Most students who do live off campus have good intentions of cooking fabulous meals but in reality find themselves sacrificing nutrition as they zap a microwave dinner or end up spending more money as they eat out more often. They are often too tired or don't have enough time to cook. These students often miss out on connecting socially as they are often eating alone in their apartment.

What is the "Freshman 15"?

Freshman 15: Potential weight gain by first year students as they adjust to college life which could be the result of overeating, lack of exercise and/or stress. You may have been warned of the dreaded "Freshman 15". The Freshman 15 could be a result of:

- All you can eat dining services with many new foods to try
- Many sedentary hours sitting in classrooms or reading
- No more high school sports or gym class to keep you active
- Consuming more food than usual due to stress of adjusting to your new environment, new schedule, loneliness, homesickness
- Late night snacking due to a non-routine schedule

How can I avoid the Freshman 15?

Adding 15 pounds does not have to be part of your college experience if you make healthy decisions. The three most important things to keep in mind to prevent the Freshmen 15 are:

1. Exercise on a regular basis.
2. Eat regular, balanced meals.
3. Being healthy is a lifestyle choice, not a fad.

It is difficult to avoid the Freshman 15 considering college life: time constraints, stress, no required exercise and lots of food.

The first step to healthy-eating is knowing how much you normally eat and exercise. Use your high school experience as a comparison. What and how much did you eat for breakfast or dinner at home? What are you eating now in college? How many hours did you spend on the practice field for high school sports? How many hours are you exercising each day in college? For more information, see Chapter 11 on Exercise.

Determine a general outline of the types and portions of food you normally eat to feel satisfied. This will help you know if you are overeating. Check out what the experts and the USDA have to offer with the new food pyramids which are individualized based on your age, sex and activity level at www.MyPyramid.gov. Here is an example based on a food pyramid you can use as a base to modify to your needs:

Breakfast: a bowl of cereal and oatmeal and/or a fruit or glass of juice
Lunch: a meat/cheese sandwich, two fruits and yogurt
Dinner: a main dish, a salad, a vegetable and/or a dessert

- Eating healthy is about choices and portions.
  - When you have several food items to choose from, consistently choose the item with the lowest fat, salt and sugar content.
  - You don't need to have full servings of every dish you choose; instead sample from a wide variety of foods.
  - You don't have to deny yourself sweets and the foods you love, the key is moderation.
- There are many menu options available to you and even more options if you are creative and make food combinations. If you find you are "tired of dining services" be aware of your own restrictions or limitations that you may be setting for yourself (that is, only eating a certain subset of foods all the time).

 Be creative by mixing foods together. For example, try a "liquid granola bar": a glob of peanut butter, some chocolate chunks (from the ice cream dessert bar), mixed into regular oatmeal. Try to convince as many as your friends to try the Liquid Granola Bar---before long, it will be the new craze at your dining center. Reflect quietly to yourself: "people are *actually* fighting over the last packet of regular oatmeal. Regular oatmeal!"

- Your body loves a consistent schedule and you will become less hungry during non-meal times. However if you are a "grazer" and like to eat continuously throughout the day with smaller meals this might work better for you.
- Snacks are a good way to take the edge off between meals. Avoid late night eating of high fat and sugar foods.
- Be careful of what you are adding to your food. Drenching your salad under excessive dressing or highly salting your food will not add nutritional value to your otherwise healthy meal.
- You might not have realized it, but drinking fountains might be your only source of water in college if you don't have a sink in your room. Carrying bottled water with you to classes is one of the easiest ways to increase your water intake throughout the day.
- Realize that pop/soda, juices and beer can be a large source of "uncounted" calories. Juices and pop/soda have a high sugar content, which can be the equivalent of eating a candy bar.
- Cakes, cookies and other desserts are always readily available. You don't need to celebrate like it's your birthday every day, every meal.

Kipp Story Box

"The Breakfast of Champions"

I'm eating breakfast one morning and I look over and there is a guy who has four glasses of pink lemonade and one donut on his tray. There are over 20 choices for drinks and he goes with pink lemonade four times! Ah, the freedom of being away from home: donuts and lemonade for breakfast. No more mom nagging about the ill effects of all that sugar on the enamel of his teeth.

If you are looking for an on-campus job to earn a little extra cash, consider working at dining services. Dining Services are very student-orientated and will be flexible in working around your class schedule. Plus it's yet another way to meet people since most of your coworkers will be college students. Since the dining hall is close to you, you won't have to worry about driving to work.

Use your meal time as a social time to connect with people. Eating meals together is a causal and easy way to strengthen friendships or meet new people. One of the best ways to meet people in college is meeting your friend's friends. Multiple meals a week gives you many social opportunities.

Not having any friends to eat meals with and sitting alone. A "shared scare" among freshmen is not meeting people or not having friends to eat with during meals. Just the thought of having to eat by yourself can give you an uneasy feeling, and you may have even considered skipping a meal to avoid it. There are two important things to realize here. First, there are many other students in the same boat as you. If you are friendly and invite other people to join in a group to eat dinner together, they will be very eager to join in--they were probably sitting in their room worrying about eating alone too. Second, even if you don't find someone to eat with for a particular meal, don't sweat it—most people don't even notice the other tables around them or that you are eating alone. The thing to realize is there will be times when this happens to you and everyone at some point. You might even find that you prefer to eat some meals alone on certain days, because it can be faster and more convenient for you.

Everyone is eager to make new friends during the initial weeks of the semester. It is usually acceptable to join someone else that you see eating alone, even if you don't know them, because they most likely have the same "shared scare" of eating by themselves. So, you finally spot that attractive person that you've been meaning to meet all week and now they are finally sitting by themselves and so you join them; but what you don't realize was all of the person's friends were just at the salad bar and you are left sitting awkwardly with a whole group of people who know each other and who are wondering who the heck you are.

Establishing yourself into a group that always eats together can provide you with security of not eating alone. However, you don't want to be an exclusive group---invite other people to join you. A good idea is to be "in" with several groups and eat with different groups depending on the meal or day of the week. This way you are not stuck with one group all the time. Most people eat in larger groups for dinner and smaller groups or individually for breakfast and lunch.

The 2-hour dinner trap:

You may be left wondering why you never have enough time in the day if you are spending too much time eating meals. There are two common traps. First, there always seems to be one *really* slow eater in every group. Second, your friends will be eating at various times for meals throughout the week based on their schedules. Just when you thought the slow eater of the group was almost done and you are ready to go, another friend joins your group to eat. Your group stays as the new friend joins because you don't want to leave your friend to eat by themselves. You have now entered the two hour dinner trap.

A few practical tips to help avoid the "trap":

- Be upfront when you sit down about your schedule and indicate when you need to leave and then leave.
- Don't talk to the slow eater. Let these people eat without many interruptions.
- Decide what you want to eat prior to arriving to the dining center. This avoids sitting down and eating, going back for something you forgot, etc.
- Be a leader amongst your friends. If you stand up and grab your tray to leave, they probably will too.
- If you are running late and join a group already eating, tell them you don't mind if they don't stay for your whole meal. This helps set the tone for others to do the same if they are ever late.

Etiquette: The Unwritten Rules

- Be nice to the people who are serving your food. It's been a long day for them too. "Please" and "thank-you" go a long way.
- If you accidentally break something (or even a whole set of dishes!) you will most likely not be charged for it. Just let someone know so it can be safely cleaned up.
- It is inevitable that all of your favorite food items will be served in one night but don't worry because menu items will repeat and come back around. You don't have to grab everything in sight that you like. Do you really need the hamburger *and* the spaghetti? Or pop and ice-cream with *every* meal?
- Try to avoid the times when the serving lines are the longest. It will take a couple weeks for lines to "settle" as people learn when the best times to come and eat and adjust to their new schedule. You can usually avoid lines by not eating on the hour or the half hour when classes let out or when popular TV shows are over.
- Don't be the nosebleed, keep moving to avoid holding up a line. Going slow through the salad bar line as you are yapping on your cell phone is

annoying to everyone behind you. Don't stop abruptly when you are walking or you might feel the food of the person's tray behind you going down your back.

- Remember you are in a public space and that your conversations can easily be overheard. You never know if the person at the next table is a friend of the person you are gossiping about.

- Expect chaos and be ready for a lot of bustle, commotion and sudden starting and stopping movements when gathering your food and drinks. You will become quite adept in predicting other people's anticipated movements in order to avoid collisions.

- In college you must remember you are much more sophisticated in your dining experience than your time with high school cafeterias; therefore, you must use a hundred little bowls and plates for every food item you put on your tray. Unlike high school you don't just slap the chocolate pudding into a compartment on your tray—put it in a bowl first, then your tray.

- Use the serving utensils to dish up your food. Never grab food with your hands.

- Making a food mess on your tray makes you look like you are in 4th grade. Besides you probably have a friend who works at dining service who will have to clean up your mess later.

- Dropping your tray is not a big deal. If someone does drop their tray you don't need to clap unless you want to look like you are in junior high.

- Sighing and bumping your tray into the person ahead of you in line will not make things go faster. Just relax.

- Taking excess food that you don't eat only drives up the cost of the meal plan.

The Cost of Taking Food:

When you are in a rush, grabbing an extra apple or cookie on the way out to class might not be a bad idea for a snack later on. However, excessively taking food from dining services can add up quickly as extra costs for the center. If each person on a 10,000 student campus were to take an item with a cost of just 25 cents after lunch and dinner each day for the semester it would add up to over a million dollars over the course of the school year. Students have been known to steal other items such as trays to use as a winter sled, forks to use as doorstops, or dishes to use in their rooms. If you are caught stealing university property, you will likely damage your permanent university judicial record. It's a numbers game and the cost is passed back onto you the student through the cost of your meal plan.

Beyond Dining Services

You may want a break from the dining center. And, often times, there is one or more meal each week that is not offered via the dining centers. If this is the case, you could try one of these options:

Eating Out:

- This is a great way to socialize with friends as you check out local restaurants. It can be fun to form a group of friends who "discover" a new restaurant each week together.
- Be adventurous by trying new foods and not ordering the same menu item each time you visit a restaurant. Go to an Indian, Greek or Thai restaurant.
- Check out local or state parks and plan a picnic or grill-out.
- Eating out is expensive, know your budget. It is standard to give 15-20% of your bill as a service tip.
- Be sure to see if the restaurant has any type of discount or specials for college students.

Ordering In:

- Ordering pizza for a late-night group study session or while watching the game is a staple of college students. Many other restaurants will also deliver such as sub-sandwiches, Chinese food or burritos.
- Always look for coupons; local businesses usually have a deal for college students. Don't forget to include a delivery tip when dividing the cost between your eating companions.

Groceries and Cooking

- There may be a small kitchen located in your residence halls that you can cook a meal to enjoy with your friends or bake a batch of cookies. Cooking supplies and space will probably be limited, however, because residence halls are designed with the idea that you will eat the majority of your meals at the dining center.
- It's a good idea to have some snack food on hand in your room in case you are hungry between meals or you aren't able to make it to a meal.
- If you have a small fridge in your room, don't forget to purchase a few items so it's not empty when you open it.

The Reality of the Situation:

Parents like to make sure their student is "set-up" before leaving them on campus. Typically this will include some grocery shopping. Some families make the mistake of purchasing bulk supplies. You almost feel sorry for the student who has those 45 cans of soup taking up space in his room all year and then having to carry 43 of them back out at the end of the year during move-out.

> **Vending Machines:**
> - You may use vending machines more often in college, because they are conveniently located pretty much everywhere, including your residence hall.
> - With all the fat, sugar and salt content, you will be sure to find a tasty treat in a vending machine.
> - Add class to your vending machine adventure by using our vending machine recipes:
>   - o Animal s'mores:
>   - Buy one packet of animal crackers, a rice crispy bar and a chocolate candy bar.
>   - Break the candy bar and rice crispy bar into small pieces.
>   - Place a rice crispy bit and chocolate piece between two animal crackers. Enjoy your Animal s'mores!
>   - o Monster Chocolate Mousse
>   - Buy a packet of small chocolate chip cookies, and a 3 Musketeers bar®
>   - Separate the outer chocolate layer of the 3 Musketeers bar® from the whipped chocolate.
>   - Melt the outer layer of chocolate (less than a minute in the microwave)
>   - Spread the whipped chocolate between two cookies and then dip in the melted chocolate. You are the envy of all around you.
>   - o Gourmet Popcorn
>   - Buy one pack of microwave popcorn and begin to microwave it.
>   - As popcorn pops, buy some M&Ms® (or other similar candy)
>   - When popcorn is done, add M&Ms® to bag...shake...and enjoy this gourmet college treat.

Your campus may have an exclusive beverage contract with a national soft-drink company. This means your university is receiving monetary funds such as revenue sharing or unrestricted cash, in exchange for the agreement to only sell that particular line of drinks through all campus venues, including dining services and vending machines.

The Reality of the Situation:

Students will come out of the bushes and line up thick for "free" campus food such as a couple slices of greasy pizza or 30-cent hotdogs. In reality though, you are probably letting a prepaid dining service meal go unused and at the dining hall you could have all the pizza and hotdogs you could want and a whole lot more.

Sure, you've heard of the Freshman 15. But what about the Freshman 45? Make it a friendly competition on your floor to see who can gain the most weight in the shortest amount of time. Pass the Crisco anyone?

- Read the menu posted for dining services silently as you run your finger across it, then turn to your friends and say, "We be eating good tonight!"
- When in line, turn to your friend, "Is this the checker girl you thought was hot?" Your friend is awkwardly left explaining that you were just kidding.
- Tuck your paper napkin into your shirt collar. Say to the people who are staring at you, "What?"
- Decorate and garnish your plate with whatever is available while at dining service to add class to your brown-yellow tray. Fill the bottom of your glass with ice tea and then add pink lemonade to create a "sunrise" drink. Add a cut lemon to the outside. Use all the cut vegetables when making your salad at the salad bar. Even put some of those cherry tomatoes on top for good measure. Make dining service into a 5-star dining experience.
- Burst out aloud during your dining experience, "DELICIOUS.....I can't help but say it, cause....mmmmm..... this cake is just soooo DELICIOUS....".
- Try to pick a fight during dinner conversation between two people talking by injecting "ooooooo" after a more or less neutral statement and continue this back and forth as the people talk.
- Eating baked beans or corn with a scooping hand is always a better idea than a spoon. It will be very messy but well worth it when the people around you look at you like you are the biggest loser they know.
- Lick all your food when you sit down to ensure no one else will try to take your food, like the days of junior high. Maybe even lick some of their food too to let them know you are their friend and you are looking out for them.

- Cut and eat a banana at lunch with a fork and knife. Be sure to open it with your utensils as well.
- Find yourself the biggest bowl you can and fill it up with corn. There is nothing better than just a very large bowl of corn for dinner. Be sure to also find a little bowl and fill it up with corn. Your friends aren't too sure, but did they even see some corn floating around in your milk?
- Tell people what you had for breakfast. Then tell them you just wasted 30 seconds of their life that they can NEVER EVER get back. EVER.
- Drink the milk from the bottom of your breakfast cereal bowl.
- When faced with below par food choices, say "What?! Did the cook sleep in today?"
- Consistently drop the large serving spoons or ladles INTO whatever is being served.
- Use a spoon when drinking water
- Make conversation at the drink dispenser.
- Throw some meat chunks into your strawberry milk.... mmmmmmm. Tell other people they are strange for not trying new things.
- As you are finishing the last couple bites of your hamburger, say aloud, "Oh shoot, I forgot I was going to start being a vegetarian today."
- Start a dining hall tradition. Inevitably, someone at your table will get up and leave their tray behind as they retrieve a forgotten spoon or help themselves to a second serving of their favorite dish. During their absence, this is where you, with the help of the others sitting with you, guzzle down ALL of the person's drinks before they return. The person might not notice at first that they have no drinks and then will become very annoyed later when they are thirsty.
- Counter strategy: If you find yourself in a group that guzzles down your drinks you can set them up—pour salt into your milk and then conveniently "forget" something.
- Amaze your friends---all you need are some grapes and a microwave. Use a knife to split 10-20 grapes down the middle without cutting through the skin on the other side and place the grapes on a plate with the cut surface facing down. Then microwave on high and watch as sparks fly out from the grapes!

Final Thoughts

Campus dining services is a very enjoyable experience and one of the best parts of college. You eat all your meals with your friends and many new social connections are made. There are a lot of choices in the variety of food. Be open to trying new foods anywhere you go. Don't be the person who always orders the orange chicken when having Chinese food. When your parents come to visit you, take them to eat a meal at the dining hall, they will enjoy seeing where you eat your meals.

Points to Ponder:

- Dining services offer:
    - a large variety of nutritious food
    - convenience for the busy college student
    - a social atmosphere to connect with friends
- Cooking on your own is time-consuming, less nutritious and less social.
- Weight gain during your first year, known as the Freshman 15, is common because you are eating more food, eating at various hours due to your busy schedule and lacking any required or formal exercise.
- Just pretend the vending machine doesn't even exist.
- It won't take long to figure the correct angle to hold your cereal bowl under the milk dispenser aka "the stainless steel cow" to prevent splash-back.
- Avoiding the Freshman 15 means leading a healthy lifestyle consisting of balanced meals and regular exercise.
- It's ok, you can sit with people of the opposite sex while you enjoy your meals—no one will giggle at you and think you like that person.
- Observe the friends you consider to be healthy and fit and see what types of food and how much of it they put on their plate in the dining center.
- Sit in a new area of the dining center you don't normally eat—it will give you a whole new perspective.
- Consider that instead of just a simple bowl of cereal for breakfast as you were heading out the door in high school, you are now having pancakes and eggs and donuts every morning for breakfast.
- Smarter choices, not deprivation.
- Grocery baggers will often say, "Have a nice day," as they hand you your groceries--you respond by saying, "Oh I will!" as you point to something in the bag, such as the milk and cereal. This is usually uncomfortable for everyone.
- You may notice there is a weak attraction between your silverware that makes them stick together. This is a result of some dining centers using a large magnet to remove silverware from trays in the dish-room leaving silverware "magnetized".

CHAPTER 11
EXERCISE
COLLEGE GYM CLASS

"Less complaining, more sweating"

In high school, you probably exercised by competing in sports, usually two seasons a year, having practices five days a week, for at least one hour each day. At the very least, you exercised twice a week with your gym class. In college, it's just too easy not to exercise; you have other distractions including schoolwork and social life, you probably aren't in a collegiate sport and you don't even have a gym class anymore where you at least got some marginal exercise. Most of your day is sedentary: you sit in class, you sit while you read and study and you sit at your computer. Your meals are prepared for you, and it's easy to overeat (see Chapter 10: Campus Dining). The "Freshman 15" is real, but it doesn't have to be part of your college experience if you make the conscious decision and effort to keep exercising from the very first day of college.

What is the "Freshman 15"?

As mentioned above, many lifestyle changes occur when you go off to college. Often times, you may pick up a few pounds here and there and this has been referred to as "The Freshman 15," meaning, you'll gain about 15 pounds. For some, this becomes more like the "Freshman 30" if not careful. But don't worry, many students are able to maintain or even lose some weight during their first year in school.

Beating the Freshman 15

First things first: go to the student health center and ask for a complete physical examination. This visit will most likely be free to you as part of your student fees. The main reason to see a doctor is to make sure you are healthy enough to start your exercise program as well as to establish baseline values for you. You will then have a record of your freshmen weight and can evaluate each year if you are controlling and maintaining your weight. Your doctor will also record your respirations, heart rate and blood pressure---all values you can use to compare your health in future years.

The main reason college students will give for not exercising is lack of time. Time management is difficult due to demanding class schedules, being involved on campus, maybe juggling a part time job and being social with your friends. However, if your health is important to you, you will give exercise a priority. Build exercise time into your schedule from the first day, and it will become a daily routine. It is recommended to exercise five days a week for 30 minutes, including aerobic and strength training.

Ways to make exercise part of your everyday lifestyle:
- Skip the elevator and take the stairs. Live on the 10th floor? Great! Even better work-out for you!
- Walk or bike to every class, every time, every day.
- Enroll in an exercise sport science class. You can enroll in an official university class, usually offered as pass/not pass credit based on attendance and participation. Benefits of enrolling in this type of class include:
  - Guaranteed work-out time built into your class schedule each week.
  - Opportunity to practice or improve your skills or to learn new skills (ex: you can take a class to learn how to play tennis or golf, etc)
  - Connecting with another social group as these classes usually require teamwork and interaction

  You will have to be your own advocate for signing up for this class. You may be discouraged by parents or your advisor that this class is "unnecessary" for your engineering major. Which is true, you won't need it for graduation credits; the reason you are taking the class, however, is for your own health and social well-being.
- Participate in a physical fitness class. You can join in a night class through the school's fitness center. Classes might include yoga, cardio-kickboxing or cycling. These classes offer the same benefits as an official university

class without the extra pressures of course credit. However, without the consequences of not attending, you may find yourself doing just that.

- Play an intramural sport. Did you play soccer in high school, didn't continue in college, but still love to play the game? Or, have you never played but always wanted to try? Sign up for an intramural team and enjoy the physical benefits as well as the comradery. If there are no intramural teams, create your own team with a sign-up sheet for some weekend pick-up games.
- Need a study break? Go for a walk around campus as you talk on your cell phone to friends or family.

Benefits of Exercising:
- Control your weight
- Increase your strength
- Increase your flexibility
- Reduce your risk of developing and dying from major medical diseases
- Increase lung and heart capacity
- Healthier bones and muscles
- Increase self-confidence and self-esteem
- Increase overall feeling of well-being

Working-Out:
- Remember to stretch your muscles out before and after your workout
- Work different muscle groups during different days; as overworked and sore muscles will cause you to give up too soon.
- Vary your workout; include aerobic and strength training activities; as variety will keep you interested.
- Learn how to properly use the exercise equipment at the fitness center so that you don't hurt yourself, and so you look capable and confident while you work-out.
- Listen to your body; allow your body at least one day of rest each week.
- Set realistic goals for yourself.
  - For example, if your goal is to have "six-pack" abs, you may never achieve this level of conditioning because you may have to reduce your body fat percentage to a level that is not healthy or realistic for you; or genetically, it may not be possible for you.

When's the best time to exercise?

In the morning:
Pros:

- By having your work out completed as the first thing you do in the morning you will be less likely to skip it as compared to night when you might be pressed for time or just feeling lazy at the end of the day.
- You can shower after your morning work out and be ready for the day.
- You can refuel with breakfast right after your work-out.
- You feel alert and refreshed, ready to start the rest of your day.
- Less people have the discipline to wake up early each morning to work out and the fitness center will be less crowded. You will be more likely to have access to the machines you want to use.

Cons:

- It can be difficult to wake up early enough to fit in your workout before your first class of the day.
- Your muscles are stiffer after waking up.

In the evening:
Pros:

- A work-out at night might be a good stress release following a long day.
- More people work out at night or late afternoon and you might be more likely to stick with your work out plan if you meet up with a friend.

Cons:

- You may end up eating a "fourth" meal after your work-out late at night.
- You may not be able to fall asleep right away after you just working out.
- You may have to get up in the middle of the night to use the bathroom if you drink a lot of water following your work-out.

Tie your room key into your shoelaces when you go out for a run. This way you can keep your room safe and not have to worry about hiding, losing or holding the key.

Final Thoughts

If you implement only once piece of advice from this book, you will not regret establishing a routine work-out. Maintaining your weight, staying fit and feeling good will carry over into other areas of your life.

Points to Ponder

- Be conscious of what you eat or you will defeat your exercise program.
- Most people "start exercising" with the goal to lose fat. By exercising you are also improving your overall health (stronger bones, increase muscles, stronger heart, etc), your ability to recover from injuries and infections and your overall self-esteem and confidence.
- Overheard in the stretching area, "I think I'm just going to lay here".
- If you use a temporary locker while you are working out at the college fitness center, bring a padlock to lock your stuff (ID card, keys, etc) to save you the headache and costs of having to replace these items.
- The hardest part of your work-out program is to show up to it. Every day.
- Consider getting a workout buddy. This accountability will do wonders in keeping you on track.
- Some people spend hours a day toning their bodies--don't try to compare yourself to them. Compete with yourself; record your improvements and personal bests.
- Calorie Balance = Inputs (Diet) – Outputs (Exercise).
- Don't skip stretching with a proper warm-up and cool-down; increasing the flexibility is one of the great benefits of regular exercise.
- There are 1,440 minutes in each day. You only need 30 of those minutes for exercise---just 2% of your day.

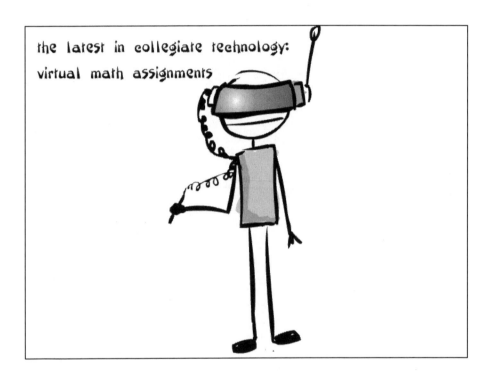

CHAPTER 12
COMPUTERS AND TECHNOLOGY
MULTIDIMENSIONAL THINKING

*"We used to use email to set up meetings;
now we have meetings over email."*

Colleges today are very computer driven. You may take a class course that is completely online. You are expected to be proficient in typing as well as using applications such as Microsoft's Word, Excel and PowerPoint. You may have to complete class homework assignments online. Important class information, including announcements, the syllabus and your professor's contact information may all be found online. You are assumed to check your email on a regular basis to receive announcements from the college and your professors. Most colleges' libraries are wired where you can access full journal articles online for research papers.

Should I bring a computer to college?

This is a matter of convenience and cost. You usually are not required to bring a computer, but you may find that you need to use a computer so often that it would be more convenient for you to have your own personal computer. If you do not have a computer, you will use "computer labs" which are rooms where multiple computers and printers are conjoined together for student use. Ask your college about the availability of the computer labs: Where are they located? How many are there on campus? What times do I have access to the labs?

The other factor to consider is cost. Computers become more affordable every year, but you may have already stretched your budget to the limit.   Check with your college's information technology services because often they can offer very favorable student discounts on computers and computer-related products, including software, that are available only to students.

Before buying a computer, contact your college to see what hardware and software will be necessary for your computer to have in order to access the university's internet.   You may need to have an Ethernet card or a wireless card installed.

Should I buy a laptop or a desktop computer?

Over recent years, more and more college freshmen students who bring computers to college bring laptops. There are several reasons for this trend. First, more and more campuses are providing wireless service at various campus locations, such as classrooms, residence halls, the student union, or the library, where it might be convenient for you to have your computer on hand to take notes, work in study groups or conduct literature research. Laptops are easy to transfer home with you during school breaks. On the other hand, laptops are more prone to theft because of this portability. You can secure your laptop with a cord that inserts into the back of the computer and then attaches to your desk or loft structure.

Protect your computer investment and buy a quality surge protector to protect it from any damages caused by electrical fluctuations.

Advantages of Computers:

Most traditional students, who enter college from high school, are very proficient at using computers. You probably have already mastered typing, using email and creating word-processed documents. Email is a useful tool to keep in touch with family and friends, ask questions (ex: financial aid, professors, etc), or communicate with your study group for class projects using a list serve group email. Access to the internet provides you a wealth of information that is quick and easy to find.   Important university information can be found online including upcoming events, the official student handbook and even nutritional information for campus dining.

Sharing photos of college life with family and friends back home is inexpensive and easy with your computer and a digital camera. Instant-messaging is also an inexpensive and easy way to communicate with your friends in real-time. Some families will choose to get webcams so they can communicate this way as well.

More and more of college is becoming digital and having your own computer allows you to keep your important documents and projects on your own computer and work on them at your leisure. As music moves to more of a digital age, one's computer becomes the storage space for music and other mixed media.

 Ask upperclassmen if they know of any local student run websites for your college. Often there are sites where you can sell or buy used textbooks, make announcements, find out about upcoming events or post your thoughts on a current campus issue.

 Instant-message your roommate while you are in your room together. Don't acknowledge them trying to talk to you, answer their questions by typing another message.

Dangers of Computers:

As mentioned earlier, theft of your computer, especially laptops, is a concern on any college campus. It is an easy, high-valued target for thieves. Protect yourself by not carelessly leaving your laptop laying around on a study table or in your backpack; make sure you know where it is at all times. Keep it locked down using a cable when you have it in your room and make sure you lock your door when no one is in the room.

Your identity or other sources of personal information can be stolen online. Be sure to protect your credit card number, your bank account number, your social security number, passwords and PIN numbers by using only reputable websites that ensure coded encryption, and by not leaving this information accessible to other people. Be cautious not to release your information to any suspicious emails that solicit or "phish" for your information. Many of these emails may look very legitimate.

It is also important to be conscious of what information is available online about you. Providing information online about your class schedule, where you live, your phone number and photos may lead to unwelcome stalkers. If possible, remove this information or set your preferences to private so that only your approved friends can view your information. Once something has been put out there, it is very difficult to remove.

Your computer and your computer files, including important papers and documents, can be infected by computer viruses. It is important that your computer is up to date with the latest computer virus software; be sure to download any new updates or upgrades. Your school may require you to have certain protection before signing into the school's computer network. Your school may offer this software as a free download or at a reduced price. You can also help protect your computer by signing off the internet and/or unplugging your internet cord when you are not using it.

Do you know what information is posted about you on the internet? "Google yourself" by searching your name on Google (www.google.com). This will bring up any past news articles about you, information your college may have released about you or any other online postings containing your name.

You can suppress information your college releases about you. You can have your phone number and address removed from printed and online phone directories. Contact the registrar's office to complete the appropriate paperwork.

College Related Computer Issues:

- File Sharing and Pirating Music/Movies
    - Sharing of any file increases your risk of getting a virus on your computer or other problems which can lead to you losing personal data or compromise the security of your computer.
    - Sharing of copyrighted material (music, movies, software, etc) is illegal. While it may seem like a good idea, your computer's identity is also "attached" to these types of files, and if the authorities found something you traded to be illegal, you could be

held accountable. It's a good idea to avoid any illegal activity with your computer.

- Plagiarism
  - o Be very conscientious to cite and directly quote any material you find and use from the internet for a college paper. It is just as easy for professors and teaching assistants as it was for you to search the internet and pull information. Colleges crack down hard on plagiarism; they will check your papers. Plagiarism is academic dishonesty and you will face serious university sanctions which could include receiving a failing grade for the assignment and class, having a notation placed on your permanent university record or being placed on academic probation or suspended from the university. Is the internet a credible source?

- Passwords
  - o Don't use important dates or numbers in your password, such as your birthday, home address, or home telephone number. (example: some college students will use the last four digits of their home telephone as their PIN because they think it is a safe, unknown number).
  - o Don't use names or words that are important to you that someone could guess such as your pets' names, siblings' names or your favorite hobby.
  - o Use a combination of words and numbers with capital letters and/or numbers inserted throughout the password (example: To make "unicorn" a safer password, replace the "i" with the number one "1" and replace the "o" with a zero "0" to spell: Un1c0rN).
  - o Use passwords that have no meaning to other people (i.e., passwords that are a random assembly of letters and numbers that does not actually spell anything)
  - o Change your password every month. A device, called a Key-Stroke Logger (KSL), can record every key you type when using a computer. Such devices can be installed on public computer lab computers. By changing your password frequently, you can decrease the effectiveness and length of time the information obtained from a KSL is useful.
  - o Use different passwords for different logins. If someone does see your password, you will limit the amount of information they can access.

- Saving Information

Save your information constantly and in multiple places.

Places to save your information:
- Desktop
- Memory stick
- External hard drive
- Email (send an email to yourself with an attachment).

Don't fall victim to losing hours of work in case the computer freezes, the computer is accidentally turned off or due to a power surge or outage.

Email Points to Ponder:
- Remember, everything you put in writing and send over the internet becomes public and a permanent written record of your words. For your own protection, do not ever threaten or sexually harass someone through emails. Use the "newspaper" ethics principle: If you wouldn't want to see what you wrote printed in the newspaper, you probably shouldn't send it over email.
- BCC or "blind carbon copy" allows someone to be copied on an email without you seeing their name. Keep this in mind when receiving emails; although you may think you are the only one reading this email addressed to you, others may have been sent the same email as well.
- Do not create fake email accounts and falsely pretend to be another person.
- Carefully consider what information you include in your email signature that appears at the end of each email you send. Sending your contact information, including your address and phone, may not be wise for all emails you send. Also, creating a "mini-resume" in your signature by listing all of your club leadership positions can be intimidating or annoying to others.
- Be sure to completely log out of your email provider if using a public computer or even your computer if it is accessible to others.
- Consider setting up an email account with a web-based, free service to use when you need to sign up for things online. This will help reduce spam email and clogging of your university email account over the span of your college career.

- Think before you hit the "send" button. Frustrated with a friend or instructor? Remember, once it is sent there is no turning back and it's officially documented.

- Sign your emails with high school year book sayings such as "stay cool this summer."
- Put quotation marks around unimportant words in your emails.
- Create false credentials for yourself (President of <insert group>, CPR Certified, Undefeated Pool Champion, Student of the Year, Intramural Runner-Up, 7th Chair Trumpet, Automobile Crash Survivor, Proficient in Email)

Social Websites:

A new standard in computing are social websites such as Facebook™ and Twitter™. These have been a welcomed addition to many lives as they allow you to share your life, your thoughts, your pictures and let your friends (and strangers) look into your life. They also allow you to stay connected with old and new friends alike in an easily managed environment. In terms of meeting new people, these environments allow you to connect based on common interests, classes, or by looks alone. With only a few seconds of viewing a friend's page, you can see what's going on in their life and leave them a short message.

In a perfect world, the above uses would be safe and the only thing these sites are used for, but that's not always the case. Anytime you place information on the internet, you are opening yourself up to the world in many cases. These sites usually have security features which limit access to those who are not your friends. It's a good idea to take advantage of the security features to protect your information and yourself. As mentioned in other sections, it's important to remember once something is "submitted," many times it is out of your control as to who sees it and where it goes. Keep this in mind when setting up your accounts.

The many advantages of these sites often times overshadow some of the drawbacks. One of the biggest drawbacks you could encounter is spending **way** too much time on these sites. It doesn't take long to have hundreds of friends on these sites. Even casually monitoring your friends pages can quickly consume hours of your time. Time is often taken at great measures by the "web" effect of these sites. You may notice a friend listed on your friends page and explore what their page has on it, then may notice on their site another potential friend, etc. and lose track of time.

Be careful of what personal identifying information you put on a page. While listing your address or phone number may seem innocent, it is actually not very wise. There are some real creeps who lurk on the internet, and you don't want to provide them with any type of information that could compromise your safety, or at the least, provide them with a way to annoy you.

There are no real restrictions as to what is posted on these sites. Someone may write a rude comment on the message section of your site and it may sit there for a day or two before you delete it. What type of impression may that leave with others who visit your site? If you attend a party, someone may snap a picture of you and others having a drink or two...or maybe not even drinking...but what impression does this send? Often, things end up on these sites which students later regret. As mentioned before, information on the internet is readily available to many people. Would you want your parents or grandparents seeing this information or photos? How about future employers? Keep this in mind as you and others post things about you. Employers **will** check and you don't want a crazy picture keeping you from getting an internship or job.

Instant Messaging (IM):

As you enter college, your list of friends on your instant messaging service will definitely grow. IM can be nice to have on your computer to have a quick conversation or to ask a quick question, but it can really take up a lot of time and keep you from forming other relationships at college. Sitting down to simply check your email could turn into a two hour talk with a couple people via IM (and sluggishly at one or two sentences per message). It can also become a burden to human interaction. Many times, college students will IM with someone two doors away when it would be easier to talk to them in person.

A good rule of thumb: IM conversations should never replace an opportunity to have a human interaction.

Music Players:

On your campus visit you probably saw many students walking around with ear buds in their ears as they went about their daily business. Many college students choose to have an MP3 player of some type for music for their walk to class, ride on the bus or for their study session at the library. If you already have an MP3 player, definitely bring it along to school with you, but don't feel like you need to go out and spend the money on one if you do not have one.

Cell Phones:

Cell phones have become an item many people have as early as their middle school years. They are a very affordable way to stay in contact with friends and family. On a college campus, you will see many cell phones in use. If you don't already have one, there are usually reasonable plans available based on your needs (local vs. national, number of minutes included, other features, etc.). One thing that doesn't typically come with cell phones is a set of guidelines on how to be socially appropriate with them. Remember, the classroom setting is not a place for cell phones. Be sure to turn your phone off when you are in class or other situations where they are not appropriate. Having your phone disrupt a class is a good way to get on a professor's bad side. Also, don't let your cell phone consume your life...unless you are a doctor who is on call or drive an ambulance, you probably do not need to be reached on a moment's notice. As many students leave class, the first thing you'll see is their phones to their ears. The same etiquette rules should be applied to texting. The constant beeping or buzzing of your phone can annoy others and shows that you are not focused on the person or task in front of you. Remember, much of the college experience is interaction with those around you.

In your cell phone's contact list, create an entry for ICE which stands for: In Case of an Emergency. If you are in an accident, paramedics are trained to look to see if you have an ICE number in your cell phone to contact someone (such as your parents) for important medical questions and insurance.

Final Thoughts

Technology can serve many different functions: from making everyday tasks easier, assisting in research for homework, gathering information, connecting with friends and various forms of entertainment. The cost and time that various technologies consume can be overlooked. Be sure you are responsible with your time and money in regards to technology. A computer that can assist in homework can also serve a great video game machine which could consume A LOT of your time. Many students find themselves addicted to one or more forms of technology.

Your computer has its own identity through its IP address and your online activity can be tracked and monitored. Consider anything you write or post online, whether it's an email, a message board post, or online application, as potentially becoming public information. Know the creditability of any website before sending information or submitting an electronic signature. Do not do any illegal activity on your computer—campus authorities may monitor the college network usage and if they suspect you are involved with these behaviors, they may seize your computer and you will be subject to university expulsion, fines and prison time.

Points to Ponder

- When the internet is "down", internal websites, such as your college's webpage may still be accessible. Information may be posted on this site concerning the internet problem, what you can do and how long it is expected before full internet is connected again.
- An electricity black out is always a humbling experience of how much of our lives involve electronics. Ouija Board™ anyone?
- Set up a "junk" email account that you can use whenever you need to list an email address for online applications. "Junk mail" could even be part of your email name.
- The next time you answer a "love quiz", consider that random surveys may actually be used by a third party (such as an acquaintance) to phish for your information.
- Clear your internet browser's cache regularly.
- Stay current on computer updates and scanware software to prevent viruses from causing havoc on your computer and files.
- Interactive and never ending video and computer games have caused the demise of many college grades—monitor your use and set your own guidelines if necessary.

there are good and bad ways to get around campus.

CHAPTER 13

TRANSPORTATION
WALKING, BIKES, BUSES AND CARS

"TOOT! TOOT!"

Most colleges are set-up as pedestrian campuses, with perhaps a student bus circulator. This arrangement allows an efficient travel system for a lot of people in a limited space. Walking from class to class gives you time to take-in the campus, enjoy nature, catch-up with your friends and stay healthy.

Walking

At college, you will most likely walk from building to building, not just from classroom to classroom. You may not be used to this amount of walking. By the end of your first week, your feet may have throbbing pain or blisters so be sure to wear appropriate footwear. Usually classes will go on regardless of the weather so be cognizant of the forecast and be prepared for hot days, rainy downpours or windy snowstorms.

Will I have enough time between classes to make it to my next class across campus?
If you scheduled two classes in a row, you will generally have about ten minutes between classes, which is usually an adequate amount of time to reach your next destination. If you have difficulty making it to class on time, consider biking (see below) instead of walking.

If you have a class late at night or find yourself studying late at the library, stay safe by walking home with a friend. If you can't find someone to walk with, find out if your campus has a safety escort service. They are more than happy to get you home safely; and when it's raining, you can stay safe *and* dry.

If you see or hear a biker, don't freeze up and suddenly stop in front of the bike or you might find yourself in a collision; bikers have a broader view of the path and base their course on the anticipation that pedestrians will keep walking.

Biking

Riding your bike became unpopular shortly after junior high when you got your driver's license; however bikes at college are very popular. Biking between your classes is much faster and efficient, leaving you more time to set up your seat and notes, ask your professor a homework question and use the bathroom before your class starts. Make sure you are current on campus regulations regarding bikes including bike registration, sidewalk usage and parking.

Buy a good bike helmet and wear it. You will look stupid if you aren't wearing a helmet. The two most likely places you will be hit by a car while on a bike are parking lots and intersections, as cars are making a right hand turn.

Theft of bikes or bike parts is present on every campus. Invest in a good lock for your bike. Lock the main frame of your bike to the bike rack. If your bike has quick-release tires, use a chain to secure your tires as well. A separate lock may be needed as well if you have a quick release seat. Only lock your bike in designated areas (i.e., bike racks) and don't lock your bike to trees, sign posts, etc. or the lock may be cut and removed and the bike will be impounded by the campus parking division depending on your college's regulations. Make sure what you are locking-to is secure and grounded and not something someone could just slip your entire lock and bike away from. If you are using a lock that uses a number sequence, make sure to scramble more than just the last one or two digits on your keypad or your bike will be more prone to theft. Be sure to write down your bike's serial number in a safe place in case your bike comes up missing.

You will need to decide where you will store your bike when you are not using it: outside on a bike rack, it is subject to rusting away in the weather as well as being more vulnerable to theft; inside in your room, will further cramp your already limited living space. If you bought a bike after you arrived on campus, you will need to figure out how you will get it home or where you can store it for the summer.

4 Great Reasons for Biking:
1. Physical exercise
2. Fast and efficient
3. Good for the environment
4. Cut down on your car usage and fuel costs

The Green Movement

Take pride in your campus and help to protect its' beauty by staying on designated paths. Hundreds of students cutting through greenery or making shortcuts leaves damaged vegetation and unsightly brown paths. Protect nature and be a member of the Green Movement.

Buses and Subways

Buses and subways are a great way to get around campus and town when it's not practical to bring your car. Not all campuses will have this service, and depending on your campus you may have to pay a separate usage fee, or it may be included with your student fees. Some campuses will offer special shuttle services to run between parking lots and campus, to circulate just through campus or at night as a "designated driver" service. One drawback to public transportation is you have to precisely plan your time around the bus or subway's arrival and departure times; missing it even by a minute will result in seeing the back of the bus as it's leaving you behind.

Let's face it: reading bus schedules, with all the different routes, times and stops is confusing; even folding the schedule back up is hard! But there is one bus you can always count on finding: the struggle bus.

Cars and Parking

Most of the time you will not use your car to drive to class. So, do you even need a car at college? Let's look at the advantages and disadvantages:

Advantages:
Cars are convenient and time-saving as you can go anywhere you want to go when you want to go there. They are great for getting around town to the grocery store, discount store or restaurants as well as mini-road trips to a favorite park. If you have an off-campus job, you may be required to have a car for reliable transportation. Cars make it easier to go home on the weekends or when leaving for school breaks.

Disadvantages:
Parking your car is a real problem on most campuses due to limited available space. Your car may not be easily accessible to you and you may have to travel (walk, bike, bus, etc) just to reach your car which is parked at a distant or off-site lot. Parking on campus is usually expensive and requires a parking permit. Cars in general will drain your budget with costs of gas, insurance, monthly payments, repairs and maintenance. Also to include in

your budget are parking tickets and towing costs, which can be quite expensive. If your friends don't have a car and they know you do, you can expect to be asked to run errands with them or even to borrow your car; this can be time-consuming for you and presents extra liabilities. It is best to have firm policies regarding use of your car set in your mind before you encounter these situations. You may also feel very frustrated not having a car when you are used to having one and the freedom to go where you want, when you want. Not having a car may mean your trips to the store will take longer, and your trips will be less frequent.

If you lock yourself out of your car, it will be convenient to have a spare set of keys with you at college. Keep a spare set at your place and if possible, keep another set on you in a billfold or purse. This way if you accidentally lock yourself out of your car, you already have a spare key in your back pocket.

The remote car door-lock opener with some cars can be used over the phone. If you accidentally lock your keys in the car, call your parents, friends or whoever has your spare key and have them hold it to the phone and hit "unlock", while you in the meantime hold the phone next to the car lock.

Keep a disposable camera in your glove compartment—it will come in handy if you need to capture a description and license plate of a fleeing car from an accident or to record damages to your car following an accident. The camera can also be used for capturing any unique photo opportunities you pass while on the road.

 Talk with your parents before you leave about what you need to do if you have car problems. Does your car insurance offer roadside assistance or towing? Do you know how to change a flat tire, change the oil or replace headlights? Learn these skills before you head off to college.

Peace of Mind Car Kit:

It's a good idea to have a winter survival kit in your car if you live in an area which is susceptible to snow or ice. Such items you may consider include: flash light, first aid kit, shovel, blanket, food, jumper cables, paper towels, duct tape, maps, matches, and toilet paper.

Scooters and Motorcycles

If you have a motorcycle or scooter, bringing it to campus can be advantageous. Often times you are able to park much closer than if you were in a car and the fuel savings is also greater. Be sure to ride safely as college campuses can be busy places and people may not see you.

Rollerblades and Skateboards

We have found these to be not convenient for college since you will have to carry your rollerblades or skateboard with you into class. However, if you have passion for either one of these, you may find this to be the best transportation for you.

Final Thoughts

Plan to stay on campus for the day unless you live close by; bring notes to study between classes, pack a lunch and/or bring workout clothes to use at the fitness center. Use your travel time between classes to socialize with your classmates and friends.

Points to Ponder

- Fend off the Freshmen 15 by walking to class.
- Tread lightly with the Green Movement.
- Bikes are cool in college.
- Think carefully before bringing a car with you to campus.
- Due to limited parking space on most campuses, you are bound to accumulate parking fines or even towing costs. You are set up for failure.
- You won't have access to a garage to park your car at college. Your car will be more prone to damages either from vandalism or from the weather.
- Visit www.4X4training.com to learn more about off-road safety and car survival lists.
- Keep a roll of quarters in your car—it will come in handy for metered parking or road tolls.
- Yes, people will actually steal your bicycle seat.
- Bring a spare set of car keys with you.

Freshmen Moments
THE FIRST WEEK

When you first arrived on campus, everything was so exciting and yet so unfamiliar. Moving to a new place can be frustrating at times as you find yourself lost, clueless to the location of local stores and your inability to find a hair stylist. It will take time just to figure out where all the bathrooms and drinking fountains are located in your class buildings as well as which direction all the building doors exit to. Give yourself time to adjust—you just moved here a week ago! Look over area maps to get a feel for the town and campus layout. Take alternate routes home when you go somewhere to explore more of the area. Soon campus and your town won't seem as big anymore and will become more and more familiar every day.

The first week you will be meeting people left and right, in your classes, people living on your floor, people who join you for meals, etc. And you'll answer the same four questions over and over: What's your name? What's your major? Where's your hometown? Where are you living? Don't worry, no one expects you to remember all these facts about them at first because they forgot your name too. People are asking these questions to be friendly and to make a connection with you. But, some are still trying to establish a "who's who" from high school and may proceed to tell you how great they are through the number of scholarships, sporting events or homecoming royalty titles they won. Also, upperclassmen may seem scary at first or like they all hate freshmen, but it is all talk. Most of them are eager to offer you advice and help you out. So don't worry, crack open the campus map—who cares if people will know you are a freshmen--1 out every 4 people on campus are, and besides you never know what good-looking Samaritan might be coming your way.

The first week is very different of how the rest of the semester will actually be. It can be misleading in many ways and does not give a realistic perception. You won't be going out every night of the week and meeting people. Your schedule will eventually calm down and you will establish a normal routine. You will start to get to know people beyond the name, major, hometown conversations. And homework and studying will increase as your first round of tests approaches.

The week is a rollercoaster of emotions, at times feeling homesick and friendless and other times laughing and thinking "this is awesome!" Yes, young grasshopper, college is a crazy time but you're going to make it, you're doing just fine. We'll leave you with this final advice for the first week:

- Free t-shirts from credit card booths may not actually be a good deal.
- Your college ID card is used for everything; protect it like you would protect liquid gold.
- It's nice to have some groceries available in your room during the first couple weeks in case you miss a meal or need a snack.
- Each day take about 20 or 30 minutes to look at your calendar, plan out your day and organize your room, your book bag and your thoughts.
- Start recording your networking connections—figure out a system to remember and be able to contact the people you are meeting today for years to come; whether it's to catch up on old times or to work a business angle, you'll be glad you organized everyone's contact information, especially email addresses.
- You just can't really walk or lay around in your underwear anymore. Unless you like to create awkward moments for other people—say where's that robe you packed?

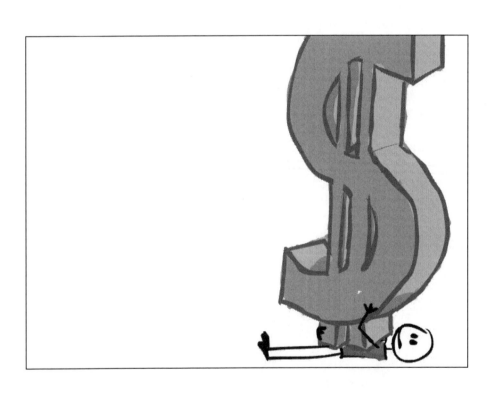

CHAPTER 14
COLLEGE FINANCES AND BUDGETS
FIND A CASH COW

"Mom? Dad? I love you"

Your education is the best investment you can make. Furthering your knowledge at a university is what you hope will lead to a fulfilling career with rewarding personal and financial opportunities. The costs associated with college, however, are a major source of stress for most students and their families. Your college education is probably the first real major investment or purchase you have made up to this point in your life; and probably the first time you will need to carry debt to your name. The financial decisions you make now will affect you in the long term, possibly for the next twenty years or longer. Learn as much as you can about how to pay for college; it's your money, your life and *you* are the one responsible to pay off the debt you acquire.

Creating a budget and following a well-thought out financial plan reduces your stress so you can focus on why you are at college in the first place, to be a student. Whether you have a partial or full ride scholarship or plan to work your way through college, everyone needs a budget. College can be a financial adjustment to your current lifestyle as you move away from the luxuries of home life and your parents. You need to form and practice good money habits and live within the means of being a college student. This does not necessarily mean that you have to be a "poor college student", but you need to make smart decisions.

For example, season tickets to your school's various sports may cost $200, but for many the excitement and memories that come from these games are truly part of their college experience. Although $200 may seem like a lot, if budgeted for properly, you can buy the season sports pass, but you may have to be flexible in other areas of your budget. But, will you be able to have season tickets to football, basketball, buy a new flat-screen TV, and dine-out every weekend? No, probably not.

Budget

When you create a budget, look at your costs and incomes for the next four years. A budget is a very fluid document and you will need to reevaluate it often to account for updated estimates, yearly inflation, and unforeseen life changes. You may be surprised how quickly "little things" add up in your budget when you multiply it out for a year. Track your expenses and income by keeping your receipts, updating your checkbook, filing your pay stubs and recording your credit card and ATM withdrawals. This will help you see how much you are spending on a particular area which allows you to make better estimates in your budget (ex: do you know how much you actually spend on gasoline in a week?). Using a computer spreadsheet to create your budget allows you to make changes easily and to experiment with various scenarios to see how they affect your financial plan.

Most of your university bill costs will be due at the beginning of each semester. Some colleges may offer payment plans so you don't have to pay such large amounts all at once, but these plans typically cost more in the long run due to interest or finance charges. Pay attention to your university bill. Many students don't even look at the itemized list of what exactly they are paying for. By knowing what you are paying for you can gain an appreciation for the services provided by your university and it may prompt you to use these services. For example, if you find that the campus bus system costs $100 per semester whether you use it or not, you may be more inclined to use this service since you are already paying for it, instead of spending money on another form of transportation. Don't just send a blind check to your university each time your bill is due without first reviewing the bill. Stay vigilant on the charges because billing mistakes occur. It will be your responsibility to address them....and errors do occur as a college may be producing thousands of these bills at one time. If you don't understand a charge on your bill, contact the university treasury office.

COSTS

Your major costs include tuition and room and board.

Mandatory University Fees:

- Tuition

  Plan on at least 5% inflation costs in tuition for each year. Some colleges can even approach 20% or more per year.

- Books and Supplies

  Books and supplies can range from $150 to $600 per semester depending on your major.

- Lab Fee

  Some classes will add a lab or field trip fee in addition to tuition, which is typically an extra $30-$75 per class.

- Activity Fee and Student Government Dues

  This one fee allows you join various college clubs. However many student organizations will also charge local or state dues.

- Facility Fee

  This includes various services and buildings on campus: fitness center, library, student union, counseling services, academic services, financial services, you name it.

- Student Health Fee

  Typically this fee will cover a physical examination and doctor visit fee; however if you need additional diagnostics (blood work, x-rays, etc.) or treatment (pharmacy, birth control, etc) you will need to pay for those services. Your school may also provide student health insurance, for a fee.

- Computer fee

  This fee funds the campus computer labs. It may or may not cover the costs to print.

- Energy fee

  Some colleges will assess this fee to help cover the general overhead costs of running a university such as the water and electricity needed in campus buildings.

- Other fees

  There may be some other miscellaneous fees appearing on your university bill with clever, smart-sounding names.

Residence Hall Fees:

- Room

  Room is your rent costs for your residence hall room and will typically include all of your utilities.

- Board

     Board refers to the cost of your meal plan. If you don't eat all of your meals at the dining center, be sure to include money for groceries, restaurants, vending machines, pizza and soda, coffee, etc.

- Laundry

     Laundry will cost somewhere between one and two dollars for each load you want to wash and dry.

     If you live off-campus you will pay for some or all of your utilities (gas, electricity, water/sewage, cable, internet, land phone line) as well any initial deposits. If you join a fraternity or sorority, you will pay for initiation dues and/or house and chapter dues.

Transportation:
- Car
     o Parking Permit

          To park on campus you will need to purchase a parking permit (can range from $50-$500 per semester).

     o Meters, Parking Tickets and Towing

          With limited parking on campus, if you have a car you can almost expect to pay parking tickets and/or towing at some point.

     o Monthly Payment
     o Insurance
     o Gas
     o Maintenance/Oil
     o Repairs
     o License/State fees

- Returning Home:
     o Plane Ticket
     o Bus Ticket
     o Gasoline

Living Costs:
- Beauty Care (haircut, tanning, pedicures, etc.)
- Health Care (dentist, optometrist, dermatologist, gynecologist, doctor exams and vaccines, etc.)
- Toiletries
- Cleaning Supplies (including laundry soap)
- Clothes
- Cell phone

Entertainment:
- Movies, Concerts
- Athletic Tickets
- Dating
- Hobbies

Set-up Costs:
- Large ticket (Loft, futon, fridge, bed sheets/towels, computer/printer, bike, book bag)
- Incidentals (tape/adhesives, hooks, marker board, etc)

Miscellaneous:

Did you account for holiday and birthday gifts? Where do stamps fall under your budget? How much do you spend on alcohol or cigarettes? Do you budget money for printer and copier costs? Are you planning any trips? How much will gas and food cost you during school breaks? What registration costs are associated with academic conferences or new student days? Will you pay for renters' insurance? What about move-in and move-out costs? Are you planning on studying aboard?

Emergency and Unexpected Costs:

When your budget accounts for every penny, emergencies and unexpected costs can cause a great deal of stress for you; leave 10 to 15% of your income unbudgeted to leave you some breathing room for these unforeseen costs.

INCOME

Your major sources of income will include scholarships, student loans, parents and working.

Personal savings:

This includes any money you have saved up from summer jobs, investments, etc.

Banking:

You may want to set up a bank account in your college town or keep both a home bank account and a college bank account. Ease of availability of money from your account is an important factor to consider when deciding if you need a bank account in your college town. If you bank with a national chain, it may be easier for your parents to deposit money into your account. When looking at a bank, look at the various benefits it offers including distance from your residence hall, ATM service, checking, online banking, withdrawal protection and student-friendly service. Ask about any service fees or possible bank fines.

Graduation money:

Although probably not a huge amount, any money you receive from high school graduation can help defray some of the initial setup, one time only costs or provide some nice extras and luxuries for college. Some people will use this money for some of the "big purchases" like a computer, dorm fridge, futon, or other large expense.

Scholarships:

You can earn scholarships for academics, athletics, leadership and involvement, community service, being part of an underrepresented group and financial need. Keep in mind the scholarships you received from your high school may only last for your freshmen year. Don't forget to keep applying for scholarships even when you are in college. There are even scholarships available when you are a college senior, but you have to constantly watch for them and apply. And remember, many of these scholarships may require a certain grade point average to renew the scholarship.

If you received a scholarship to compete in a collegiate sport, it offers many other benefits besides its monetary value including staying in shape, prestige, belonging to a group and making close friends. However, keep in mind why you are going to college; if sport practices take up so much time that your grades suffer or that you end up at college for an extra year, the sports scholarship may not have been worth it, especially if you are entering a career that does not involve that sport.

Tips for Scholarship Applications:
- Send in more information than requested.
  - Let the scholarship committee decide what to do with the extra information you submitted—having five recommendation letters when you only need three will not hurt you.
- Go way above expectations.
  - Spend more time on your application than you think you should--make it an easy decision for the scholarship committee to select you.

- Tailor your application and resume to the scholarship.
  - For example, if you are applying for a campus involvement scholarship, place more emphasis on your campus organization leadership and community service activities.
- Report the positives
  - Don't be afraid or shy to speak highly of your accomplishments. Be confident.
- Keep a consistent story.
  - Explain any time gaps in your resume. "Tell a story" by demonstrating the natural progression of your leadership, involvement or community service.
- Have solid examples.
  - Don't spread yourself thin—stick with two or three main activities you are actively involved with.
- Have multiple people review your application.
- Conclude your essay with a well-thought reason why you should be selected for the award.
  - "As demonstrated through my leadership in the university, our community and academics, and exemplified through my commitment and dedication to initiatives to help fellow students and the community, I hope you recognize I would make the best representative for the.......scholarship-award."

Financial Aid and Grants:

Your school may offer you money upfront as a lump sum or as a reoccurring yearly amount based on your past accomplishments. You may also qualify for additional funding from your school or major department based on your continued success in college. Many scholarships are contingent on you maintaining a certain GPA and keeping a clean university judicial record.

There is also money available for students with financial need, such as grants or work-study (see Chapter 39: Spring Introduction for more information on the Free Application for Federal Student Aid, or FAFSA).

Summer Job:

Including the summer before your freshmen year, you will have a total of four summers during college during which you can earn money. Summer jobs and internships are also a great way to gain experience in your field of study. When figuring out an estimate for this category, don't forget to take into consideration taxes (Federal Income Tax, Social Security, Medicare and State Income Tax) which can amount to almost a third of your total gross income. However, you may receive most of this money back through a tax refund in the spring.

Part-time School Year Job:
There are many on-campus and student-friendly jobs that you could work part time during the school year. Having a job during school can help you manage your time, if you remember to keep academics and studying as your main priority. Most on-campus employers understand this and will work around your class schedule; as another bonus, your job will probably be within walking distance of your residence. Some jobs may allow you to work on your own time and you can usually find a job that will allow you to work ten hours or less per week. Another option is to work full-time during school year breaks.

Some students work within their major department to gain practical and resume experience; others will work any general job so they have extra spending cash for incidentals and going out with friends. Others choose to work as a way to network to lead to other opportunities or as an outlet to meet people and socialize.

There are many types of jobs on campus that typically employ students such as undergraduate lab researcher, computer lab monitor, tutor, teaching assistant, parking enforcer, or working in the residence halls as a resident assistant, hall desk worker, student security, student janitor, maintenance or dining services worker (see Chapter 7: Campus Housing).

 Direct deposit of your paycheck into your banking account can save you time and most university employers will offer this option. You may also be able to link it to your university bill so that if you have any charges your paycheck will be applied to those first before being deposited.

Medical Studies:
You may be able to participate in a medical study for payment. The study could be as simple as answering some questions about your habits or be more extensive including blood draws and urine samples. Studies are typically two weeks in duration, but can range from one day to a semester. Some students will also sell their plasma on a regular basis to earn money. Be sure you understand any health risks associated with "selling your body" to science.

Remind people they are lucky to have a job to complain about.

Military Money:

At some point you will hear about a branch of the military that has an offer to pay for college in exchange for enlisting either part time or full time. This can be a great way to pay for college and receive leadership training, but be sure to carefully consider all of the commitments and associated risks. The Reserve Officer Training Corps (ROTC) is an excellent program where students attend college and part of their curriculum is serving with a branch of the military. Joining the military often requires a multi-year commitment after graduation. Again, just be sure to consider all options and don't make any snap decisions.

Parents:

Don't forget your grandparents or any wealthy relatives!

Cash Cow:

You're a college student, you're smart. Look around you--what opportunities exist. Think of the hundreds to thousands of students on campus and now multiply that number by $5 each. What need is currently not being met on your campus? Think, think, think....

Birthday Money

Hey, this is a comprehensive list!

Loans:

There is a good chance you will need to take out loans during college and that's ok. Use your loan money for investment in your education (i.e., direct college costs such as tuition, books, fees, etc.), not for day to day living expenses and luxuries (i.e., car payment, gifts, etc); use your other sources of income (such as a part-time school or summer job) to cover these indirect college costs. Although it is tempting to take out more loan money than you need, it is wise to only borrow the minimum amount that you actually need to reduce your total repayment amount. Think of a loan as pre-spending your future salary. You don't want to be writing a check at age 30 to cover the money you spent on pizza and a car that no longer exists.

After completing your FAFSA form (see above), you will be notified of what loan programs you qualify for and the total amount you can borrow. The most common loan is the Direct Stafford Loan Program, which is a direct loan from the United States Government through the Department of Education. The loan is available as either a subsidized or unsubsidized loan. Subsidized means the government pays your loan interest until you enter repayment and this loan is awarded based on financial need. Unsubsidized means you must pay the interest; while you are in school you can choose to pay this interest or let it accrue and capitalize on your principal amount. All Stafford loans (as of July 1, 2009) have a fixed interest of 6.8% or lower. You are also assessed a loan fee upon each loan disbursement up to 4% of the value of your loan. The loan is distributed to your college and is applied to any university costs first; if any money is left over once your university bill is paid, you will receive the remaining amount. You must sign a promissory note, a binding legal document, agreeing to the repayment conditions, which usually start six months after you graduate from college. You can also take a loan out from a private lender such as a bank, but interest rates and terms are usually not as favorable as federal loans.

Spend Less:
Although not a source of income, the less you spend, the less money you need.

Credit Cards

College may be the first time you obtain a credit card. A credit card serves many useful purposes but also carries a lot of responsibility. Some college students end up in major credit card debt because it is easy to overspend using credit (since you don't need to have the actual money up front), combined with high interest rates and no full-time job or any job at all to pay off the credit card. But when used correctly, credit cards can help build your credit score and reduce the amount of cash you need to carry on your person. Credit cards can also be useful during emergencies, such as your car breaking down. The best way to manage your credit card is to not spend money you don't have, that is, make sure you can pay off your credit card completely with each billing cycle. You may consider a debit card instead, which is like a "check card" because it automatically deducts money from your bank account. Like everything else involving your money, make sure you educate yourself and understand all of the fine print.

 While it may seem like a good idea to sign up for a credit card to get a free shirt or mug with your school's logo, remember opening an account opens up a line of credit. And simply cutting the card up when it arrives does not close this line of credit.

Credit Report

The Fair and Accurate Credit Transaction Act (FACT Act, a federal law), allows you to obtain one free credit report from each of the three national credit reporting companies (Equifax, Experian and Trans Union) once every 12 months. The only official website where you can get a free credit report is from www.annualcreditreport.com. The information on your credit report determines your credit score, which translates into your creditworthiness for future lenders and the amount of money (and at what interest rate) they are willing to lend you. Therefore, it is wise to know what is on your credit report and monitor it for any fraud.

Understand how interest works. Yes, you could get a new big screen TV, DVD player, and surround sound speaker system with no payments, interest-free for six months, *but* you still will have to pay off that $4,000 debt. As enticing as it is to only have to pay $25 a month "minimum payment," with interest, that $4,000 set-up can easily become a $9,000 set-up that you'll end up paying off for years!

Final Thoughts

Planning a budget for college at first can be overwhelming and frustrating. In the end though, things will work out. Going through the process of creating a budget allows you to appreciate the value of your education as well as encourages you to develop good money habits. You don't have to be a cheapskate to get through college, but it's important to stay on top of your finances, record your expenses and live within your budget. The decisions and habits today will affect how much discretionary income you will have later. Although student loan repayment seems like a far away thought, graduation day will come faster than you think.

As you can see, college is costing you a lot; keep this in mind if you are considering skipping your next 8 AM class. Using very conservative estimates, each class session costs about $20. Would you skip a concert or going to a movie after you bought the tickets?

Points to Ponder

- Watch for student discounts, special events and college coupon books.
- There are many free campus events where you can have fun; some events have low turn-outs and you can rake in the door-prizes.
- Everyone and their brother brought DVDs with them to college; peruse their collection, microwave some popcorn and skip the movie theater.
- Think creatively. You don't need to spend much money to have fun with your friends or go on a date.
- Ride share.
- Use the campus resources you've already paid for (student health, fitness center, library, finance center).
- The price you pay for a product all depends on where you want to live on the fashion and technology curve.
- Don't sign up for a credit card just because you want the free shirt; opening and closing multiple credit cards can affect your credit score.
- Live the student life style. Buy generic. Buy used. If you live like you are a young professional with a full time job while you are still in college, you may have to buy used and generic when you actually do have a job because the you in the future will need to be supporting the you from the past.
- Don't always be the cheapo; take your date to a nice meal and pick up the tab.
- Anything you buy on a daily basis, such as vending machine snacks, coffee, pop, etc., will add up quickly over the course of a year when multiplied by 365.
- Buying from the grocery store will be cheaper than purchasing convenience snacks and soft drinks.
- Record, review, and reflect on your budget. Align your budget with your priorities.
- Think in the long term, and don't throw things out. For example, it might be better to buy a more quality, expensive couch that can last throughout college and beyond than to buy a cheap couch every year that you throw away. Also consider, how many wall posters and plants make it to a second year?
- Think about security; where can you keep your cash in a safe spot?
- When ordering merchandise online, if you notice a field for "coupon" or "promotion code" during the check-out process, you may be able to save

yourself money by searching the internet for that coupon code—type in the company's name and/or product with the words "coupon" or "promotion code".

- Don't wait until it is too late; make sure you understand what you're signing, what you're borrowing and what you'll need to pay back.
- Set achievable estimates and goals.
- Save more, spend less.
- Evaporation without explanation: Keep track of ATM withdrawals.
- Like at home, having back-up supplies, such as extra laundry soap, is nice and convenient as it cuts down on trips to the store, but it is also expensive to store extras and space in your room may be tight.

CHAPTER 15
ALCOHOL AND COLLEGE PARTIES
IT'S DRINKING TIME!

"But MOM!.....if I were truly an alcoholic, don't you think my dorm fridge would be empty, and not full of beer?"

In some form or another, alcohol and drinking will be present during your freshmen year. Realize though, there is no "freshmen expectation" that you have to drink once you are at college. By providing you information on common alcohol policy myths, the pros and cons of drinking, some situations you may find yourself in and what to expect and not to expect at college parties, you will be able to draw your own conclusion if you want drinking to be part of your college experience.

Real Peer Pressure

Do you remember in junior high health class where you were taught about peer pressure? It probably involved some video or other scenario where your friend (who, as it turns out later, really isn't your friend) offers you some sort of drug or alcohol in the school parking lot or playground. The person seems to come out of nowhere interrupting what you were doing, you politely say no to their offer and go back to your game of Four-Square. Unfortunately this is not a realistic perspective of peer pressure. In college, *real* peer pressure might look more like this:

It's your first weekend at college. You are excited to be on your own, exploring new freedoms and meeting lots of new people. It's Friday night and you hear a knock at the door; it is a couple guys you met earlier this week at the dining center. They want to know if you would like to go out with them to a house party tonight. Even though you don't consider yourself a "drinker", you don't want to sit in your room alone on a Friday night, and so you decide to join them.

You will quickly find yourself in many situations in college like this and you need to decide *beforehand* whether you want drinking to be part of your college experience. Knowing who you are and what type of college experience you want will help you make decisions. Otherwise, although subtle, this seemingly simple invite shows how easily it is to be influenced by peer pressure by playing on the shared scares of every freshmen student: feeling alone and isolated; not wanting to miss out on a "college experience"; and feeling there are no other acceptable social alternatives to drinking.

Peer pressure is tough. You should know what you will do or say when alcohol is a choice before you are in that situation.

Many habits are formed in college. The choices you make in college will continue in your life even after you leave the university. How big of a role do you envision alcohol to play in your life?

Perspective

You aren't missing out on any opportunity or college experience if you choose not to drink. The majority of any college population is made up of freshmen and sophomores, who are typically under the age of 21. This means there are more people on your campus who can't drink alcohol legally than those who can. Simply stated, the majority of people at your college are under 21. Everyone is NOT at the bars and you can find other people and other things to do for fun that does not involve drinking.

What are you missing by not being at the bars? Expensive drinks, smoky, crowded atmosphere and loud music that makes conversation difficult.

Be creative in the fun you have and surround yourself with people who don't need to involve alcohol in everything they do. Envision you are sharing a photo album of your first year of college with your family or high school friends, what pictures do you see in that album? Would you rather have: One where you spent most of your time and weekends being wasted at parties, and trying to avoid the police? Or one where you went to collegiate sporting events, participated in club activities, attended campus events, enjoyed local parks, volunteered in the community, attended concerts and plays and watched movies and hung out with friends?

You are not socially inept if you do not drink. You don't have to drink to be social and to have fun. People will recognize and respect your decision not to drink.

Know the Facts

Myth #1: College campuses have special regulations that allow you to drink even if you are under the age of 21.

You will hear many variations of this myth, but here is the concrete fact: If you are under the age of 21, it is illegal for you to possess and consume alcohol in the United States. End of discussion. You may be confused later by what upperclassmen tell you or what your cousin tells you, but always keep the above statement in the back of your mind. The National Minimum Drinking Age Act, [23 U.S.C. § 158], was passed by Congress in 1984 and requires that States prohibit persons under 21 years of age from purchasing or publicly possessing alcoholic beverages as a condition of receiving State highway funds.

Why is there confusion?
- Some college towns have bars that allow people 18 years and older to enter. However, you still must be 21 to possess or consume alcohol in the bar.
- During sporting events such as football games, there may be special rules allowing consumption of alcohol in designated areas such as the stadium parking lot. This is an exception to the public open container law, not to the minimum age to consume alcohol. If a law enforcement officer witnesses you possessing alcohol while "tailgating", you will be issued a citation for Minor in Possession (MIP) and possibly public intoxication.

Mike Story Box

A freshmen student who lived on my floor was upset because she was issued a MIP while tailgating. She did not realize it was illegal and stated everyone else around her was also drinking underage. She had to call her parents because she was not able to afford the $125 fine.

- College students underage studying aboard or spending spring break in a foreign country may be able to consume alcohol under the foreign country's law. Be careful though because United States or your university policies concerning alcohol may still apply to you while you are visiting these places.

Myth #2: *If you live in the dorms, it is ok to drink alcohol.*

A change in location is not an exception to the federal law stated above. Remember: If you are under the age of 21, it is illegal for you to possess and consume alcohol in the United States. No exceptions.

Why is there confusion?

- Read the Terms and Conditions of your residence hall contract carefully. There may be a difference in the judicial process if you are documented for having *empty* alcohol *containers* in your room (such as an empty wine bottle) versus being documented for having actual alcohol in your room (a half-full beer can in your hand). The empty alcohol container may result in a break of residence hall contract and your judicial review will be at the university housing level with a professional staff member such as the hall director. The case with having actual alcohol in your possession will be in violation of student conduct of your University's Student Handbook and your judicial hearing will be held at the university level with representatives from the Dean of Students office and/or public law enforcement officials. Sanctions from either example can result in monetary fines, required alcohol education class attendance, recording on your permanent university record, university probation status, disqualification from athletic teams or scholarship funding, ineligibility to apply for student university jobs, difficulty in applying to graduate or professional schools, unfavorable letters of recommendation, required community service or university suspension or expulsion.

    Example:
    Some students create "glow lamps" by placing the dye from a highlighter into a bottle filled with water—the bottle will then glow under a black light. If you choose to make a glow-lamp from an empty wine bottle and you are under 21, you may be violating

your residence hall's terms and conditions contract (stating you will not keep empty alcohol containers in your room), even though there is no alcohol in the bottle.

- Another area of confusion in the residence halls regarding alcohol policies is the situation where one roommate of legal drinking age shares the room with someone under the age of 21. It will again depend on the specifics of your residence hall contract (Terms and Conditions), but usually the person who is 21 or older retains the right to possess and consume alcohol within the room. As you can see this often creates a gray zone that can lead to trouble for the person under 21 since alcohol can be found in the room. If you find this to be your housing situation and you are under 21, be sure there is no confusion of the ownership of the alcohol in the room (i.e., don't allow the alcohol be stored in your refrigerator on your side of the room.) Have a discussion with your roommate about where the alcohol will be kept in the room, if and when the alcohol can be consumed in the room and about having parties and guests over who are drinking.

Most residence halls will also have a policy that restricts alcohol consumption to residence hall rooms only, which means you cannot drink alcohol in the hallway, common floor spaces or bathrooms.

Mike Story Box

One Saturday morning I was brushing my teeth in the community bathroom when another student came in drinking from a beer can. He then proceeded to take a shower with his beer. *If you drink while you shower, you have an alcohol problem.*

Your university housing department may have alcohol-free housing options that prohibit alcohol within the building by anyone regardless of age. Whether you choose to drink alcohol or not, there are many benefits of living in a wellness environment including: returning home to a clean, quiet, safe place; avoiding alcohol-related behavior such as noise and vandalism; surrounding yourself with positive people who can find fun without involving alcohol. You will more fully appreciate the benefits of an alcohol-free community if you ever live on a non-alcohol free floor where the bathrooms are not useable on the weekends because puke is splattered on the toilet seats and shower stalls.

Myth #3: Everyone else is drinking at the party, so it must be ok.

Nope, if you are under 21, it is still not legal to drink alcohol, no matter how many other people under the age of 21 around you are drinking alcohol. In fact, even if you aren't actually drinking at the party, you could still be cited for minor in possession. You may not get caught the first time you drink underage, but everyone eventually does. You are not immune no matter how many times you drank before without being caught. Little, simple mistakes will lead you right into the hands of a residence hall staff member or public law enforcement officer when you least expect it. If you choose to drink underage, you must be willing to accept the consequences of your decision. Besides being cited as a minor in possession (MIP) of alcohol, your trouble with the law may not end there. Other associated citations may include:

- Public intoxication and lewd behavior
- Public urination
- Open container in public or in your car
- Driving under the influence (DUI)
- Vandalism of personal or public property
- Noise violation
- Using false identification
- Rape
- Possession of drugs or drug paraphernalia
- Resisting arrest or fleeing from police

Mike Story Box

A very bright, friendly and ambitious student lived on my residence hall floor one year who made one poor decision regarding alcohol one night that changed the rest of her life path. Her night started with using a fake ID to enter a bar with a friend. After becoming inebriated they came across a running, parked car that had keys in it. She and her friend thought it would be fun to drive the car five blocks back to their residence hall. She was still drunk and was talking loudly to a neighbor about the night's events. A student security officer overheard the conversation and reported it to law enforcement. The police arrived shortly thereafter and arrested the student. She spent the night in jail before her family posted bond. She and her parents spent a lot of time and money on lawyers and legal fees. In the end, she was charged with possession of fake ID, underage drinking, driving under the influence, and grand theft auto (felony). She had to complete extensive community service hours, attend alcohol education classes, pay fines and damages and went on probation. She was expelled from the university.

> **Mike Story Box**
>
> A student one year ahead of me in veterinary school changed his entire life after one night of drinking. He was partying in a nearby town and at the end of the night drove home. On the highway he crossed the median, struck another car and killed the driver. On charges of involuntary manslaughter, he will spend at least the next decade of his life in prison. The driver he killed was just 26 years old, and his fiancé had just bought her wedding dress the day before.

Don't think these situations or other similar devastating events will ever happen to you? I promise you these two students did not plan on these events, would not have predicted it would have happened to them, and regret every minute of their choices.

Myth #4: It's not a big deal if I get caught, no one will find out, and I'll just pay the fine.

As we discussed in Chapter 2: Orientation regarding FERPA, the law and university will treat you as an adult and will most likely not directly notify your parents about judicial violations (unless, of course, you signed an information release form, you are under the age of 18, or in some other circumstances). However, city or university newspapers have the right to put your name in print and the alleged violation from police reports and logs. It is hard to keep public information private, including any future internet searches of your name. Information will travel quickly back to your hometown and family. Imagine the disappointment of your family, after being so proud of sending you off to college to be responsible and on your own, to then find out about your poor decisions leading to you being arrested. Your professors will be reading the same newspapers as well.

You and your friends make a night of drinking. Around midnight, you think one of your friends has had too many drinks and may be suffering from alcohol poisoning but you are afraid to seek help because you all have been drinking underage. What should you do?

Call an ambulance or police immediately. Tell them you need a wellness check on your friend that you suspect has alcohol poisoning. Alcohol poisoning can be a fatal condition and every year college students die from it. **Police are more concerned about helping someone get the medical attention they need than citing them for underage drinking.** Be up front and honest with all facts that will help the professional staff make decisions for your friend including the amount and type of drinking and any drugs used.

Even if you aren't sure your friend is suffering from alcohol poisoning (see below), but something tells you something is not right, seek help immediately. Notify a resident assistant or someone else who can get help for your friend. Don't hesitate and wait to see if the condition will improve. It won't.

Signs of alcohol poisoning:
- Unconscious; Unable to wake the person; doesn't respond to you pinching their skin
- Paleness, bluish skin color, feels cold to the touch
- Slow breathing; irregular breathing
- Vomiting while asleep
- Seizures

This is a real situation you may find yourself in, whether you drink or not. While you are waiting for professional help, turn your friend to the side in case they vomit to prevent them from swallowing the vomit and it entering their lungs (aspiration pneumonia). Don't leave your friend, stay with them until help arrives.

Confrontation:

If you are confronted by a police officer or resident assistant for underage drinking, the best thing to do is to be honest and cooperative. Being a responsible decision-making adult also means accepting responsibility for your actions and any consequences. At this point, you have been caught and you have to accept this fact; the best thing to do to help keep yourself from getting into more trouble by not doing something irrational. If you cannot accept the consequences of drinking, then don't drink. Don't try to give a false name or try to run away, you will only get yourself into more trouble.

The biggest clue to your resident assistant that you may be having a party is having loud music coming from your room. In fact, your RA may just knock on your door to ask you to turn down your music as a courtesy to your neighbors, only to discover you have alcohol in the room when you open the door. An RA will also be suspicious of you having a party if there is a lot of activity around your door, with people coming in and out. The last tip-off would be the sound of glass bottles clinking or the sight of people entering your room with square backpacks (cases of beer) late on a weekend night.

Guilty by association. Even if you are not drinking, you can be cited for minor in possession for being at the party. Why even put yourself in that situation?

To drink or not to drink?

For each person this is a very personal, complex choice that is the result of many factors including beliefs, values, religion and upbringing. This section will compare some of the pros and cons of drinking for you to ponder.

Pros:

- Drinking can be a way to be social. You can meet a lot of people at parties and interact with people whom you may not have otherwise interacted.
- Drinking can be a distraction from your normal routine. It may provide you with a way to escape stresses of your regular week.

- Drinking can be fun way to connect with your friends. Drinking parties may revolve around card games or party themes where you have the chance to dress up.
- Drinking can be educational. You can learn a lot about yourself, others, group dynamics and social interactions. You can also learn about the various kinds of drinks and mixes.
- You can be a responsible partier and role model for your friends. You can help keep your friends safe and be a designated driver.

Cons:

- Drinking can lead to relationship problems. Increased incidents of arguing, unexpected pregnancies, date rape, sexually transmitted diseases and physical abuse may occur when alcohol is a factor.
- Drinking can lead to financial problems. Liquor is expensive and will quickly affect your limited budget. You may be surprised how much you actually spend on alcohol by keeping track.
  If you are strapped for cash, reduce the amount of money you spend on alcohol.

To promote better health, what if someone offered you $1,000, which you could spend on anything you wanted, on the first day of every summer if you agreed not to drink alcohol during the school year, would you do it? Calculate how much you spend on alcohol in a year---you could be that person who makes this offer to yourself—a healthier and wealthier you, every year.

- Drinking can lead to academic problems. Staying out late on a Thursday night may make you miss your Friday morning classes. Being too sick and hung over for the weekend will decrease your effective studying time. College classes are already hard enough without the added dimension of being hung-over.
- Drinking can lead to legal issues. Besides the obvious of drinking underage, you could also find yourself in trouble for: using false identification, public intoxication, destroying public or personal property or driving while under the influence. If you are caught, you may damage your university record, have to pay fines and attend an alcohol class.
- Drinking can lead to health problems. You are adding unnecessary calories to your diet, the reason why they call it a "beer gut". You are ingesting a toxin that your liver has to detoxify and overtime will cause liver damage. There is nothing fun about laying next to a toilet all night vomiting and then still feeling sick in the morning and wasting away your day.

Some people are misled to believe avoiding beer and only drinking hard liquor will reduce their calorie intake while drinking. If you want to be a healthy person and maintain your weight, decrease the amount of alcohol you drink or don't drink at all.

- Drinking can lead to personal problems. While under the influence, you may do something embarrassing, hurt yourself or make unwelcomed sexual advances. Habits form in college and you may find yourself dependent on alcohol. Drinking excessively may lead to depression.

The atmosphere of parties encourages people to fake their behavior and act more drunk than they truly are. Fake behavior allows people to justify their actions, in case they do something embarrassing or sexual, by chalking it up to the excuse, "Oh I was drunk." This usually leads to the one or two "crazy stories" that people tell the next day about what happened at the party. An example would be: "The party was so crazy! People were dancing on the table!" But what they don't tell you is that only happened for about ten minutes and for the rest of the 3 hours they spent standing against the wall or walking around. People will often create or do something silly so that they have a story to tell later. An easy way to tell if someone is putting on a show is to tell them the police just arrived and observe if they suddenly have dramatic control over their actions.

 Coffee houses are a great place to be social and get lost in conversation. You don't even have to drink coffee; try some of these tasty drinks: Chai tea, milk steamer, fruit smoothie or milk shake.

The Reality of the Situation:
- Ask yourself *why* you drink:
- Is it because you are socially awkward otherwise?
- Do you drink because it's the only way you can relax?
- Do you drink because you can't make conversation with the opposite sex without first "inhibiting" your fears with alcohol?
- Do you drink because you are uncreative and this is the only thing you know how to do?
- Do you feel out of place everywhere unless you have a drink in your hand?
- Do you feel nothing is fun unless alcohol is involved?
- Do you like having slow reflexes?
- Do you like feeling nausea or the aftertaste of vomit in your throat?
- Do you sometimes just like to pass-out for the night and not really remember where you were and who you were with?

Some words that describe people who choose not drink: health-conscious, confident, high self-esteem, loves life, likeable, fun, responsible.

Dangers of Drinking:

- Date Rape:
  - o You are more likely to be raped by someone you know, often in a social setting. Involving alcohol increases your risk of this danger.

If someone is intoxicated they cannot consent to sex and you can be charged for rape if you have sex with them. The "I was drunk, too" excuse will not protect you from charges. For your own protection, don't even put yourself in a situation where you could be accused of rape. Protect your own future. When someone tells you no, **it absolutely means no**.

Date Rape Drugs:

Date rape drugs, commonly Rohypnol (a.k.a. Roofies), Ketamine hydrocholorine (a.k.a. Special K) or Gamma Hydroxy Butyrate (aka GHB), are tasteless, odorless and colorless drugs that can be slipped into your drink and will cause you to act without inhibition, decrease your ability to think clearly and cause you to have no clear memory of what happened. The drugs can take effect within 15 minutes and you can be disassociated from your surroundings for several hours. Traces of the drug will exit your body within about 72 hours.

How to protect yourself:

- o Don't accept open drinks. Choose bottles or cans that you open.
- o Never leave your drink unattended or out of sight.
- o Don't go to secluded areas with someone you don't know.
- o Stick with your friends at parties. Keep tabs on your friends to make sure they are ok.
- o If you suspect you may have been raped after usage of a drug (memory lapses, waking up in an unfamiliar place, missing clothes, soreness or bruising of your genitals, used condoms or seminal or vaginal fluids), go to the student health center and tell them you want to be tested for the presence of date rape drugs. Don't

delay as the drugs will decrease in your system over time. Don't urinate and don't change your clothes or shower as there may be more evidence collected.

- Binge Drinking
  - o Binge drinking means drinking an excessive amount of alcohol in a short amount of time (typically this means five or more drinks for men and four or more drinks for women). Activity that can lead to binge drinking may include: card games, taking shots, funnel shots and keg stands. Vomiting, loss of perception and blackouts are common adverse effects of binge drinking. It can also lead to alcohol poisoning.
- Alcohol Poisoning
  - o Alcohol is a toxin that can overwhelm your liver. It can make you unconscious and can be a fatal condition if immediate medical help is not sought.
- Physical Harm (driving, walking, puking, loss of control, slow reflexes)
  - o Alcohol slows your reflexes. There is nothing neat about not having control of your own body. No one likes the sensation of nausea and vomiting. You can hurt yourself just by walking. If you drive you could kill yourself and others.
- Altered Behavior
  - o Alcohol can make you act without inhibition and cause you to commit crimes with which you normally would not be involved. Common altered behaviors associated with drinking include noise and vandalism.
- Poor Decision Making
  - o Alcohol inhibits your ability to think clearly and can result in making irrational decisions. Poor decision making while under the influence can lead to physical harm to yourself or others, destroyed relationships and friendships and legal problems. Decreased inhibition can lead to unprotected sex and contracting a sexually transmitted disease (STD).
- Alcoholism
  - o Habits form in college. Alcoholism is a disease that will affect every aspect of your life: family, friends, finances, schoolwork and career. Alcohol is addictive and impairs your control of your body and your thoughts.

College Parties

What to expect:
- If you are hosting the party, something of yours could be broken or stolen.
- Your initial plans being interrupted by group processes: trying to get everyone together in one place, helping your friend who is puking,

mediating between two friends who are yelling at each other, having to collect money for the alcohol, presence of police officers dispersing a party, etc.

- Majority of your time is spent standing around, awkwardly making small talk conversation.
- Alcohol costs money, and you'll probably have to pay (even if you don't plan on drinking).
- Conversations are harder to keep because it may be loud, and the people may be intoxicated.
- A "huge party" could be eight people or 100. Walking into either could be awkward.
- More men than women present.
- People not knowing when to say "no" to alcohol, and thus, drunken behavior.
- Someone crying for some reason.
- Fights do happen and you could get caught up in one.

What not to expect:
- Never being caught or cited for underage drinking.
- Free alcohol.
- Group sex orgies.
- Engaging conversations.
- Everyone you meet remembering who you are the next day or later in class.
- Finding the love of your life.
- The party scene you've seen on countless movies.

Don't brag about the number of beers you drank or how wasted you were over the week. It's basically like saying, "hey everyone, I'm a tool".

Safety Tips for going to a Party:
- Go with a group of friends and watch out for each other. Make sure everyone gets home safe; don't leave any of your friends behind.
- Plan ahead and have a plan B to exit the party. You don't need to stay at the party the whole time; it's ok to leave whenever you want.
- Know your alcohol limit. You should not have memory black-outs. If you vomit, your body is telling you it can't process the amount of alcohol you have consumed. Don't let your friends keep drinking if they have vomited.
- If you don't know what is in a drink, don't drink it. Keep your drink in your sight at all times.
- Don't ever get into a car with someone you don't know or someone who has been drinking. Even if the person has only had "just one" drink, you are endangering your life. Have a designated driver if you need a ride.

- Dress appropriately. Wear comfortable shoes in case you end up having to walk home or have to leave a party quickly. Leave extra accessories at home that you may lose or forget at a party such as purses, jewelry, expensive cameras or coats.
- Avoid secluded areas with someone you just met. Don't be afraid or shy to leave someone who makes you feel uncomfortable.
- Draw attention to yourself by yelling, kicking and screaming if someone makes inappropriate sexual advances.
- Don't drink on an empty stomach.
- After a night of drinking, reduce your gravitation potential by sleeping on your futon or couch. Alcohol inhibits your reflex control and falling out of your loft while you are still drunk can cause head concussions and other major harm to your body.
- Time is the only way to sober up. Coffee and cold showers will not speed up the process. Alcohol causes you to become dehydrated ("dry mouth") and drinking water will help keep you hydrated, flush toxins out of your body faster and improve your headache. Drink water throughout the evening to stay well-hydrated.

The Reality of the Situation:

Why do you have to urinate so much when you drink alcohol? Alcohol inhibits the antidiuretic hormone (ADH) which acts on the kidneys to conserve water. Without ADH, fluids pass right through your body causing you to urinate more and become dehydrated at the same time (which is also why you get a headache and feel thirsty the next day). You may find the urge to urinate to be so strong as to override your better judgment leading to a public urination citation.

Drunk Dialing:

This is where your friends might call you late at night after an evening of drinking. They are drunk and won't remember the conversation in the morning so feel free to hang-up and go back to sleep. If this is a common problem, turn off your phone before going to bed on the weekends.

 The walk of shame occurs when you wake up the morning after a night of partying in an unfamiliar place and must then walk home. You may wake up next to someone who you do not know and do not remember if you did anything sexually with. You may or may not have to find some or all of your clothes to put back on. The walk of shame is so named because you look out of place in the morning as you are walking home because you will still have your wrinkled party clothes on and your hair is messed up. You may also still be wearing make-up and you may have a confused look on your face, perhaps even stumbling, as you are still waking up and are hung-over. Where is that struggle bus to give you a ride now you wonder...

Incriminating Photos:

Inevitably, someone always has a camera at parties and is taking pictures and you might find some very "interesting" photos have been taken on your camera if you lose track of it during a party. These pictures can then be, and commonly are, posted on the internet on popular social and networking websites and can be viewed by anyone including your parents, residence hall staff and the police.

Questions to Ponder:

- Does alcohol have to be part of everything you do to have fun?
- What positive stories have you heard from people who drink? Was that truly a positive story?
- What negative stories have you heard?
- Is drinking alcohol the most fun social activity for you? Do you truly enjoy drinking?
- Have you ever met someone who wished they drank more alcohol? Have you ever met a smoker who wasn't trying to quit?
- What type of person do you envision yourself as? How do you think other people view you?
- What type of people do you want to be associated with? Who do you want your friends and acquaintances to be? Are they the same people who talk about being wasted on the weekends?
- Do you think alcohol could play a role in your own personal death?
- How would your life change if you: contracted a STD? killed someone while driving under the influence? were charged for rape? were raped? had to call your parents because you needed someone to post bond to get out of jail? Weren't accepted into graduate or professional school due to charges on your permanent university record from your freshmen year?

Personality Line-Up: Common "Drinker" Personalities @ a Party

- The Uninvited Guest: This person just shows up and no one knows who they are.
- The Fighter: This person is ready to rumble if you look at them wrong.
- The Alcohol Snob: This person "only drinks hard alcohol" or shuns at beer which isn't of the highest quality.
- The 8th Year Senior: This person should have a degree in partying. They've been doing it for years and just can't seem to finish out their degree program.
- Mr./Mrs. Naked: These people somehow always end up taking off some of their clothing sometime during the event.
- Mr./Mrs. Make-Out: They've come to this party with one goal in mind...making out with other people. Also seen at the student health center with STDs.
- Cry Baby: This person is crying about something, and their solution is alcohol tonight.
- The Storyteller: Always one upping others stories, lots of stories about running from the cops. Most of this is made up.
- Mr. Passed Out: This person has no idea how to drink and is passed out on the couch by 8 PM...usually with phallic symbols drawn on their face.

Final Thoughts

At some point, alcohol will enter your freshmen year. There is a good chance it will even be present the first week or first night you are at college. You can choose whether you want drinking to be part of your college experience. Think carefully about the information in this chapter when making your decisions.

While drinking and the college life seem to go together, there are a lot of dangers and myths many forget to acknowledge. When people think of someone with an alcohol problem, an image of a middle-aged man sitting at his kitchen table opening a can of beer for breakfast are what many people picture. However, alcoholism doesn't start then, it starts at the college level (if not before). College students will try to justify how "cool" drinking is but is doing the longest keg stand really going to advance your life goals and be seen by the general public as a noble thing? Is spending more on alcohol than on your textbooks in a semester really something to brag about? Many college students convince themselves (and others in their situation) this is the way life should be lived. But what happens when college is over.

If you've decided alcohol is how you need to have fun, you start believing this yourself. All of a sudden you find yourself not having fun at the family barbeque unless you have a six pack at your side. These decisions will negatively affect your health, your relationships with others and your ability to be successful in many areas of your life.

Points to Ponder

- You are an adult. You know how alcohol can affect your body. You know the consequences of choosing to consume alcohol.
- You're not a loser if you don't drink.
- Know your stance on drinking before you're in the situation.
- There will be more than one opportunity for you to drink your freshmen year.
- Know what's fact and what's fiction when it comes to alcohol policies.
- If you can't think of anything else to do but drink, you're lame.
- Know how to be safe and how to keep your friends safe if you do drink.
- In a drinking card game, is the point to win or lose?
- Be the designated driver for your friends.
- You can drink responsibly.

CHAPTER 16

RELATIONSHIPS: DATING AND BREAKUPS
THE "MRS. DEGREE"

"There are two general paths in life: the path of love and the path of logic. Both paths are correct, and that's why it's so hard."

Dating

College is probably the one time in your life where you will not only live in an area with the highest concentration of people within your own age-group, but also where you find people who want to interact and have fun getting to know each other. You can't plan on finding love at college, but fate encounters abound from your chemistry lab partner, who makes even lab goggles look fashionable, to your good-smelling friend, who shares their laundry soap with you. Explore the college dating life by getting out and dating a variety of people--it may be better to *not* be in a serious relationship by Homecoming to be free to have fun with all of your new friends. Keep in mind there's no set quota of hook-ups, sexual experiences or number of people you date needed to live the college experience. Be happy being you and enjoy life; when you least expect it, someone will be falling for your smile across the dining hall.

There is still life after college. Don't feel pressure as though you need to meet "the one" at college. Many will graduate without their "MRS." degree.

When you do find that someone special you feel an amazing happiness, and love seems to be everywhere around-- even the campus squirrels seem to be a little more playful and frisky on your walk to class. You feel butterflies in your stomach and you get a huge smile just thinking about that person. Even their quirky habits, like keeping their pencils in the fridge or insisting on using only Spiderman bandages, makes you giggle. You become each other's number one fan wanting to learn everything there is to know about each other, sharing your feelings, thoughts, dreams and fears. When someone else is excited about you, it makes you feel special and loved. As your relationship develops you feel relaxed, safe and close. You have a best friend to share your college experiences and struggles with.

 It's good to have certain expectations for your relationship. Don't change who you are for someone else. Your new love should sweep you off your feet. If you need to constantly make reassurances or excuses for someone else and their behaviors, it's probably not a good match.

Before you will have success at dating, you have to know and love yourself first. If you are confident and loving life, people will be drawn to you. If you are having a good time other people will want to join in your happiness. You're not going to find a central hook-up place in college that everyone goes to find their boyfriend or girlfriend. The best way to "find" that someone special is just to do what you already love doing, such as playing on an intramural flag football team, going to church or volunteering with the environmental group. You'll meet a lot of compatible people because you already know these people are interested in some of the same things you are. Just make time in your schedule to be active meeting people and be open to various opportunities. Don't discount your everyday interactions with your classmates in study groups or your coworkers at work either—your significant other may have been right there all along.

The best pickup line ever
You need to know someone, through an initial connection or previous introduction, before asking them out or you will be rejected with a safe "no". But, if you really want to meet someone, but don't have a way to connect with them, try this: when you see them at a study table or eating alone, lift up a nearby empty chair, point to it, and say "Excuse me, is this chair taken?". If they laugh, you've made yourself a five second window to start talking. If they give you a blank stare, back up slowly, put the chair back and then run, far and fast away and hide.

There is a really fine line between being romantic and being creepy. The main difference between the two is whether or not the other person likes you. For example, you may send flowers to your secret crush, and if she likes you too, she's going to think it was romantic; but if she doesn't, you just creeped her out.

You may be perplexed how a "loser" guy ended up with the prettiest girl on campus. How does this happen? The reason can be explained by the "pretty girl syndrome" where a lot of guys are attracted to her but never ask her out, they assume she already has a lot of guys competing for her attention, so they don't have a chance or they are afraid of the fear of rejection. But the "loser" guy has nothing to lose so he is he bold enough to ask her out; before long these two opposites have fallen in love. The moral here is to take a chance and ask your crush out on a date. You will never know how they feel unless you take the risk. Even if they are not interested, they will probably be flattered that you asked. So you don't need to feel awkward afterward. But, that's assuming the worst case scenario; of course they may have been thinking the same thing and are absolutely thrilled and excited for your date this Friday.

 When most people think of an idea for their first date they think "dinner and a movie"—boring! During the first half you have the dinner where you try to fill any awkward pauses by asking questions, and you soon feel like you are in a job interview. Then the second half you are silently sitting next to them at the movie not interacting and left wondering what they are thinking. For a better first date, plan an activity you both can enjoy; check out our Creative Date Ideas below. You'll have plenty of opportunities some other time to ask them over dinner about their grandmother's dog, but for now, play, laugh and have fun as you sled down the hill towards the snow ramp you both made together.

 Everyone is pretty much in the same boat in college with no full-time job or large bank account. With a little creativity and thought, you don't need to spend a lot of money to plan a fun date; in fact, probably some of your best dating memories will come from creative dates you didn't need to spend any money on at all; your date will probably be more impressed with your originality and thoughtfulness than your checkbook. For example, going to watch a college sport is an inexpensive and fun date where you can also share your school spirit. Packing up your thermos and a fleece blanket to share at the game is just one of the creative date ideas below:

Creative Date Ideas:

- Go to a college basketball game, soccer match or gymnastics meet
- Go to a hockey game
- Go ice skating at an indoor or outdoor arena
- Tailgate at a football game
- Rollerblade together on a walking path
- Go out for ice cream
- Enjoy hot chocolate at a coffee house
- Cook an exotic dish or your favorite meal (no spaghetti!)
- Go to a new restaurant each week
- Grill-out at a state park
- Go for a hike through the woods
- Rent a campground, make a bonfire and have S'mores
- Feed bread to ducks

- Go geocaching
- Go off-roading or mudding
- Go on a night-hike and then find a clearing to look at the night sky
- Check out a butterfly garden, arboretum or lawn garden
- Visit an animal shelter and play with the animals
- Make some animal friends at the zoo
- Go for a drive in the country
- Drive around and look at neighborhood holiday lights
- Visit each other's hometown and meet their family
- Explore a small town nearby
- Take a weekend road trip to visit one of your high school buddies or to visit a big city
- Dress up for a "dinner and movie" date
- Plan a movie night—break out the classic trilogies and order in a pizza
- Go to a movie premiere; camp out in line even if unnecessary
- Late night pillow talks
- Play card games
- Play board games
- Get to know each other more through using the The Book of Questions by Gregory Stock
- Go for a bike ride
- Check out the local Farmer's Market
- Wake up early and go to Saturday morning garage sales
- Be creative with an outdoor photo shoot of each other; use black and white film and develop it in a dark lab
- Volunteer together
- Carve a pumpkin
- Take a class or seminar together
- Go to a concert
- Register for a run together
- Practice your massage skills on each other
- Watch the sunset
- Watch a thunderstorm
- Go shopping
- Do nothing together, absolutely nothing and just be with each other
- Bake cookies
- Watch the game on TV
- Play with kids (nieces/nephews, church group, babysit, etc.)
- Plan a camping trip
- Go skiing
- Go canoeing or tubing down a river
- Go to church or a church outing
- Sing karaoke

- Go to the state fair
- Play an intramural sport together or join in a weekend pick-up game of volleyball, soccer, basketball, dodge ball, etc
- Go swimming at the community pool or local lake
- Develop a small business idea
- Listen to music together
- Attend celebrations together (graduation barbecues, weddings, etc.)
- Go to a playground
- Go see or listen to stand-up comedians
- Check out an art festival
- Listen to outdoor concerts
- Enter a contest
- Help each other with a project or with cleaning

Keep the conversation going! There are basically three types of conversations: small talk (ex: can you believe the football team lost again?), the basics (ex: where did you grow up?) and opinions (ex: so what are your thoughts on...?). Have some questions in mind from each of these categories in case you hit a lull in the conversation.

PDA: Public Displays of Affection

Some couples find it necessary to show their affection in a physical manner and do so in a setting where others can see it. While some may argue "young love" is a cherished thing, "young love" attached at the mouth can be a bit much for others to watch. Be respectful of others if you are in a relationship. People don't want to see couples being overly touchy and making out. It's probably a good idea to keep the public affectation limited to holding hands and the occasional kiss on the cheek. You don't want to be the couple that everyone in your class or residence makes jokes about.

Kipp Story Box

There were a couple of residents in my residence hall who were ALWAYS together and would sit outside and kiss and touch WAY more than people liked to see. They became the joke of our building. One day someone was so fed up at their constant public displays of affection (PDA), they flung an alarm clock out the window and hit the guy on the top of the head...one of those old alarm clocks with the bells on top! The lesson: people are watching and would rather see you just hold hands, not doing things that belong behind closed doors.

Dating tips:

- The traditional classics still melt hearts: open doors, offer your coat and give a goodnight kiss.
- Don't rush things. It's ok if your second date has to be postponed a couple weeks due to busy schedules.
- Give them time to miss you; resist spending 24/7 together.
- Offer to pay for a date; show your appreciation when someone pays for you with a thank-you.
- Be a positive person to be around.
- Don't bring up past relationships.
- Give them your full attention. Remember details.
- Ask them questions about the important people in their life and their class work.
- Leave them little reminders for them to find later about how much you care about them.
- Don't talk about yourself the whole time.
- Smell good.
- Don't lie.
- Be excited.
- Get to know their friends.
- Be gentle.
- Respect their feelings.
- Alcohol and relationships don't mix well.
- Follow through on your promises.
- Learn all of their favorites.
- It's essential to attend the other person's important events.
- Don't be a jealous person.

Advice commonly given is "break with your high school sweetheart before you go to college." Why do high school relationships always get a bad reputation?

- In college you discover more about yourself and may grow in different directions.
- You may lean on your high school sweetheart as a security blanket instead of facing uncomfortable situations to meet new people during the first few weeks.
- It's difficult to date long distances. You may miss out on the college experience if you are returning home on the weekends to attend home football games and prom by reliving the high school experience.

This advice is typically ignored by those in high school relationships because they love their significant other. There is no single black and white advice that can be given for this situation. Although from past experience the majority of these relationships do not work out because of the reasons above, there are some high school relationships that do have a good thing going on and later get married. Keep the reasons above in mind and perhaps consider a "break" during your first year of college---if you are truly meant to be with the person for the rest of your life, a couple semesters apart while at college will only be a small fraction of your total relationship.

 The best way to ask someone out is in person. This can be hard and takes a lot of guts. An indirect approach to "save face" is to have your friend ask your crush if they like you. A twist to this common strategy is to have your friend talk to your crush with your friend suggesting to them, "well, hey, if you want I can find out if my friend (that's you) would be interested in going on a date with you". Now your friend has become your crush's messenger to find out if he or she likes you---brilliant!

Relationships are a balance of compromises. Although everyone has their quirks (some of which are more lovable than others), you need to know your own values well enough to know what you are and aren't willing to compromise on. Don't try to fool yourself into thinking you can overlook someone else's behavior that is not compatible with what you believe ("oh, he just drinks every weekend because we're in college; he said after four more years he won't drink anymore"). Habits form in college and what people value and spend their time on usually continues after college.

People cheat for different reasons; if someone cheats on you, it's not your fault; it's their own character flaw. Once you are in a relationship you build upon a base that you have created through feelings, memories, and understanding. If your significant other has cheated on you the relationship trust has been broken, and it's time to move on.

The Single Life

Of course when you're not dating, the single life has its own perks to offer:

- You're free to flirt.
- You're a free agent on the weekends.
- You have more money in the bank.
- You have more time.

- You're not going to get dumped.
- You get all the bed, blanket and pillow you want at night.
- You can wake up in the morning in a ditch and no one will care.

Breakups:

When you are in love, it's as though the entire universe bends to your will, welcoming you with opportunities and excitement. You feel bold, confident and unstoppable: you are loved. Your relationship becomes your world, consuming your time and thoughts and soon your friends, schedules and even your stuff becomes intermingled. In exchange for this connection, you have entrusted another person with your heart. And with that trust, the other person can turn your whole world upside down one day without notice if they decide to end the relationship, leaving you heart-broken and crushed. A break-up is often a one-sided decision--a decision made by someone else without your input or control but that dramatically impacts your life. This is especially tough when you still want to care for them. Breakups are even more difficult if caught by surprise as you go from a gleeful bliss to a desperate sadness, leaving you a faucet of emotions you don't know how to turn off.

Following a break-up, you feel vulnerable, hurt and extremely sad; it can cause you to feel sick with a nausea feeling, anxiety before sleep and not even wanting to eat. Schoolwork is hard to concentrate on and seems unimportant. You are emotionally exhausted. You may feel confused as to how someone so close to you who you love and loved you could now cause you so much pain and seemingly not care. You try to reanalyze the past few weeks of what you did and what was said with questions racing through your head, trying to think of any signs you missed. You long for everything to go back to "normal"; you long just to hear their voice again on the other end of the phone. You cry because the love you felt was pure.

You are sad because you have lost a love, someone you are close to, someone who you care about, someone who understands and knows everything about you. It hurts *because* you were so close to them. You try to block out all the memories and moments shared with them because it is too painful to think about. Your head spins with all of the "should've", "could've" and "what-if" scenarios you create in your mind. You regret not doing the things you planned or wanted to do with that person and regret not being able to do everyday stuff with them anymore. It seems as though there are constant, little reminders everywhere of places, people and things that make you think of them. You want to tell them about your day or to tell them an inside joke only they would understand. It hurts to think that person won't be in your future plans and life.

Breakups can progress through similar patterns including: shock, pleading, sadness, hatred, rebound and acceptance. Your emotions will feel like a rollercoaster ride, at times feeling strong and hopeful and at times breaking down and crying again. It's ok to feel sad and show your feelings. And it's ok to be alone. Allow yourself time to grieve and mourn. You lost someone you really cared about, and it will take time to heal. You lost your best friend.

Unfortunately, the majority of your dating relationships will end, until you find the one you both know is a match meant without an end. As you date in the meantime you learn about yourself and share in other people's stories as you figure out what you want and don't want in a significant other. You grow and take something with you from every relationship. Each relationship gets you closer to finding what will make you happy in the end. Everyone has at least one major heartbreak; it's part of living and opening your heart to be loved. From this experience you value and appreciate your next love that much more.

Loss of familiarity (such as the nightly phone call before bed, or guaranteed plans for Friday night) can leave you with a lost, empty feeling. Because you were made vulnerable, you want to hold onto something that was once familiar, comfortable and safe, even though you know the same person is the cause of pain. You may be upset that the other person was able to get over it so easily. Although this may not be true but rather they had more time to think about and prepare for what would happen after the break-up since they were in control of the breakup and its timing. Everyday will get a little easier for you; here are some coping strategies:

- Find a friend who will listen to you share your feelings. You will be reminded that you have some really great friends.
- Take time to reflect within your own thoughts. Find your inner peace and be happy with who you are. Be confident in yourself.
- Your friends may be able to offer you some advice or pointers that helped them cope and move-on. Listening to their stories may help you realize you aren't alone and that other people know what you are experiencing. They may have had some of the same questions, doubts and feelings you have.

- Fill the voids by redirecting your energy into new activities. Instead of thinking about how your phone is silent at 9 PM, go down the hall instead and join your friends in watching a favorite TV show together.
- You may have idolized the relationship. Even if you were to get back together, it probably wouldn't be the same anymore because now doubt has entered.
- Stop trying to win them back. They have already moved on.
- Get away from old memories and things that trigger these memories.
- Get out, meet people and do things.
- Don't regret the past; life happens for a reason and this could be the start that leads to a happier ending.
- Sometimes it is too hard to deal with and you just need to block them out of your memory in order to move on.
- You don't need to start seeing someone else right away to "prove" you're over your ex.
- When you are ready, let yourself be available by opening your heart again.

Even though you don't want to hear it right now, things will get better with time; know that in the end you *will* be ok. Things are worse right now because a large part of your life, including your time, energy and emotions, went into this relationship; but later down the road this relationship will not be as large of a portion of your life. And by then you will be ready for the next person to walk into your life, and you can show them the cool and happy person that you are.

The person may have broken up with you because they no longer feel that special connection with you or feel you are not a good match for them. It's a feeling they have and not a concrete problem that you could work out together; which can also be frustrating because you may think there is something wrong with you and they are just using this as a nice way to break-up. But in reality as you date someone you either fall more in love with them or you fall out of love with them as you spend time together or maybe you never truly loved them in the first place. As hard as it is, you just have to accept this fact and let the person go. Your instinct will be to find out why they no longer want to date you but the "why" is no longer important and not really up for debate anyway. When a person breaks up with you, they have already thought it out and agonized over the situation, and you probably won't be able to convince them to change their mind through arguing. They may become irritated and defensive towards you. Even if they tell you the "why", it may be sugar-coated and not the real reason behind their decision; the real reason may be too hard for them to tell you, because it could be a petty, selfish or hurtful reason. Prying for this reason will only lead to more hurt feelings for you (and your continual pestering eventually crosses into the realm of creepy) and prolongs your own healing time. You need to take steps in the direction that will help you recover.

Some reasons why relationships end:
- The person was never 100% into the relationship to start with; they still had their guard up to opening their heart completely after being hurt in their previous relationship.
- Not spending time together either due to distance or schedules
- Realizing this isn't the person you are meant to be with
- Money arguments
- The other person is cheating.
- The relationship is no longer what it used to be; arguments have replaced the fun.
- Feelings change and no longer feel a connection

 Your ex-sweetheart may have borrowed some of your stuff such as DVDs, a favorite sweatshirt, etc. Trying to recover these items is usually futile and painful after a break-up; consider their non-recovery as part of the "collateral damage" from the relationship.

Having to be the person who breaks up with someone is also very hard. Even if you are the one who is breaking off the relationship, it doesn't mean you don't care about the person or don't think they are a still an amazing person. It is not easy to do because you know that you will be the cause of hurt and pain to the person you once loved. Because relationships involve so many intense emotions, it is important to have thought out your decision carefully. All relationships will have some bumps in the road, but if you feel there is nothing to be saved from the relationship, it is best to be honest about your feelings sooner than later. Be sensitive to their feelings, but make it clear you are no longer interested in continuing the relationship. You will need to then stay firm in your decision and be prepared for possible begging, crying and screaming. Although it may be tempting to try to smooth things over by telling the other person you may be open to dating them again in the future, if this is not your true intention, do not give the other person these false hopes, because it only delays emotions to be hurt again later. Within reason, it can be helpful for you to answer any questions they have for you following the break-up to help them bring closure in their mind to the relationship.

One of your friends may reach out to you for support following a break-up. The best thing you can do is just listen. Even though it's true, they probably don't want to hear that things will get better with time; that future is too far away for them right now and all they know is that right now they feel really sad and hurt. You can provide the voice of reason when they have irrational thoughts involving the numerous ways they plan to "get back" at their ex. Welcome them back to the single life and plan something fun together.

A rebound is when you hook-up with someone soon after a break-up. Rebounds occur because you are depressed and lonely and want to feel a connection again with someone, or you just want to feel desired, or you want to "get back" at your ex. Rebounds could happen with your ex as well because you both don't know how to act around each other outside of a relationship and you both probably have some residual feelings for each other. Although this may offer a short term solution to your empty feelings inside, only the passage of time will help mend your heart.

Be sure to send your high school friends at other colleges cards for Father's Day, signed by their "4 year old kid" that they don't know about. Use crayon.

- After just meeting someone, as you are hanging out, say "this is the best blind date I've ever been on".
- When leaving someone you *just* meet, be sure to hand gesture a phone to your ear to indicate they should call you.
- Give awkward hugs.....you know, the kind where you don't let go after the other person does; just keep holding.
- When your friend looks over at you in class remind them: "I'm out of your league".
- When leaving the computer lab before the rest of your friends, call out to one of them and say "ok *friend's name*, I'll see you at home". Wink as necessary.

- Ask the cute worker at the movie rental store what would be a good movie to ask someone out who you like but don't know very well. Go and find their recommended movie and ask them what they are doing tonight.
- On the back of your homemade cards, be sure to draw in a pathetic looking crown and write underneath it, "Hallmark".
- Tell your friend things are going to be so different when you're dating their mom.
- While your roommate is nervously awaiting their date to arrive, invite your buddy over. Turn on some soft music, light some candles and strip down to just your towel as your friend gives you a full body massage. Act 'surprised' when your date arrives "early" and finds you in this situation.

When visiting their parents:

Sleep-in late into the afternoon, rolling over when they try to wake you up to join in the family activities; moan and tell them to let you sleep.

- Send mail to the parent's house addressed to you so that it arrives during the weekend you are visiting.
- Take a long bath. Have a good time and slosh around in the water. Get real quiet if someone knocks on the door to see how you are doing.
- Add a bag of kiwi to their refrigerator without them knowing. At some point they might say something like, "feel free to make yourself at home. If you want something to eat or drink, don't be shy and just help yourself". Open the fridge and say excitedly, "oh look KIWI!!!" and ask if you can have one.
- Leave your toiletries out on the bathroom counter. Have different foot disease medications and bottles for plantar's wart, athlete's foot, etc. overflowing from your bag. Walk around the house all weekend barefoot. Insist on it.

Finals Thoughts

A relationship is defined by the connection two or more people develop over time. Connectivity is the sharing of reality and is directly proportional to the strength of a relationship.

One must understand reality before one can understand connectivity. Reality is how we define the truth as our life unfolds. The truth, however, is determined by our perception. This is why many eye witnesses will have different versions of an event. Perception is based on previous experiences. Your mind automatically fills in gaps based on these previous experiences whether or not it actually happened. For example, think back on the last time you saw someone that you thought you knew and it turned out to be someone else. Your mind wants to make sense of what it perceives and in doing so projects previous experiences.

To recap, connectivity is the sharing of reality. Reality comes from our perception of truth. Perception is the sum of our experiences. Therefore, connectivity is the sharing of our experiences with another person. As your relationship with another person grows, the more experiences that are shared, the greater the likelihood the two of you will have the same mental projections of previous experiences. This is why a couple can know at times each others' thoughts or complete their sentences. Couples with this kind of insight of each other are involved in a very deep relationship that typically takes a very long time to reach. However, connectivity is present at all stages of a relationship even from the first time you meet. Some individuals have had so many similar previous experiences that it is as if they shared them together. These individuals have a head start in the connectivity process and will perceive love at first sight.

The closer you are to someone and the more connected you are with them, you can now see how this connectivity effects everyone around us. We live in a spider web of connections. With individuals at each point of intersection, any perturbation of an individual will ripple through the web of connections and be felt most significantly by those closest to the disturbance. A positive attitude will have a positive effect on those closest to you. A negative attitude will have a negative effect. Be optimistic. Be happy. And those around you will feel your energy ripple through them.

Points to Ponder

- Nothing is more attractive than self-confidence.
- "Do you want to come over to watch a movie?" is code for a lot of things.
- Only you know the whole story of what happened---and everyone has their side to it.
- Endings hurt.
- One of the worse things about breakups is having to tell your friends, family and Facebook™ about it.
- January is known for its break-ups.

- When someone breaks up with you, you feel as though they are saying, "hey, I think I can do better than you."
- How is it that within one day you can go from sharing your intimate secrets with someone to never talking to that person again?
- It's not going to work out if one person likes the other person more.
- If a relationship does not work out in the end, you haven't lost time, because a certain percentage of your life is dating or seeking if you are not dating.
- When you feel vulnerable, you branch out to others; when you feel on top of your game, you might not take other peoples' feelings into consideration.
- Your thoughts on how you feel about certain things will change with time; it's ok sometimes to make a decision that goes against the "rules" you have in place in your mind.
- Signs that you have gone from "dating" to "serious relationship" may include saying 'I love you', planning an event several months in advance or visiting their parents.
- Knowing someone's middle name somehow has become a measure of how close you are to them.
- It's always an agonizing time waiting for the response to the email you sent to the person you like.
- Start simple—see if they want to join you for lunch on Thursday.
- Compliment your date.
- If you're on a date with someone, give them your full attention; turn off your cell phone.
- Don't cheat.
- If your date is on Friday, you better start doing pushups no later than Wednesday.
- It's ok to be alone.
- Every girl should have at least one vase at college, you never know when someone will want to give you flowers.
- Pass out classroom Valentine cards; just like in elementary school, make sure *every*one on your floor receives one—for some people, it may be the only valentine they receive and they will always remember your thoughtfulness.
- You always need to work on your relationships--don't take it for granted.

 A great way to meet a lot of other people is through a Speed Date event. You know that everyone at the event is single and looking and with mutual matching there is no fear of rejection. Speed Date events are great for busy college students to go on many dates all in one night. With three-minute conversations with all sorts of 'characters' you know you will have a good time. Instant-Dating can also serve as a fundraiser for a student organization or for a sponsored charity.

CHAPTER 17
SEX
BREED ME!

"Let's get naked!"

At college, the opportunity to have sex increases as you are constantly surrounded by hundreds to thousands of people your age of the opposite sex who live, sleep and eat in close quarters. Sleepovers are no longer under the watch of your parents as you have more privacy and control of your own space. Although there is an increased probability to have sex at college, it does not necessarily need to be part of your college experience, and it is not a measure of college success. In reality, a lot less people than you think are actually having sex.

It is *your* choice whether you will have sex or abstain. Many influences will factor into your decision such as your religious beliefs, your family upbringing, your personal values and morals, love and finding the right person, your desire to save yourself for your future spouse, your past sexual history, your sexual interest, your readiness to support an unexpected pregnancy and the risk of sexually transmitted diseases (STDs). You should not let your decision be influenced by having the opportunity, alcohol, pressure from your significant other, trying to "keep-up" with the sexual experiences of your peers or being caught up in the heat of the moment.

You need to be able to have a conversation about sex with your significant other long before it happens. Questions to consider:
- How will this change the relationship?
- Should we have sex?
- Do we both want to have sex?

- How will you feel if you have sex but are no longer with the person later in life?
- What protection will you use?
- Do you know the sexual history of your partner?
- Have you and your partner been tested for STDs?
- How will you cope if you do contract a non-curable STD?
- How will things change with an unexpected pregnancy?
- How many sexual partners do you want to have in your life?
- How will this affect your relationship with your future spouse?

The most important part of the conversation is honest and open communication. Reflect on your own thoughts; know your partner's feelings and make sure both of you feel comfortable about any decisions.

There are many other ways to become close and intimate with someone without having sex (see Chapter 16: Relationships and Dating). You can have an active sex life without having intercourse. However, with the new freedoms of being away from home, entering adulthood, changing personal views about sex and being in love (and possibly your first true love), you may decide to have sex as a freshman. Sex adds a dimension that changes relationships. Pleasure and curiosity can lead you to desire more and more sex until it can become the focus of the relationship. Relationships centered only on physical activities usually do not fare well in the end. If this relationship ends, you have now crossed the bridge between not having sex and having sex, and you will be more likely to continue having sex in future relationships since you will want to share this level of intimacy with your new love. Also, during the rebound period, you may seek out sex with different people to help replace your feelings of being sad and heart-broken following the break-up, to feel the pleasures and closeness of being intimate again and to just check out what it's like to be with other people. Your number of sexual partners can then dramatically increase from zero to multiple once you decide to have sex, a side effect of your original decision you may not have anticipated.

As big as college is, it's small. You can quickly be labeled with undesirable terms such as "easy" or "player" based on your actions. You also live in a small, densely populated area; the people who live close around you know (and hear) what you are up too. There are few things in college more uncomfortable than walking in on your roommate having sex or vice versa. This situation can create a very awkward dynamic in your relationship with your roommate unless you have a conversation about it. We're all interconnected through people who know people and even *years* after college you may be reminded of a random hookup by someone else making a connection between you and that person, a connection you would never see now.

Contraceptives

It's beyond the scope of this chapter to review all of the contraceptives available, their advantages, disadvantages and costs, but the two most commonly used contraceptives, the male condom and female birth control pills, are highlighted below. Before you are sexually active, talk to your doctor about which contraceptive is the best option for you.

The pill:
The birth control pill is an oral contraceptive that commonly contains a mixture of estrogen and progesterone hormones that regulate the menstrual period. When used consistently, the pill approaches 100% efficacy against pregnancy. The pill does not protect against STDs. The pill is obtained with a doctor's prescription.

Condoms:
A properly used, quality condom used with a spermicide approaches 100% efficacy against pregnancy and sexually transmitted diseases. Try different brands and styles of condoms to decide which ones you and your partner prefer.

Failure of condoms result from:
- Using an expired condom
- Improperly storing a condom (exposure to heat, light)
- Using an oil-based lubricant (Vaseline, hand or body lotions, cooking oils)
- Failure to leave space at the tip to collect the sperm
- Using a condom after contact is made between the penis and vagina

How to use a condom:
Use a condom when the penis is erect, before any contact is made with the vagina. Make sure the rolled up ring is placed in the correct direction to roll it down, over the shaft of the penis. Leave a space at the top for semen collection. After ejaculation, hold the condom in place at the base and pull out carefully. Properly dispose the used condom and wash your hands. Only use water-based lubricants (K-Y Jelly, spermicides).

 Practice how to put on a condom.

You may be able to receive free condoms through your Student Health Center. There are often various campus events throughout the year where free condoms are handed out. It's smart to keep some condoms on hand.

Emergency contraception, obtained from your doctor, the Student Health Center, or other clinics such as Planned Parenthood, prevent pregnancy after unprotected sex by either inhibiting ovulation or preventing implantation of the egg into the uterus.

STD Testing

Safe sex means being smart, staying healthy, and not acquiring STDs. You or your partner may have an infection you don't realize you have. It is important to know the status of your partner before you have sex (see chapter 18: Health and Safety, to read more about STDs and testing).

Random Hookups and Friends with Benefits

Random hookups often occur at parties involving alcohol (see Chapter 15: Alcohol and College Parties on the Walk of Shame).

Friends with benefits (a.k.a booty-calls, sexualized friendships, etc.) involve physical intimacy (ranging from making-out, foreplay to sex) purely for sexual purposes without any expectation of a formal relationship. This type of agreement is used by college students who seek a sexual outlet without the commitment, stress, time or money involved with dating. These agreements are usually short-lived as one of the parties may become involved in a committed relationship, becomes jealous or wants more from the other person or feels used.

Most people desire their first sexual intercourse experience to be in a loving, committed relationship. In either case (random hookups or friends with benefits) you may be cheating yourself of finding the right person for you and devoting your energy to a relationship with them.

Date rape

You are more likely to be raped by someone you know, often in a social setting. Involving alcohol increases your risk of this danger. You can help protect yourself by establishing a buddy system and knowing your alcohol tolerance limit.

If someone is intoxicated they cannot consent to sex, and you can be charged for rape. The "I was drunk, too" excuse will not protect you from charges. For your own protection, don't even put yourself in a situation where you could be accused of rape. Protect your own future: when someone tells you no, **it absolutely means no**.

What to do when a rape occurs:

Being a victim of sexual assault or rape is a very scary and traumatic event. It occurs on many college campuses, usually by someone you are familiar with and often involving alcohol. It is never your fault if you are sexually assaulted, you did not do anything to deserve to be sexually assaulted and you have the right to not be the victim of such attacks. As soon as you can after a sexual assault or attack occurs, get away from your attacker and go to a safe place. Typically a sexual assault victim will have three main resources available from either the university or community including emotional support, medical help and legal options. You are in control of which support resources you want to utilize and to what extent.

Emotional Support:
- Go to a place you feel safe, away from your attacker following a sexual assault or rape. Call a friend you trust to stay with you.
- Contact sexual assault resources provided by the university or community to talk to an advocate who will help you process your options. The advocate will act in your best interest, will not pressure you and will support you throughout the process, making sure you are well-informed and comfortable.

- Insecurities and emotional fallout may continue for a long time after the attack. Consider visiting with a counselor on a regular basis and/or joining a victim's support group.

Medical Help:

- In most cases this service will be provided at no cost to you.
- A medical examiner will make sure you are healthy, give you options to prevent pregnancy and information concerning STDs.
- If you consent, evidence will be collected during the medical exam as well.

 Don't eat, drink, brush your teeth, use the restroom, douche, shower or change your clothes. Traces of date rape drugs or semen could be lost during urination. This will help preserve evidence if you want to pursue legal action.

Legal Action:

- Even if alcohol was involved with the sexual assault, the attack is not your fault. Don't let the fear of the consequences of underage drinking prevent you from filing a police report after being raped or sexually assaulted—the police and legal prosecution will be more interested in helping you and filing charges against the attacker. It's likely that no underage drinking charges will be filed against you.
- Even if you are not sure if you want to press charges, if you file a police report after the attack and allow the medical examiner to collect evidence now, it will give more options at a later date. Physical evidence of the assault may only last hours to days after the attack, but your option to pursue legal action may last for years.
- Write down any details you can remember about the attack (description of the person, how it happened, etc).

If someone comes to you after being sexually assaulted, first and foremost make sure they feel safe. Be a friend for them. Believe them. Realize this was a very traumatic event. They may be very scared and not be able to think rationally. You can help them by informing them of the three support services available to them (emotional, medical and legal). Although most victims will naturally want to cleanse their bodies afterwards, inform them that evidence may be lost if they urinate, douche, shower, brush their teeth or change their clothes. Let them be in control of the decisions; this is very important to a victim whose control was taken away from them during the assault.

Voyeurism

Look outside your dorm window, how many other windows can you see? Keep this in mind when you are changing in your room with the blinds open. This is even more important when you live on the ground level, especially near entrances.

Protect yourself and your housemates by not allowing people of the opposite sex into the restroom or shower area intended for one sex. Find out where your guests can use the appropriate bathroom. Strictly guard your privacy and report any violators.

If you decide to enter the adult porn industry, it is best to make this decision when you are sober and well-educated on the topic. Remember, porn is life-long and widely distributed throughout the internet. You will not be able to keep your appearance on Girls Gone Wild, Playboy's College Coeds, or Amateur Night at the local strip club a secret from your friends and family. Any "home-made" videos or digital pictures of you in a sexual nature can also be easily posted on the internet.

Streaking in a group is a tradition at some colleges but has decreased in popularity in recent times due to stricter laws (ranging from indecent exposure to being charged as a sex offender). If you are going to streak, it's probably best late at night as opposed to a sporting game. Be cautious of posting pictures or movie clips on the internet.

Coming Out

For many, college is a time for sexual self-discovery and exploration. College can provide an atmosphere that is more accepting of different sexual orientations. For some, who were isolated in their closed-minded home town, find support through meeting increased numbers of non-heterosexuals and/or increased numbers of heterosexuals supportive of different sexual orientations. Most universities have support groups for people who are gay, lesbian, transsexual, transgender, intersex or questioning. Some students "come-out" during their freshmen year after realizing they are not heterosexual or are more comfortable with their identity given the supportive college atmosphere. Coming out is not an easy thing for someone to do as they are often unsure how others will react.

If someone comes out, realize this was hard for them and they trust you by telling you.

If someone comes out to you:
- Don't judge.
- Respect their confidentiality.
- Let them know you are still friends.
- Include them.
- Ask questions.
- Learn how you can be an ally.

Universities do not tolerate harassment or discrimination of any protected group. You may not even have realized you use words or phrases that are derogatory until someone at college points it out to you especially if you came from a closed-minded family or community without much diversity. For example, you may have become desensitized to the phrase "that's so gay" or thought it was an innocuous term; but as the world of college broadens your horizons, you will discover more about yourself, how your upbringing has shaped you, how to be more open to groups you are not familiar with and how to be more sensitive in your words and actions.

Final Thoughts

Sex in college can be more causal. You could even find yourself in a situation your very first weekend at college where you need to make a decision to have or not have sex—are you ready? What's your plan? Many times these situations involve alcohol—do you want to have sex when you are drunk? You will meet people who are only after sex, and they know exactly what to say and when to say it to influence you to have sex with them. Don't let these people get to you—you have the right to say no. Also, don't be this person—no means no.

Curiosity, temptation, pleasure, desires and hormones---a powerful blend of factors that places sex on your mind. There is no need to rush into sex. Once you lose your virginity, you can never go back. Based on pop culture, you may feel like there must be something wrong with you if you aren't enjoying an active sex life, but there's not, and contrary to the common perspective, everyone else around you isn't engaged in a sexual relationship. In fact, many college students don't have extensive sexual experience. Your energy may be more focused on other things like making friends, getting involved with your college and making the grade in your classes. When you find the right person, your experience level does not matter. Ask yourself this: who would you rather be with, someone with lots of sexual experience or someone with limited experience? Would it be more fun to explore sex together with your future spouse or having someone who has already done everything you can think of? And which one do you think your future spouse would prefer?

Points to Ponder

- Seriously, is this the only chapter you're going to read?!
- Don't be naive, STDs are out there.
- Your significant other isn't going to think less of you if you haven't had sex; in fact, they may respect you more.
- How many people do you want to have sex with in your life? Write that number down and hold to it.
- Safe sex requires planning.
- Advice in a student health pamphlet read, "Don't reuse used condoms". Are there really people who would consider reusing condoms?
- Don't be gross (see above point).
- Contraceptives are the responsibility of both individuals. It's your health and future, protect it.
- It's ok if your thoughts on sex have changed since high school.
- Love your body.
- Drunk sex is for dumb people. Don't be a dummy.
- Don't collect STDs at college. Do what you need to do to keep yourself free of disease.
- Lofts are squeaky and wobbly.
- Sex produces babies. Don't have sex with anyone you wouldn't want to have a baby with.
- Remember the dorm room walls are thin and the showers aren't private.
- Too much of a good thing can be a bad thing.
- Asking someone to be tested for STDs isn't about lack of trust, it's about staying healthy.
- Was it what you thought?
- It's not just the number of sexual partners you have, but also the rate at which that number increases that can be problematic.
- If your entire relationship is based on sex, you are missing out on a lot of other cool benefits of being in a relationship.
- If you are going to streak, make sure someone you trust is on the other end waiting with your clothes.
- Sex can have plenty of its own awkward moments.
- Enroll in a college human sexuality course. It probably won't be required for your major, but it will be a class you won't skip. Heck, you'll even read the textbook *and* show up early. Anyone need a study partner?

CHAPTER 18

HEALTH AND SAFETY
DON'T TOUCH ME

"Maybe a cookie will help my sore throat?"

Health

College can be the perfect breeding grounds for infectious diseases to spread. With a high density of people living in a small space, increased contact occurs as hundreds of students share everything from breathing space to door handles to eating- utensils. At any given time the people around you have less than ideal health to fight off infections due to lack of sleep, stress, lack of exercise, not eating nutritiously and not drinking enough fluids. Combine all these factors with those that don't wash their hands regularly and you create the "mini epidemics" that periodically sweep through residence halls where it seems like everyone you encounter is sick.

You were probably assessed a student health fee with your other university fees. This fee typically covers the office visit fee with your doctor and general physical examination, but if you need further diagnostics, such as blood work, or x-rays or need treatment, such as pills or minor surgical procedures, you will need to pay for these services. Typically you can apply these charges to your university bill and some charges may be covered by your health care insurance. Without your parents around, you will need to fill out the doctor's form when you visit the health center. Do you know your own health history? (What was that you had when you were six and you had to be hospitalized for a couple days? What was the date of your last surgery when you had your wisdom teeth removed?). Do you know your family history? (Was it grandpa who has the high blood pressure? What type of cancer does your aunt have? And doesn't someone have diabetes?). You will also need to know who your health care provider is and what they cover. If you are no longer covered by your parent's health insurance you can typically obtain student health insurance from your university. It is a good idea to have your insurance information on record at the Student Health Center before you visit for your first time.

When you turn 18 you acquire additional rights and protections by federal laws. Your parents will not be able to access certain information regarding your student health records unless you sign a specific authorization for release of medical information as protected by federal confidentiality laws. This release is generally valid for one year from the time it is signed.

List for College Medicine Kit:
Without the family medicine kit or medicine cabinet available to you at college, here are some items to consider for starting your own collection of supplies:

- First Aid Manual
- Thermometer
- Instant hand sanitizer
- Antiseptic towelettes
- Antibiotic ointment
- Bandages
  - Bandage strips (Band-Aid™)
  - Elastic wrap roll (Ace™)
- Gauze pads, roller gauze
- Cotton balls, cotton tipped swabs
- Scissors, tweezers, needles, safety pins
- Sterile eyewash (saline solution)
- Instant Cold Packs
- Disposable latex gloves

Medications:
- Antihistamine (Benadryl™)
- Pain relievers (aspirin, Advil™, etc.)
- Sinus and cough relief (Sudafed™)
- Anti-diarrhea meds (Imodium™)
- Hydrocortisone cream
- Any personal prescription medications, inhalers, epinephrine-pen, etc.

Miscellaneous:
- Sunscreen
- Flashlight with backup batteries

When living in a new area keep a list in a handy location of important emergency numbers such as:

- Local emergency services
- Ambulance
- Police
- Fire
- Police, non-emergency number
- Student Health Center (and name of your doctor)
- Poison Control
- RA on duty
- Campus Safety Escort
- Maintenance

College vaccines
Required:

For public health control measures, you will need to provide your college documentation of your past vaccine history demonstrating coverage of all required vaccines; otherwise your college will require that you receive these vaccines upon arriving at college and could put a "hold" on your admission until this requirement is completed. It is common for the Measles, Mumps and Rubella (MMR) vaccine to be required of all people over 18 years of age if they have not previously had the disease or been vaccinated for it. You may be required to booster your Tetanus/diphtheria vaccine if you have not done so in the past 10 years.

The Meningococcal Meningitis Vaccine is a *highly* recommended (and sometimes also required) vaccine for college students: freshmen who live in college dorms are an increased risk group for this disease. Meningococcal meningitis is a rare but rapidly fatal bacterial infection, spreading among the spinal cord and cerebrospinal fluid. It is transmitted through direct contact and oral secretions (coughing, kissing, etc.). A small number of freshmen students die every year from this disease. Although a vaccine is never 100% efficacious, it will reduce your risk of infection. If diagnosed early, it can be treated with antibiotics; however, common signs of high fever, headache, stiff neck and sleepiness can be confused with flu-symptoms, which occur during the same time of year (late winter, early spring), causing delay in its detection and early treatment. People infected also complain of light-sensitivity. The vaccine can be expensive.

If you plan to study abroad or travel abroad for spring break there may be additional vaccines required before your departure. Some vaccines, such as Hepatitis A and Hepatitis B, require boosters separated by six months and thus early planning is important.

Mono and the Flu

Both infections are spread among college students; and both infections can drain your energy levels and thus affect your performance on schoolwork.

Mononucleosis:

Infectious mononucleosis is usually caused by the Epstein-Barr virus and is spread in adolescents and young adults by intimate contact involving saliva (a.k.a. "the kissing disease"), but otherwise is *not* highly contagious. Common symptoms include fever, sore throat, swollen lymph nodes and extreme fatigue. The general treatment is symptomatic care such as adequate rest, increased fluids, pain relief pills, etc.

Do all you can to fight off disease and stay healthy. Getting something like Mono your first semester or any semester can really put a strain on your academics if you're unmotivated to even walk to class.

Influenza:

The flu is caused by the influenza virus and is spread through the air through coughing and sneezing. Common symptoms include fever, headache, sore throat, runny nose, muscle aches and tiredness. The two best prevention measures against the flu are to wash your hands often and to get the flu vaccine. The best time to obtain a flu vaccine is in October through November. There are two types of flu vaccines:

Inactivated vaccine containing a killed virus given in your arm muscle through a needle.

Attenuated vaccine containing a live but weakened virus given through your nose in a spray.

Shower Foot Diseases

You can pick up infections from your dormitory community shower because infectious agents thrive in warm and moist conditions, especially in poorly cleaned areas such as the shower floor. Some common infections and their symptoms include:

- Plantar Warts (caused by a virus, human papillomavirus)

Typically occur on the bottom of feet, alone or in clusters; usually white with black specks (blood vessels) and are covered by a hard callus of skin.
- Athlete's Foot (caused by a fungus, *Tinea pedis*)
  Typically occurs on the side and toes of feet and presents as cracked, blistered skin with an itching, burning sensation
- Onychomycosis (caused by a fungus, *Trichophyton spp.*)
  Typically occurs under nails causing toenails and fingernails to be yellow and brittle

Some of these diseases are not easy to treat and require long-term medications. To help prevent acquiring these infections, follow these practices:
- Always wear sandals while showering.
- Keep your feet dry; change your socks if they feel damp.
- Most dorm bathrooms are cleaned once a day. If your schedule allows, plan to take your shower shortly after the bathroom has been disinfected.

For some reason some college students forget to keep up on their personal hygiene. **Remember it's still important to take a daily shower, even when you are in college.** Doing your laundry and wearing clean clothes also helps your appearance and social standing.

Sleep

The common recommendation calls for eight hours of sleep per night but this can be hard to achieve for the busy college student. However sleep is an important part of your health and if you make a conscious effort to go to bed at a decent hour on a consistent basis you will have more energy and feel more refreshed when sitting through lectures. If you have trouble sleeping at night, try to go to bed at the same time, block out extraneous light and noise and reduce your caffeine use. Napping during the day is a popular activity of college students and can help replenish your "sleep debt". Pulling an all-nighter is usually never beneficial as your mind will not be as sharp and alert for the exam; you will do better on an exam with some sleep rather than no sleep.

Exercise

See Chapter 11: Exercise. Exercise helps you stay in shape, reduces your stress and makes you feel good. Learn how to properly use the equipment at your college fitness center; improper use will led to injuries and make you look foolish. Don't be embarrassed to ask someone how to use a weight or aerobic machine you aren't familiar with. Remember to stretch before and after exercising to help prevent injuries. Exercise results are daily, they occur over time. Keep in mind you probably aren't exercising as much as you were in high school, so it's important to incorporate exercise into your routine and to make lifestyle changes such as taking the stairs instead of the elevator, walking to class or joining intramurals.

Water

Staying well hydrated is important to your health and can help prevent headaches. Drinking water is especially important in college as you might not have a convenient access to water with no kitchen sink and drinking fountains serving as your only source of water. Carrying a water bottle with you to class is an easy way to help increase your water intake.

Eating Disorders

Eating disorders often do not fall under the classical descriptions (see below) and many people do not realize or want to admit they might have an eating disorder. People with eating disorders often have a distortion of reality and what constitutes a normal body image and healthy weight. Eating disorders can develop in college as students adjust to new stresses and pressures. Having control over eating may be compensating for not having control over other areas in life. You can help a friend you suspect has an eating disorder by 1) learning about the disease 2) talk openly and honestly about your concerns 3) show that you care about them as a person 4) help them find professional help.

Anorexia: self-starvation leading to emaciation
  Signs: thin, general weakness, cold hands and feet, constipation, ketotic breath, weak heart

Bulimia: "binging and purging" leading to rapid weight gains and losses
  Signs: dental problems from vomit acid, digestive disorders including ulcers, muscle weakness and heart irregularities

Compulsive overeaters: overindulgence leading to obesity
  Signs: shortness of breath, high blood pressure, diabetes and joint problems

Sexually Transmitted Diseases

Web of Sex Partners:

Before you have sex you should know the sexually history of your partner for your own health protection. This means you and your partner should have STD testing (usually a blood or urine test but can also include a mucosal swab). Asking your partner and actually going in for STD testing may seem unrealistic, but the reality will set in when you have unexplained painful bumps on your genitals and every time you urinate you have a painful, burning sensation.

STDs are transmitted through bodily secretions and contact through the penis, vagina, anus *and* mouth. Many people don't even know they have a STD because infections can be latent or asymptomatic. Some STDs are treatable, and some are life-long infections. Here are some common STDs and their clinical signs you should know about:

Bacteria:
Gonorrhea (Neisseria gonorrhoeae)
Women can experience difficulty urinating and have vaginal discharge. Men can experience painful, burning urination and may have a copious (pus) urethral discharge.

Chlamydia (Chlamydia trachomatis)
Chlamydia can cause pelvic pain by infection of the uterus, fallopian tubes and ovaries, causing difficulty in becoming pregnant. Men can have abnormal urethral discharges, painful urination and swollen, tender testicles.

Syphilis (Treponema pallidum)
Primary syphilis is characterized by a painless skin ulceration (sore or chancre). In secondary syphilis, a red non-itchy skin rash develops over the body, including the palms and soles. Tertiary syphilis has tumor like skin growths and systemic effects (nervous and cardiac symptoms).

Viruses:
HIV (human immunodeficiency virus)
HIV suppresses the immune system and can lead to AIDS (acquired immunodeficiency syndrome).

HPV (human papillomavirus)
HPV is common in women but only certain types lead to disease. HPV is a highly communicable disease and both men and women are carriers; condoms are not 100% effective against transmission. Some type causes genital warts while another type can cause cervical cancer (a good reason for a Pap Smear). Women should receive the HPV vaccine, which is

effective (about 70%) against the two most common types that can lead to cervical cancer.

Herpes (herpes simplex virus-2)
Herpes virus-2 can cause a tingling, itchiness and burning sensation of the genitals as well as blisters and sores. These outbreaks are reoccurring and there is no cure or treatment for herpes.

Herpes simplex virus-1 most commonly causes fever blisters or cold sores in the mouth. However, it can be spread to the genital area from an infected person engaging in oral sex. HSV-1 is most contagious and infectious when the person is showing signs but it can also be spread when the person is asymptomatic.

Hepatitis B
Hepatitis B can cause inflammation of the liver (hepatitis) with signs of general ill-health (loss of appetite, nausea, body aches, etc.) and jaundice (yellowing of the skin and mucous membranes). There is a vaccine available for Hepatitis B.

Parasites:
Pubic lice (Phthirius pubis)
These parasites live on hair follicles and can cause skin irritation. They can spread through sharing bedding and clothes as well as through sexual contact.

Your college might offer free HIV or STD testing.

Molluscum contagiosum, a contagious pox virus, can be transmitted during sex even when using a condom since it only requires skin contact. The virus causes small raised non-itching and non-painful bumps (white-head like appearance) on the genitals, and inner thighs. The papules can increase in number and spread to other parts of your body. The bumps take 10-24 months to disappear and in the meantime you should avoid sexual activity to prevent spread to other people. Liquid nitrogen can be used to remove the bumps but it can leave scarring.

See Chapter 17: Sex for information on Contraceptives.

Safety

Fires, Tornadoes, Hurricanes, Blizzards, Earthquakes, Terrorist Attacks:

When you are in a new location, familiarize yourself with emergency plans. Make sure you know where the emergency exits are, especially if you live in a high-rise dormitory. Where's the nearest fire extinguisher? Where can you go to get away from windows or find a safe shelter?

Campus Shootings:

Campus shootings are extremely rare when you consider the thousands of colleges and millions of college students. However they occur without warning, you have little to defend yourself and multiple students are left injured or dead. Typically a campus shooting is carried out by a single individual with multiple guns and is over in a short amount of time. If you find yourself in this unfortunate situation, there will be little that you can do; however, some students have survived by laying motionless by pretending to be already dead, hiding behind a barrier (such as a support beam or behind a desk), or stealthily leaving through an exit (make your move when the shooter stops to reload weapons). Where you choose to sit in the classroom at the beginning of the year (such as close to a second exit or near a barrier) may play out to be a huge factor for your survival in these situations.

Tattoos and Piercings:

Separated from your parents and of legal age, you may decide during your freshmen year to get a tattoo or body piercing. When making your decision, consider:

- Will your appearance affect your future job or career?
- How will your future partner react?
- Are there any social situations you will be in that the body art may be inappropriate?
- Will this still be the same statement you want to make 25 years from now? Have you considered a temporary tattoo?
- How do you deal with pain?

Evaluate the studio and artist performing your piercing or tattoo:

- Is the studio an established business? Is it clean? Are new containers of ink and needles used for each procedure? Are latex gloves used? Can you look at a sample book of actual customers and final products?
- Does the artist belong to a professional organization? What education does the artist have related to this practice? How much experience do they have? Does the artist make you feel comfortable and answer all of your questions?

Tattoos and piercings can take weeks to months to heal. Be sure to follow all home-care instructions to prevent infections. If signs of inflammation persist (redness, heat, swelling, pain, and loss of function), seek medical attention.

Tanning

Tanning beds are used mainly during winter or spring months, often before spring or summer break, by some college students for the perceived cosmetic affect. Tanning beds may also be used by students who suffer from seasonal affective disorder, insufficient vitamin D, acne or muscle aches. However, tanning can also lead to sunburns, premature aging (including wrinkles), eye problems such as keratitis and skin cancer, especially melanomas. If you tan:

- Only use reputable tanning solons that have well-maintained and properly sanitized beds to prevent spread of infections.
- Always wear FDA approved tanning goggles to protect your eyes.
- Wait at least 48 hours between tanning sessions.
- Plan a shower after tanning to reduce the "after-tanning smell".
- If your skin becomes dry, red or burned, stop tanning.

Stalkers

A stalker can be anyone on campus including classmates, acquaintances or friends who repeatedly harass you through invasion of your privacy, unwanted contact or mental abuse. If you feel as though you are being stalked here are some things you can do:

- Firmly and directly tell the person no further contact is allowed.
- Do not engage in any further communication with the person (talking, visiting, emailing, phone calls, etc).
- Save all letters, emails, phone messages, gifts, etc. sent by your stalker.
- Inform your Resident Assistant and campus police about your concerns.
- When out in public, stick with a group of friends.
- Monitor the information available about you on the internet. Remove contact information, class schedules and pictures. Make sure to inform your roommate and friends to not give out your cell phone number or inform others about your whereabouts.

Final Thoughts

College may also be your first real exposure to drugs. By now you know the adverse side effects and the legal issues of drug use and as an adult you are capable of making a decision concerning your use and accepting any consequences of your decision. Our best advice is to avoid even being around illegal drugs, whether you are doing them or not, to avoid trouble with the law. You have too many other things going on in your life and you have too much at stake such as your scholarship funding, your enrollment in college and your integrity. Universities take drug use very seriously; if you feel there is a casual environment around drug use on your campus, take a closer look—where are those pot smokers by the end of the semester?

College may also be your first exposure to caffeine. Some students at first don't really like the taste of coffee, but with enough added sugar, grow used to the taste until eventually they are addicted to the caffeine. If you take care of your body (exercise, eat right, get enough sleep, etc) you won't need the effects of caffeine to get through college.

Points to Ponder

- Washing your hands is the number one public health preventative you can do to prevent spread of infectious diseases.
- Be ready. Educate yourself by taking a First Aid and CPR course offered through the American Red Cross.

- Meningococcal meningitis is rare but fatal. If you are a freshmen living in the dorms, you are at a highly increased risk of contracting this disease. Invest in your health and get the vaccine.
- Ah, how can you *not* get a disease at college?!
- www.cdc.gov
- Coffee is a gateway drug.
- Habits form in college.
- Drink milk or other calcium containing products to help prevent osteoporosis later in life; this is especially a concern for women.
- The most effective weight loss pill is one with a label that reads "exercise for one hour after taking pill".
- If something is painful or you find something abnormal on your body, have it checked out. Don't ignore it.
- You might not even know a campus shooting occurred at your college until hours after the fact because of the size of the campus grounds and the size of the student population.
- Focus on being healthy and the weight loss will follow.
- Gardasil vaccine for HPV is about 70% effective in preventing cervical cancer and about 90% effective in preventing genital warts. Call student health today.
- If nothing else, use the campus safety escort program for a free, warm & dry ride.
- Press the test button on the smoke detector---working?
- Have you ever met a smoker who wasn't trying to quit? It's easier to quit by not starting.
- Some people can develop an anemia with inadequate iron levels.
- Washing your bed sheets and having to remake your bed when it's lofted is a pain. For this reason some college students wash their sheets once a semester, if that. Keep this in mind as your head hits the pillow at night next time you sleep over in someone else's bed and remember pubic lice can be spread through sharing bedding. Whoa, we were just saying, are you really going to make them wash their sheets now at 2 am in the morning?
- Coffee houses have a variety of non-coffee drinks; try a milk steamer, chai tea or other flavored drinks.
- If you see a friend at the Student Health Center, respect their confidentiality; they probably don't want you to ask why they are there.
- Tattoos are permanent and painful. Meaning, full of pain.
- Remember, Stop, Drop and Roll. Practice if necessary.
- What's your plan for a tsunami?

Freshmen Moments
LIVING GREEN:

There are many ways you can improve your ecological footprint while at college. Listed below are realistic and simple ideas you can implement immediately and will hopefully inspire other ways you can help mother Earth. Some college students will use a lot more energy in lights and heating and cooling since you don't pay a monthly utility bill; develop energy conservation habits now before you do have to pay the bills. Think of every item you place on your tray as having a cost to you to help reduce food wastage in the dining hall.

For the truly ambitious, you may consider starting a recycling program in your residence halls if there is not already a program in place; you may be

surprised how easy it can be to start a recycling program that can be quickly scaled up; any profits from your efforts could be used for additional green projects such as planting trees, gardens or other landscapes around your college. And don't be shy about promoting your efforts as others will likely volunteer to help or provide donations; you may even receive special awards or scholarships for your efforts.

- Turn off lights in your room when you're not there using them.
- Turn your computer to sleep mode when not in use.
- Unplug your cell phone charger when not in use.
- Keep showers short.
- Turn off the water when not using it.
- Don't waste food at the cafeteria.
- Don't buy bottled water; use a reusable container instead.
- Only take the napkins and condiments you will use.
- Pay bills online.
- Search online for ways to remove your name from junk mail lists.
- Support environmentally conscience groups and companies.
- Don't drive if you don't have to; most campuses are set up for walking or bicycling.
- Recycle: paper, cans, bottles, magazines.
- Recycle: batteries, cell phones, glasses.
- Use reusable grocery bags.

CHAPTER 19
ACADEMICS INTRODUCTION
INVESTMENT AND PURPOSE

"It's strange, mom, at college you are still expected to do work, turn in assignments and all that stuff."

When you first arrive on campus in the fall, you are very busy making new friends, exploring your new surroundings, setting up your room, and going to parties and welcome-week activities. It is easy to forget the main reason you are at college: to learn.   The first semester is a transition as you learn to make the initial adjustment to college and find a balance between social and academic environments.   The most important thing to remember is to keep your focus on academics.   If you let your primary focus slip, you will become part of the percentage of first year students who drop out or fail out their first year in college.   College is not meant to be easy.   You should and want to work at your major as you prepare for your career.   Really focus on your classes during the first few weeks of the semester.   You will start college off on the right foot and it will set the tone for the rest of your academic career.   **The more you put into your learning over the next four years the more you will gain from your college degree when you graduate.**

Will freshman year be difficult?

Your first year of college can be difficult if you aren't aware of how to avoid some of the common freshmen pitfalls.   Your priorities need to include academics at the top of the list.   Your first year is manageable and it is within your reach to succeed.

There are several reasons why freshmen year is difficult.   Classes that are at the 100 to 200 course level are labeled introductory or general but do not be mislead by equating introductory or general with meaning "easy". These classes are not always easy because often the class is a rapid *survey of many disconnected topics that give you a vague overview and little in-depth understanding*. You can be deceived by the first couple weeks of class as well because often it is review material of basic concepts from high school and you might begin skipping classes because you think you already know the material.   However, you will soon be caught off guard as the material rapidly becomes new and unfamiliar.   It is not uncommon to be intimidated to seek out individual help in a very large lecture course where you are one of 400 students in the class. This is combined with your lack of general knowledge of available college resources for academic help as well as the falsely conceived stigma that if you succeeded in high school but now need tutoring or other campus resources you must be a college failure, preventing you from seeking help before it becomes too late.   And combine all that with the fact that there will be plenty of other things that will distract you beyond homework and the classroom.   You will have to master time management skills in order to survive your first year in college (see Chapter 26: Time Management and Scheduling).

Be cautious if you are told one of your classes is an "easy A". It might be an easy class or more likely it will be a very vague overview class that just scratches the surface of a bunch of unrelated topics which can make the class hard to understand.

There is one other point that will help you understand first year classes---that is the "purpose of learning." Introductory level courses are not necessarily to teach you actual pertinent material for your major but instead to develop critical thinking, logic, methods and other skills that will be needed as you advance through your curriculum. For example, in organic chemistry you need to know and memorize the details and rules of many different chemical reactions. This knowledge is then applied to problem solving questions to solve synthesis problems or to draw an organic molecule based on lab data sets. Remembering the details of those reactions is not important once the class is over; but what is important is developing and demonstrating your ability to apply that information to the problem or task at hand. So, if you find yourself complaining about how you "don't understand why you have to take a particular class" and that you "will never need calculus for your job or career", then you have missed the point. *The purpose of learning might not be the actual material.* With this concept in mind, classes will be more of a challenge than a burden.

The Reality of the Situation:

You want to enjoy the pleasant fall weather and decide to study outside under a tree, setting up on a blanket, with your apple next to you; the perfect stereotypical "college experience" scene from a movie. The reality of the situation: insects and bugs biting, the sun beating down causing your shade to disappear and you to sweat, the ground is uneven and wet, wind blowing your papers, forgetting things and have to make multiple trips back inside, being distracted by everyone walking by.....until finally you decide to just back inside to study.

Top Ten List: How to be successful in your classes

10. Go to class every day.
9. Be on time or early for class.
8. Complete all assigned homework.
7. Don't be afraid to ask questions.
6. Actually pay attention during class to what is said.
5. Make sure you understand *all* homework and why *that* particular homework was assigned.

4. If possible, try to re-read everything.   Reading the textbook chapters at least twice and the lecture notes as many times as possible will help better commit the material to your memory.

3. Expose yourself to the material in as many ways and forms as you can (go to review sessions, form a study group, take practice tests, talk to the professor etc).

2. Be aggressive about studying. Make it your "job".

1. Don't settle for anything less than your potential.

Final Thoughts:

If you were to view your life as one big pie chart, then the next four years of college education is only a small slice of the total.   Make the most of the opportunities you have now.   Take extra electives, learn for the sake of learning, and don't limit yourself.   These are your academic years.

Points to Ponder:

*   Having to retake a class is a waste of your time and money—plan to pass every class the first time.
*   Paying for college is like purchasing a new car or in some cases, a new home—make the most of your investment.

CHAPTER 20
MAJORS AND ADVISORS
YOUR COLLEGE SCHEDULE

"What the hell kind of major is that?!"

Majors

One of the first questions you will be asked is, "what's your major?" You will most likely choose a major based on something you find interesting or have a strong background in. If you have not decided on a major, you can enroll in college under "general university studies" or "undecided" until you finalize your plans. Choosing a major should involve appropriate research and reflection, as your major will lead into your career field. Find the answers to these questions:

- What types of jobs are available for people with this major?
- Are these jobs in demand? What percentage of recent graduates with this major obtained jobs upon graduation?
- What exactly do people in those jobs do on a day to day basis?
- What is the average salary of these jobs? What is the starting salary? Will this salary justify and enable you to pay off your student loans?
- Will additional education be required for your job beyond your 4-year degree (i.e. graduate school, specialized training programs, continual education, etc.)?
- What are the required classes for this major? How many credits on average will you need to take each semester? Can you finish the degree in four years? Will you need to enroll in summer sessions?
- Will you need to complete other requirements such as research or an internship?
- What types of people will be your classmates in this major and thus will become your future co-workers?

- Can I see myself in this career and being happy?

Majors are formal organized programs of study that lead to a university degree. Majors are commonly grouped together under one department with several departments composing a college within the university. For example genetics, biology and zoology majors may be grouped under a Life Sciences department which is one of several departments within the College of Agriculture at your university.

 One of the most popular majors coming into college and even through the first year is "undecided." Unless you've done a lot of research in high school and taken some classes similar to what you want your major to be, it's ok to hold off declaring a major. While you may feel "behind", you may actually come ahead by completing general university requirements first rather than students who change their majors two or three times. Be patient and learn more about your options.

There really is no such thing as an "easy" major to choose because it depends on your passions, strengths and goals. For instance, someone who has excelled in science in high school might find a major in aerospace engineering "easier" than enrolling as a music major, while someone who has a passion for creativity and art might find being a graphic design major "easier" than being a physicist.

Some majors have a required introductory class for students in that particular major. The course is designed to explain the requirements expected of you and explores the opportunities available to you while in college as well as once you receive your degree. These classes are typically for "R" or required credit, which means you are not graded but are expected to attend as part of your major curriculum. Pay attention in these seminars, because they are often packed with useful information, giving you insider advice, resources and connections. They will also inform you of important deadlines you need to meet for your major. The class may also present information about similar majors and job opportunities; keep an open mind because you might discover something else along the way you didn't even know was an option that is more in tune with your planned goals.

There are positions and jobs out there you don't even know exist; keep your mind open to these opportunities.

Attending introductory classes related to your major is a great way to start making initial bonds with other students in your major as well as faculty.

The Reality of the Situation:

Marketing major
Thinks they will be in downtown New York City creating the next marketing campaign for a Fortune 500 company that creates an instant best-seller. Reality is they are marketing nuts and bolts on a flyer to advertise to a hardware store in a strip mall.

Geology major
Thinks they will be uncovering dinosaur bones and traveling to Egypt. Reality is they will be a college professor educating more anthropology majors.

Psychology major
Thinks there must be lots of job opportunities since so many other students have decided on the same major. Reality is they are unemployed following graduation.

Physical Therapy
Thinks they'll be nursing NBA and NFL athletes back to health and making millions. Reality is they will be working in a nursing home helping elderly learn to navigate their new walker or wheelchair.

Theater major
Thinks they'll be choosing between a broadway debut or reading screen plays upon graduation. Reality is they are working at a Blockbuster™ video store and sharing some stage time at their local community theater's production of "Oklahoma."

You might have also chosen a major without really knowing much about it because it sounded good when you chose it from a list--what exactly does a zoologist do on a day-to-day basis anyway? You may decide to switch your major at some point during your four years and that's ok. Of course, the earlier you make the switch, the easier it will be to complete your degree within four years. Before you switch majors you should reflect on *why* you want to switch majors (see introductory questions above). If you are enrolled as an undecided major during your freshman year, you will complete "gen-eds", which are general education courses required by your university for graduation of all students, regardless of their major. If you know what general field you want to enter, you can enroll in courses that apply to the majority of the majors in that category (i.e. if you know you will most likely enter a science-related major, you will most likely enroll in introductory courses in biology and chemistry).

Don't opt out of a major just because you think a particular course or professor will be too hard. You will be able to find the resources you need to triumph over one or two "hard-spots" in your program if you are committed to your goal.

Advisors

You will be assigned an academic advisor during orientation who will meet with you at some point during your first semester. Academic advisors are college faculty members or professors within your major department. He or she will help you plan and approve your course schedule each semester during class registration in order to help you stay on track to complete your major. Academic advisors are not like high school counselors, because they typically advise a small group of students and have other university responsibilities beyond advising such as research or teaching. However, some advisors are more involved than other advisors and may help you out in other areas besides academics such as networking and job opportunities.

Now is the time to also clear any holds on your record that will prevent you from registering on time. Holds can include unpaid parking fines, overdue library books, inadequate vaccination history, etc.

If a class you want to take is full, you may be able to get into the class at a later date as other people add and drop the course---keep checking, even through the first week of class, to see if any seats have come available.

When you are planning your course schedule with your advisor, only you know yourself well enough to know what you are capable of (i.e. can you make it to class at 8am three times a week?). You are the one who has the most vested-interest in your schedule and path. You should know what classes are required for your major, what choices you have, classes you would like to take, and roughly how many credits you are comfortable with. Don't blame your advisor for having to take a particular course or not graduating on time. You need to take charge, look after yourself and make the final decisions.

Degree Audit

Your academic advisor will print your "Degree Audit" each term to help you monitor your academic and course progress. Your audit sheet provides a "snapshot" of the courses you have completed or are currently taking (including corresponding grades for each class), and the required courses you still need to complete your degree. The audit sheet will help you plan your class schedule each semester.

When people tell you their major, no matter what it is, your reply should always be, "What the hell kind of major is that?!"
When people tell you their major, look concerned and ask, "Does our college even offer that major?"

Final Thoughts

Selecting a major requires research. It's important to carefully think about this decision because your college major leads into your career. Think in the long term—where are you heading?

Points to Ponder

- When you choose a major make sure it can lead to a job—you don't want to graduate to find out there is no market for your major.
- The requirements specified in the course catalog (used to map out the requirements to obtain your major) you received as a freshman should not change even if the college later decides to change course requirements.

CHAPTER 21

CLASS
YOUR ATTENDANCE COUNTS

"WHAT?! We have something due today?!"

College classes are taught in many different styles. Some of your classes, such as an English literature class, might consist of small group discussions with constant back-and-forth interaction between the teacher and students; other classes, such as a required general education class, might be a very large lecture class where the teacher talks in front of 100 or more students. Generally lectures last about one hour and the class meets several times a week.

Some large lecture classes will have a designated additional class period called a recitation. A recitation is generally taught by a teacher assistant (TA) or graduate assistant (GA), instead of the professor. There are multiple recitation sections so that you meet with a smaller subset of the larger lecture class. Recitation classes are intended to provide you a time to ask homework questions, seek clarification on your lecture notes and discuss concepts you did not understand during lecture time.

Recitation classes are known for pop quizzes.

In a lab class, such as a chemistry lab, you are usually working with a partner on a step-by-step lab procedure. Lab classes generally require concurrent enrollment in the corresponding lecture course. They generally have a pre-lab time to allow for instructions on the week's lab. Labs may require a pre or post lab write up and you may have a quiz during the pre-lab time. Generally, labs meet once a week for three hours. A variation of a lab class is a studio, for an art or architecture class. In this type of class you generally work alone on large, hands-on projects and will spend many hours in the studio completing your project.

As compared to your high school schedule, your classes might not be one class after another. Most likely, you will have extended periods of time between your classes. Your classes might start as early as 7 am or go as late as 10 PM. Some days you might only have a couple of classes or no classes at all, and other days your schedule might be packed with lectures and labs.

Contact hours are the number of hours actually spent in class each week (lecture hours and lab hours). This number can be different from the number of credits you are taking. Credits are units applied towards your degree and each course has a certain number of credits based on the class's contact hours. Generally a three hour lab is one credit while a lecture class that meets three times a week for one hour each time is three credits.

Online classes are becoming more and more a part of almost every student's college experience. There are varying degrees of online classes. Some classes are entirely online, including lectures, notes, and even discussion boards required by students to read and respond to. Some classes will have a couple of components which are online, but tests and quizzes are completed in a regular classroom. If you have a choice to take a traditional class versus an online class, be sure to think through the benefits and drawbacks. While an online class may seem like a great idea because you can complete the work anytime, anywhere, it also requires a lot of self-discipline and motivation. There also is a level of disconnect with personal interactions with classmates and the professor with an online class. Questions are asked via email and can't be answered on the spot during the lecture. But, as your college career continues, online classes can be a great way to squeeze in a class which wouldn't fit anywhere else in your schedule.

It seems most classes will have some type of online component, even if as small as online grades. Be sure to learn and understand how the online portion works. Often times you are able to track your grades and other scores much more easily online and also have access to class materials.

A five credit class will have more effect on your GPA than a one credit class, even if you get a better grade in the one credit course (see Chapter 24: Grades).

A general rule of thumb is that one contact hour equals one credit except for lab classes.

Definitions

Drops:
You can usually remove or "drop" a class from your schedule before a certain date each semester. After this cut-off date for drops, you can no longer withdraw from the class without a resultant failing grade and/or financial penalties. The number of drops you are permitted throughout your degree program may be capped. If you drop a required class, you will need to take the class during another semester. Dropped classes may be recorded on your transcript as having been dropped. Don't get 'drop happy' though!

Audit:
You can audit a course which means you are signed up for the class but you do not receive credit or a grade for the course. You might decide to audit a class you are interested in learning more about for the sake of learning without having to worry about turning in assignments for grades.

Course Number:
The first digit of a course number corresponds to the typical year a course is completed, that is a 100-level class is intended for first-years while a 400-level is intended for seniors. Because classes in a series progressively become harder, the level indicated by the course number *usually* also indicates the difficulty of the course.

Instructors use many forms of media to teach a class such as PowerPoint, overhead transparencies, writing on the board, or leading class discussions. Your class notes will also vary in form. You may be expected to copy down what the teacher writes on the board or talks about during class; you may be given an outline of the notes to fill in as the teacher lectures; or you may be given an exact copy of the notes. If you are given an exact copy of the lecture notes that is pre-bought or posted on the web, it is still important to go to class to know what the teacher emphasized in the notes and to add any new material.

Going to class is getting the summary (that is, the lecture) of the summary (that is, your class notes) of the story (that is, the book chapter). Therefore reading your textbook will give you the full story behind the lecture material.

Note Taking in Class

The challenge of taking notes in class is knowing what are key concepts to write down and what is not important. Good note taking involves being able to paraphrase main ideas efficiently and still be able to understand what was being conveyed when you review your notes later. This skill will come with time and experience as you become more familiar with the teacher's style and what is emphasized on tests. Here are some helpful pointers:

- When you have a set of prepared notes in front of you, underline the points talked about in class. This will help you remember what was and wasn't talked about during lecture. This will help you later while you are studying, especially when you are behind in a class and don't know what is going on at the time of the lecture.
- Develop different signs (such as stars or boxes) that you consistently use in all of your class notes to indicate the degree of importance of a point emphasized by the professor or the length of time spent on a main concept.
- Make a note next to anything that is unclear or confusing. Be sure to follow up later and find the answer (ask the professor, talk with classmates, read the book chapter).
- If you have a difficult time discerning what you should and shouldn't take notes on during a discussion type class, one method you can use is to watch your classmates. If you notice or sense that a number of people around you are taking notes, then it's a reasonable bet something important was said and you should take some notes at that point, too.
- Teachers can cover a lot of information when using PowerPoint because they can quickly click through slides. To encourage students to come to class on a regular basis, the teacher may not make these slides available to you for printing or viewing on the web. This can be frustrating if you aren't quite able to copy down all the information from one slide before the next slide is presented. A little preplanning is required for these classes: have a

friend copy the slide from the bottom up as you take notes from the top down and then compare notes after class.

Asking questions in class

It's useful to ask questions during lecture for clarification and further understanding, especially if you have a "mental block" when it's important to understand the information before being presented with the next topic. Don't be afraid to ask your question because generally you will not be the only one confused. In some cases it may also be more appropriate to ask your question after class when your professor can be more attentive and provide you a more thorough, interactive explanation.

Personality Line-Up:
- The person who doesn't really have a question but wanted to share their life story with the class.
- The person who loves attention and tries to dominate class time.
- The person who comes in late and asks a question within five minutes about information that was already covered.
- The person who asks a question because they had no clue what is going on and they are hoping asking *any* question will help clear things up.
- The person who asks a question they already know the answer to, letting the instructor know they read the material.
- The person who took a similar class in high school and constantly brings up points trying to "stump" the professor.

Pearls of Wisdom:
- A well timed and appropriately placed snapping of binders, ruffle of papers, and zipping of bags can help speed-up the end of class.
- Expect to have homework your first day of class.
- Classes don't have assigned seating like in high school. But, normally where you sit the first week is where you'll probably sit all semester because people become very territorial over "their seat". Sit in the front of the class, so you can hear better and see pictures more clearly. Plus if someone asks a question, you will be able to hear it. On test days you'll get your test first which means you'll have more time to work out the questions and you won't have to wait while the teacher runs off more test copies if they come up short. Try to sit near an exit so that you don't waste time waiting for the lecture to empty out following class. Seating in the back can be distracting, although funny, because of the many side comments or conversations from the "back row students".

- Meet as many people as you can during the first couple weeks of class. This will help you later to form study groups to prepare for tests. Invite people to be part of your group and exchange phone numbers or email.

- Choose your lab partner carefully, because you will be working closely with that person and they can affect your grade. You want someone who will do their fair share of the work, is positive and someone who is at your level or slightly above your level of understanding. People who don't care about the lab do not make good partners, because they will slow you down. People who seem to know everything also don't make good lab partners, because they will go so fast they won't have time to clue you in and you won't know what is going on.

- Go to class every time, including the Friday afternoon before a long break. When teachers planned out their syllabus for the semester they didn't factor in for your Friday afternoon plans. You may even be rewarded if attendance is low by attendance points or test question hints.

- Arrive to class early. If you arrive late you might miss important announcements or class handouts. Also, some teachers will begin to write notes on the board before class in order to save time. Allowing yourself a few extra minutes before class starts also gives you time to use the restroom, get a drink of water, find a good seat, situate your notes and bag, and make small talk with your crush.

- If you are late to class, don't make a big scene about it and sit in the nearest seat you find.

- When you hear or ask for advice, it is important to evaluate the source it came from. A student who got a C on a test after not studying very much might tell you the test was very easy while a student who got an A on the test might tell you the test was hard because they missed a perfect score and were hung-up on a handful of difficult questions.

- The "10-Minute Class Rule", which is not an official rule, states if a professor does not show up after ten minutes from the start of the class period, then lecture is cancelled. Of course, you can leave lecture anytime you want because taking attendance is uncommon in college classes, but there could be a number of reasons a teacher is running late who still plans on having lecture. Just keep in mind the '10 minute class rule' is a myth.

Mike Story Box

I have had professors show up when more than half way through the class time and start lecturing. Even if other people start leaving, stay and go over your notes.

Cover all your books using brown paper grocery sacks and bring them to class.

When the teacher asks if the class can hear them ok, say "YES!" very clearly, *especially* when sitting in the front row.

- When someone coughs or sneezes during class, look over and give them a very angry, "SHHHH!!"
- When someone sneezes say "easy there killer". If someone sneezes twice, tell them to knock it off.
- In a smaller classroom, pass around a National Geographic and open to a story that roughly corresponds to something being covered in the current unit of material with a small note that reads "pass around". Someone will eventually be caught for reading a National Geographic magazine in class when the teacher spots them not paying attention and takes it away from them. Try not to giggle.
- When someone drops their pencil, pick it up, don't acknowledge them or their persist tapping your shoulder, and start using it. As far as you're concerned you've always had this pencil.
- With 90 seconds of class left, raise your hand and say you have two questions. You will never hear so much groaning from your classmates except at that very moment.
- Ask your friend, "will you carry my books for a just sec? (implying you need to tie your shoe, put on your coat or something like that), let out a sigh, and continue to walk with the person, showing no interest in taking the books back anytime soon.
- When the person sitting next to you in class unzips their backpack to get out their class notes, reach into their bag and grab for stuff.
- Ignore your ringing cell phone in your backpack; when someone around asks if you're going to do something about it, say "nah, I'll call them back later. I want to pay attention to the lecture".
- Point at people when the teacher is discussing cheating, giving them the, "This means you, are you paying attention, no more cheating!" look. Be obvious to everyone around you that you have identified the class cheater.
- When the teacher announces there will be no class the following class period because he or she needs to attend a conference out of state, raise your hand and accusingly ask "Are you really going to a conference? or is that just a cover because you are interviewing with another university?" Stare intently as though you know something. Follow their answer up with a "uh-huh. Right. I guess we'll see then."
- When the teacher poses a question for class discussion be sure to offer your thoughts on the topic. Wait a little bit, then raise your

hand again as though you have something to add, and repeat *exactly* what you said the first time.

- During pre-lab, when the TA is talking about how some students typically make a mistake at this point in the experiment, and thus ruining their lab results, point your finger directly at your friend with a reassuring nod of the head, as though to be saying, "You. That's who he's talking about." This also applies whenever the professor is talking about human diseases, especially STDs, identify your friend with the point of the finger again as though you are say, "You. You have the disease he's talking about! Share your story with the class."

- When your teacher tells the class to pass an assignment to the left, be the voice in the background that can be heard saying, "WHAT!" We have something due today?"

- Take notes when note taking is not appropriate. This will worry someone in the class.

- When a classmate looks over at you in class, cover up your notes in an obvious manner.

- Pass around a sheet on the first day of class laying out the plan for a 45 second standing ovation for your teacher at the end of class.

- Pass around a sign-up sheet during lecture for future social events with a specific time and location. Never mind the events you create don't really exist, your fellow classmates can't resist signing their name on a sheet promising them a free 30 cent hotdog or some greasy pizza. Be sure to include other information categories that don't relate to the event or otherwise don't make sense such as "What college do you attend?" or "Are you single?" Put a note at the bottom to return the sheet to your favorite nosebleed in the class.

- Crowd into the door as the other class is trying to leave.

- Be the kid in class who has seen or done everything in class that the teacher asks, whether the teacher asks if you know how to do something or have visited somewhere, etc. Always volunteer your hand consistently even if you can't follow up with the claim. Be sketchy on the details if called on to relate your experience to the class.

- Say "PSSSST!" and call the person's name who is sitting in front of you. When they turn around, tell them they should be paying attention and point towards the front of the room (same for a car in front of you at a green light: wait just for the moment as the light turn green, honk your horn, and when they look back at you, point at the now green light and act angry, with an angry fist in the air and your best psycho face).

- Be a nosebleed by raising your hand in the affirmative whenever a teacher poses a rhetorical-hypothetical type question.

- Answer a question with the answer to another question that wasn't asked.
- Always start answers with, "Well I think the answer is in the question…".
- Run between your classes—be sure your backpack is fully loaded. Bump into people on the sidewalks as you run.
- When leaving a class-building, act like you haven't seen sunlight in days and that it is burning your eyes. Also, complain about the reperfusion injuries of the fresh air to your lungs. Sit on the ground and let everyone else walk around you.
- During finals week, as you are handing in your final, IMMEDIATELY take out your notes for your next final and begin studying as you are walking out of the classroom.
- Play Hang-Man in class. Use H-A-N-G M-A-N as the word that your friends are trying to figure out.
- Write a message on a classroom board with SAVE next to it and see how long it will last. If you can't think of a clever message to use, save your Hang-Man game.
- Give people "gifts" such as rocks, leaves, twigs as you are walking to class. Act offended and upset if they drop it.
- Wink at people you pass as you walk to class.
- When someone is getting a drink at the drinking fountain, nub in next to them and try to get a drink of water at the same time. When they stop holding the fountain button and give you a look, ask them if they could turn it back on because you are still thirsty.
- Blurt out answers confidently and if you are wrong, still say, "Yes!" and be adamant if people challenge you and say that's not what you said.
- Anytime it snows, post a sign on random class room doors that reads, "NO CLASS TODAY".
- During a really boring lecture ask someone for a fork. Because, as you explain, digging your eyeballs out with a fork would be more stimulating than the lecture.
- Ask clarification questions during an oral quiz that don't make sense. For example, in a world religion class where the answer might be Jesus, ask the teacher if the person's first and last name will be needed for full credit? This will make other people in the class think twice about their answer.
- During a PowerPoint presentation, ask a couple of questions about a topic that was already covered in the previous slides. Have your friends sit in other sections of the classroom and have them ask more questions about the same topic so that the teacher has to keep back tracking to the same slide. The teacher and the rest of the class will wonder where this extreme curiosity on an otherwise neutral topic came from.

Final Thoughts

We're going to assume you are taking a 15 credit load this semester and the semester is 16 weeks long. Consider your three credit course that meets Mondays, Wednesdays and Fridays for a total of 48 times in one semester. Assuming your tuition costs $10,000 per year, *each* lecture for this class costs about $20. Pretend someone is collecting a twenty dollar bill every time you walk into a lecture. Make sure you receive your money's worth by not skipping class.

Points to Ponder

- Review your notes during the first 5-10 minutes of class as the teacher sets up for the lecture.
- When a teacher shows a complicated diagram and says don't copy this down, it doesn't mean just sit back--listen for the main points and write them down.
- Even if the lecture makes sense at the time, jot down some notes.
- If your friend starts dosing-off in class, give their cell phone a ring; the quick, frantic search to the bottom of their book bag is just the adrenaline rush they needed to stay awake. You are a true friend.
- Don't skip class. Weather is not a reason to miss class.
- If someone tells you a class was an "easy A", it was probably a general topic class. The depth of class material covered in these classes is usually vague because of all the topics covered, and it might not be so "easy".
- Pay close attention the very last two minutes of class as everyone else is packing up; during this time key information is usually given in the form of summary points and this information could make the difference between an A or a B on your next test.

CHAPTER 22
PROFESSORS
DOCTORS WITHOUT MEDICINE

"This person has A LOT of letters after their name!"

Professors have many responsibilities at universities including teaching, research, academic committees, student advising, supervising graduate students, and administrative responsibilities. Many college courses are "team-taught," and you could have multiple teachers throughout the semester for one class. Many professors are passionate about their work and are committed to helping college students. They are often excited when you show interest in their course material or stop by during their office hours to discuss a homework problem.

Connecting with professors on a more personal level can be challenging in large lectures. Realistically, you won't need to know the majority of your professors outside of the classroom but it is important to establish relationships with a handful of professors, especially those related to your major. Ways to connect with your professor may include: active participation in class, visiting during their office hours, enrolling in other courses taught by them or learning more about their research. Cultivating this relationship can lead to more than just classroom success as the professor may be able to help you gain outside experience, write you an academic reference letter or provide you advice as an "unofficial advisor".

Professors hold different positions depending on their education background, experience and career objectives:

Teaching Assistant: often a graduate student who serves a supplementary role in class instruction (example: A T.A. may teach the lab component of a class or recitation)

Assistant Professor: "entry-level" position for professors with a masters or PhD

Associate Professor: usually a professor who has earned tenure through academic creditability, teaching excellence and research publications. Tenure is a contract clause allowing the professor academic freedom to pursue original lines of thought (even when contemporarily controversial) without fear of losing their job.

Full Professor: senior position for professors; the top few will be honored as "distinguished professors". When a full professor retires but continues to teach in some capacity then they are given the title "professor emeritus".

Adjunct or Visiting Professor: These professors are not hired on a permanent basis by the university and teach a special course or seminar.

Professors may perform differently in their ability to teach as depending on if they were hired solely as an instructor or if teaching was "added on" to their research assignment.

When Teachers Say: It really means:
Please ask a lot of questions, I want class to be more like a discussion than me just up here lecturing to you.
> There is so much material that you are responsible for, I'm not even going to *try* to get through all the notes; you'll have to cover it on your own time outside of class.

Have you gone over this review material in another class?

Yes? No? I'm not sure why I just asked that, I'm still going to cover it anyway.

You'll get out of class early today.

I think I have extra time today, so I'm going to take my time. I'll probably need to rush the last ten minutes just to get you out five minutes early like I said I would; Oh, and if everyone could stick around after class for a few minutes, I can hand back your tests.

For the first ten minutes of class I'm just going to tell you what we will be talking about today.

My outline is exceptionally clear, but none of this will make sense. I've meshed all of the topics into one, and the lecture is not really going to follow the outline; I may have left out a few topics as well; don't forget you have homework due tomorrow on this.

I was working on grading your quizzes last night.

I almost got three of them completely graded; you'll forget you were even waiting for these results before you see them again.

Any questions?

No questions? I will assume then you understand all of the material I just presented to you that you are still trying to copy down.

Class, class, please, let's get started, we have a lot to cover today.

I amaze even myself sometimes how much information I can cram into these PowerPoint presentations. I need you all to quiet down because I'm attempting a new personal best today: 15 slides per minute.

Calcium is important for bone growth, nerve conduction and enzyme reactions. Can anyone tell me one important role of calcium in the body? Yes, that is correct. You all are great! Classroom learning is fun!

I'm not sure why everyone felt the test was so hard, you all seemed to understand the material so well in class. Obviously it must be your fault for not studying.

We'll get back to this if we have time at the end.

the sound of crickets chirping

The Nosebleed:

This is the kid who quickly responds "no" whenever the teacher asks if they should cover a review-topic. This person is annoying because you doubt even they fully understand the concept in question but spoke on behalf of the class leading the teacher to assume everyone completely understands the concept.

Mike Story Box

I was having difficulty in a large-lecture advanced math class due to the pace of the course. My strategy to excel in the class was to make sure I understood every homework problem assigned. To accomplish this goal, it often consisted of me seeking my professor out during office hours, and asking questions in class. By sitting in the front of the room, my professor knew I was attending class every day. Halfway through the semester my professor knew my name and called on me in class. My efforts paid off in the end when my final percentage was used in the curve as the last cutoff for the "A" grade even though my percentage was in the typical B range.

Mike Story Box

During a genetics lecture my professor collapsed and fell on the floor. Paramedics arrived on the scene and assisted the teacher over the next 35 minutes as she recovered from a hypoglycemic attack. With half of the class gone and only 15 minutes left of class, the teacher went ahead with the lecture. In retrospect, I'm not sure which part of it was more shocking: the fact the teacher collapsed or the fact that we still had class. Nonetheless, it shows how dedicated professors are to making use of every class minute.

Final Thoughts

Professors vary in their ability to teach—you're going to have some awesome professors as well as suboptimal ones. Your challenge to be a successful student is to adapt and excel in the class regardless of the professor's teaching ability. Part of earning an A grade is figuring out your professor's teaching style to maximize your learning.

Points to Ponder
- Don't blame the professor—learn the material on your own if necessary.
- The translation for when a teacher says, "A way you can remember this", is "You're going to see this on the test".
- Amazing, you often ponder, how every topic covered in every class every day of every semester every year lasts exactly the time allotted for that class period.

- By the time you graduate, you will probably have been taught by over 100 professors.
- Do teachers really believe they are relating to you by putting something in terms of beer or pizza?
- Email is one of the best ways to get a hold of a professor.
- Don't be afraid to see your professor during office hours; a lot of students don't, and it will show an effort on your part to do well in the class.

CHAPTER 23
CLASS SYLLABUS
MAPPING OUT YOUR CLASS

"I've got a lot ahead of me this semester."

A syllabus is a very important class document, usually one to four pages long, that outlines the course's:

- lecture and topic schedule
  - what will be covered on each day of class and possibly corresponding reading assignments. It will also list the dates of tests, midterm and the final for the class
- policies and rules
  - attendance policy, disability accommodations, cheating, etc.
- grading rubrics and grading scale
  - states what percentage of your final grade will be comprised of tests, papers, projects, quizzes, homework assignments, class attendance and participation, etc. Also, if a standard grading scale is used as well as the cut offs for each grade, in total points or by percentages, including pluses and minuses for each letter grade
- required textbooks or supplies for the course
- professor's contact information
  - office location, office hours, email

As you can see a syllabus contains a lot of useful information. You will receive a syllabus for each of your classes during the first week. It is not something you will need to memorize for a test, but it's important to carefully analyze it. By the end of the week you will have a hard time keeping everything you are expected to do for each class straight; therefore it is critical to have a method to organize all of this information.

Dissecting a syllabus

Once you have all of your classes' syllabi in front of you, the first thing you should do is map out your entire semester on a schedule or planner. This is critical and will help you visually see in a week to week format the overall timing of your tests and other deadlines for projects. You will find very quickly that tests in college will come in clumps and you will have two to four "rounds" of tests throughout the semester.

Be aggressive and get projects and papers done early in the semester. When you look over your syllabi you will notice some projects or papers that won't be due until the end of the semester. Don't leave these for the end of the semester; however. If you can start them now, you can use that extra time to study for finals. You will have a lot more time in the beginning of the semester than you will at the end and completing these tasks now will pay off in large returns.

Next, look at the components that will determine your final grade. In some classes, tests may not be as important as papers, projects, group work, etc. if tests compromise a smaller percentage of the total points; while in other classes you may only have a couple of tests and a final. Your success in the class depends on your knowledge of this break-down so you know where to focus your energy. Take note of the cumulative effect of what seems to be "minor" 5-10 point attendance or pop quizzes because these points can add up to a significant portion of the total grade and are an easy way to maximize your total points. This is one of the biggest mistakes of students who skip class and justify missing those quizzes as, "It's just a ten point quiz". There is no excuse for not receiving a 100% on attendance quizzes.

Look to determine which of your classes are "front-end heavy" with the majority of tests and points before midterm versus those that are "end heavy" where the majority of points come after midterm such as the final or semester projects. This will also affect how you divide your time among classes.

Definition:
Midterm: 1. designates the half-way point in the semester. 2. refers to a cumulative test given when the class is about half-way completed. 3. refers to a notification from your college that you are in danger of failing a class with your current graded material for the class.

It will help to make yourself a spreadsheet for each class that lists the individual components and associated points that will determine your grade so you can chart and keep track of your progress. This is most useful when you are half way through the semester. You can then calculate how many of the remaining points you need to earn to achieve your desired grade. Another way to think of this is to determine how many points you are "down" (missed points) from the amount of points you can miss to still be in your desired grade bracket.

Finally it is also important to look for any special caveats the professor may have inserted in the syllabus that could affect you later, such as "professor reserves the right to lower or raise the grading scale based on class performance" or "pop quizzes may be given" or "your lowest two quiz scores will be dropped". The latter may not actually benefit you if those are simple attendance quizzes and you have earned full points on them; if this happens to you, calculate the difference in your grade from dropping points versus not dropping points and talk with the professor. For those classes that have pop quizzes it is imperative to stay on top of the current material for that class and come prepared ready to take a quiz when you go to lecture.

Mike Story Box

Be sure to explore any websites listed on the syllabus. I had an English class where the teacher referred to the book website three times during the first class and then never said anything more about it after that. It made me curious, so I explored the website and found that the weekly quizzes with the answers were on the site. At the end of the semester the teacher asked if anyone had discovered the "secret" to the quizzes. I and two other people raised our hands. Our classmates were not too happy but the teacher told them that sometimes in life it pays to go the extra step.

Cheating in College

In some high schools, cheating is often rampart and common place. However in college this is not the case. You are now in a point in your academic career where **you need to know this information** for your future. What does cheating say about you and your character and integrity? You have too much on the line with creditability, respect and professionalism to be embarrassed by cheating. If you are caught cheating, the consequences can range from receiving a zero for the test or assignment to being expelled from the university (depending on the nature and severity of the cheating). The reprimand could appear on your permanent record and follow you for many years.   You should know your college's honor code policy.   In any case, you should be proud of a hard earned C compared to a dishonest A. The consequences versus benefits of cheating in college are just not worth it!

 On the first day of class the teacher will go over the syllabus and class rules. If the attendance policy states attendance is not required and will not affect your grade, stand up and leave just as that part is read.

- On the first day of class, be sure to ask the professor for his or her home phone number.
- From day one, clap when the teacher is finished lecturing, causing other people around you to clap. People will start to think it is normal to clap when a teacher has completed a lecture.

Final Thoughts

Think of a syllabus as the blueprint of how to start off college on the right foot.

Points to Ponder
- Not all classes are created equal—use the syllabus to figure out where you need to focus your efforts.

CHAPTER 24
GRADES
YOUR COLLEGE REPORT CARD

"Another day, another A"

If you set out to learn and understand the course material, academic success will come natural to you; that is, learn for the sake of learning, not just to earn a letter grade.   In the long run, you will surpass your colleagues by delving deeper into your studies to satisfy your inquisitive mind rather than restricting yourself to only what's required by the class.   Grades, however, are also important, but achieving high grades encompasses more than just knowing and understanding the course content.   Going to class, completing homework assignments and reading the textbooks are major parts of "getting an A," but other factors involved include:

- Knowing the teacher and their background; especially knowing their research focus can help give you insights into what material they will think is important for tests.
- Knowing the level of depth the teacher expects you to understand the material after taking your first test and seeing old test files to determine the format and style of the questions you will be asked.
- Knowing the material when you need to know it.   Any difficult course is easy if you have all of the time you want to study for it; thus the success of an "A" student is knowing how to balance time management correctly to maximize your efforts to your most demanding classes.

A "shared scare" among freshmen is whether or not they will be prepared for college level material. You may have been told that college is a lot harder than high school and to expect many more hours of homework. This is probably true for most students, but there are other factors that play into that statement as well such as adjusting to college life and finding balance in your schedule. One of the keys to college is time management and knowing how to prioritize. If you did alright in high school, you should be prepared for this next step of education. At times you may even find that some of the material is material you covered in high school; at other times you might panic because you have no idea what is going on. The basics to earning an A in any college course:

- Know the class material. This means anything in the class notes, anything said during class and anything in the homework or reading assignment. (see Chapter 27: Studying and Study Groups)
- Know what your professor emphasized during class and what your professor views as important.
- Know what the format of the test will be. Studying for a recall type test, such as short answer essay, requires a different studying strategy than studying for a recognition type test, such as multiple choice. (see Chapter 28: Tests, Papers and Projects)
- Know the material when you need to know it. The challenge is when you have multiple tests in a given time period and knowing how to prioritize what you need to study and for how long before moving on. College would be so much easier if you only had to worry about one class. (see Chapter 26: Time Management and Scheduling)
- Retain the information. That will make earning an "A" in a later class easier if the subject matter is similar.

GPA Goal Setting

When setting your GPA goal there are many factors to consider such as:
- Do you have any scholarships that require you to maintain a certain GPA level to continue your eligibility for funding?
- How much of a role will your grades play in your future plans when you are applying for a summer internship or job following graduation?
- If you plan to attend professional or graduate school, what is the average GPA of accepted applicants?

- How competitive is your major? Will a high GPA provide you other opportunities (Dean's List, Scholarships, Honor Societies, Honors Program, Campus Jobs, etc.)?
- What expectations do your parents have for you?
- How important is school to you? What letter grades would you personally be satisfied with?
- What are reasonable grades for you to achieve? What is your tolerance for stress? Are you willing to study long hours?

With these factors in mind, you can set a feasible GPA goal; you might strive to keep high grades in any class related to their major, (your "major GPA"), or to stay eligible for a scholarship or to qualify for the Dean's List (see below) or to achieve a 4.0.

Kipp Story Box

Setting your goals for a GPA can be a self-fulfilling prophecy. I told myself I wanted to get all A's my senior year. I found my mind frame was changed and in each class I was looking at how to get an A. I've heard many people say, "I want to get all B's" and they find themselves giving up when they reached B's when they *probably* could have earned an A or two in one of those classes.

GPA Calculator

Most university use a four point system when calculating your grade point average (GPA), with an A given the maximum four points and decreasing points for subsequent letter grades (i.e. 3.6 points for an A-, 3.3 points for a B+, 3.0 points for a B, etc.). To calculate your GPA, take the number of credits for your course multiplied by the value for your letter grade, known as quality points, based on the chart below. Add up your quality point total and divide by four times the number of credits you completed.

Letter Grade to Quality Point Conversion Table:

A: 4.00	B-: 2.67	D+: 1.33
A-: 3.67	C+: 2.33	D: 1.00
B+: 3.33	C: 2.00	D-: 0.67
B: 3.00	C-: 1.67	F: 0.00

College grading scales can be more liberal or more stringent than the grading scales you are familiar with in high school. For example, in some college courses the cut off for an A could be as low as an 83% or has high as a 94%.

Some students are mistakenly led to believe their grades during their first year are not important and will be able to later excuse any poor grades as "freshman inexperience". However, no job, scholarship or application has a freshman inexperience clause used when looking at your grades and GPA. Therefore, you should be extra conscientious to earn good grades your first year so that you aren't later left saying "if it wasn't for that one D my freshmen year, my GPA would have qualified me for...". It is equally important to do well your senior year because some applications will ask for a separate GPA that takes into account only your last 45 credits of classes (in addition to your cumulative GPA).

Your GPA will tend to fluctuate during your first year until you accumulate more credits which will help stabilize any outlier grades.

The Dean's List

Universities commonly recognize high academically achieving students each term by publishing a Dean's List, composed of those students who meet a certain GPA cutoff point, typically a 3.0 or higher (similar to the "Honor Roll" used in high schools). If you make the "Dean's List", you will typically receive a letter from a representative in the Dean of Students Office congratulating you on your achievement. Although no financial award is tied-in with being on the Dean's List, achieving high grades can open doors to other opportunities including scholarship qualification, campus jobs, Honor Society invitations or coveted space on your parent's refrigerator.

Honor Societies

Joining an Honor Society is typically by invite only for those students who meet certain minimal scholastic criteria such as having a B+ GPA average or higher or being in the top 15% of your major. If you decide to accept an invitation to join an honor society, you will usually partake in a formal induction ceremony before you are recognized as a full member. Honor Societies are similar to other campus organizations with governing officers and hosting events including guest speakers, special topic lectures and community service projects. Be aware, though, some honor societies are not as legitimate and serve to do nothing more than collect money from you. You are better off not spending your money to join these "paper honor societies". The value added to your resume for such inactive honor societies will only be marginal and redundant, because your other academic achievements will already be shining through.

Honors Program

University Honors Programs allow students to individualize their studies in the pursuit of additional knowledge or a more challenging curriculum. This might include courses specifically designed for Honors students, taking graduate level courses, conducting research or attending special seminars or topic lectures. Honor students may be given additional benefits such as priority class scheduling, increased maximum credit loads, extended library loan privileges, access to the honors building or study space or grant money for projects. The Honors Program is a good way to network within your college as well as connect socially with other academically focused students. To qualify for the Honors program you will typically need to maintain a certain GPA as well as fulfill other requirements as set out by the program such as taking a certain number of Honors designated courses or completing an Honors research project. Universities will denote participation in the Honors Program on your official academic transcript as well as recognize students in the program during graduation ceremonies.

Grade Reports and Transcripts

Much like high school, a grade report will be available for each term you complete. Your grade report is typically found online after a certain date following the end of the semester. Your parents are typically not mailed a copy of your grades.

Your grade reports are all compiled onto your official university transcript with your current cumulative GPA. You can request, usually for a fee, to have your official transcript mailed to employers, graduate schools, etc. If you print your transcript yourself, it is regarded as an "unofficial" transcript since it does not have the official university stamp that signifies the document's authenticity.

Students with high GPAs will be recognized at graduation ceremonies by various levels of distinction on their college diplomas:

- *Cum laude*: "with honor"
- *Magna cum laude*: "with great honor"
- *Summa cum laude*: "with highest honor"

Perfectionism:

It's ok to have high standards and goals; however perfectionism is a self-defeating frame of mind of some college students who set unreasonable and unrealistic goals.   These students are afraid to fail or make mistakes. Failing to reach these excessively high goals can then lead to anxiety, depression, stress and low self-esteem.   Others may view perfectionists as pretentious or distant since they do not disclose their mistakes or feelings. Keep the big picture in mind—will one low exam score or one B on your report card really matter in five years?   Are you missing out on other opportunities by not taking risks?   In college, there is always going to be someone else who excels more than you in any given area.

A letter grade is an absolute entity, meaning once you meet the minimum cutoff for an "A", you have an "A"—so whether you achieved a 93% or a 99% in the class, the final record will only indicate "A".   Therefore, if your only goal is achieving an A grade, you may be wasting your time to perfect a project to earn a higher A if you don't need the extra points.

On the other hand, if you are borderline between two grades, one or two points are well worth the extra time and effort. Professors have to make a cutoff for each letter grade and it can be very frustrating to be only one point away from the next higher letter grade.   However, the cutoffs are strictly followed, even if it's only one point, because otherwise when the cutoff is dropped to include your grade, then someone below you is now just one point away, and then they too would like the cutoff lowered...

If you find you are someone who is usually on the borderline cutoffs for grades, it is important to attempt to regain any missed test points throughout the semester. Here is how you can correctly argue missed points back:

- First step is to add up the number you got wrong on the test and subtract from the total. Sleepy grad assistants who are grading hundreds of tests can make a simple math error.
- Resist the urge to run up to the professor immediately after the tests are handed back. Your argument will only be drowned out by the other 50 students who ran up before you. If you cannot resist this urge, ask a question that seems unrelated ("leading question") before you ask your test question. The answer to your leading question should be yes, and that answer supports your argument, thus trapping your teacher into rewarding your points back.
- Check your answers with the posted answer key. If you still believe you are correct, prove it. A professor has very little leverage not to award you the points if you can provide why another answer was right by citing the appropriate reference.
- Write your name, test question, reference, and reason why you believe you are correct into a memo or email to the teacher. Let your teacher know you are not necessarily seeking points back but would like clarification in preparation for the final. This strategy will demonstrate you care about the class and put thought into your argument, as well as provide the teacher time to consider it and also serve as a written reminder to change your grade if the teacher agrees with you. Even if you don't receive any points you have gained useful feedback and left a favorable impression upon the teacher.
-

Most professors have office hours as part of the class. If you have well-thought out questions, stop by during these hours. By showing them you have an interest in learning the material, you may benefit later if you are really close to a higher grade, etc.

Some professors will include in the syllabus a statement similar to "your lowest two quiz scores will be dropped from the final grade". This is invariably to help those students who need to miss an occasional class or forget to study for a particular quiz.   But, if you attend class regularly and do well on quizzes, this policy can actually hurt your final grade.   To help illustrate this paradox, consider this example:

Assume there are 100 points total in your class, half of which come from two, 25-point tests and the other half from five, 10-point quizzes. You find the tests to be harder and earn 35 out of the possible 50 points but the quizzes are much easier (based on attendance or less material covered) and you earn 48 of the 50 points (your lowest two quiz scores were two 9 out 10 scores and you earned 10 out of 10 on the remaining three quizzes).   If you calculated your grade at this point ((35 + 48)/100), your final grade would be an 83%. But now, if you drop your lowest two quiz scores, (35 + 30)/80, your final grade would be an 81%.   The difference is small but in this case the policy meant to help you actually lowered your final grade, enough to possibly lower your class grade from a B to a B-. Check any of your final course grades in any course with a similar policy by calculating your grade with and without dropping your lowest grades; if you find that dropping your lowest scores also dropped your letter grade, talk with your professor about your concerns.

The larger your class, the greater probability there are "low achievers" on the fringes. These students are actually really valuable to your grade because they help reduce the difficulty level of tests and are the ones who help drive the class curve average lower.   Next time your classmate skips class or ignores a homework assignment, tell them "thank-you".

When the teacher announces there were only 4 A's on the test, start "air counting", point to yourself, your friend and then look puzzled as you turn around and try to figure out who the other two people are; don't even consider the people sitting directly behind you.

- When a large crowd is gathered around the hallway sheet with posted test scores/grades, push your way to the front, then in a very obvious manner to the people around you, follow the highest score back to "your" ID number and say, "Alright!"
- Same situation as above and as you struggle to see the list, say aloud "can someone just tell me what the high score is so I know what my grade is?"
- In class when the teacher tells the class the high score for the test, turn to the people around you and mumble that you wish the teacher wouldn't announce your grade to everyone; or say, "What, how did I miss two points?!"
- Things to say to people in your class after tests are handed back:
  - Good luck this Saturday at the test retake. Later the next week, ask them how the test retake went.
  - Hand them an employment application for McDonald's.
  - Will you be needing your college books anymore? Can I have them?
  - What are you still doing here? I thought you failed out last semester; who are you trying to kid here?
- After a test is handed back, a group of students can be found around a professor trying to argue points back. This is where you randomly join this group and listen just long enough so you can say to the people nearest you, "Yeah! See? I told you!"

Final Thoughts

You need to answer for yourself the question: What is the reason you are studying at college? This is a fundamental question. Is it for good grades? Is it to prepare for your career or a specific job? Is it so you can enter graduate school or a professional program such as medical school? Is it so you become a well-rounded individual in society? Is it because your parents thought it would be a good idea for you and the next logical step after high school? Achieving high grades will open doors for you with job interviews or acceptance into graduate programs as well as invitations into honor societies, your college's Honors Program or qualification for scholarships and awards. However, learning and understanding *the* course material for the bigger picture is even more important than the grade. Now is the time to soak up as much knowledge as you can. College is meant to be challenging and you should push yourself to find out what you are capable of; don't avoid a hard class or take less credits just to achieve a high GPA. Learn to learn.

Points to Ponder

- It is true that some employers do not care about your grades. It is also true that for some jobs you didn't even need your college degree. It is also true that some jobs are better than others.
- A "D" student wishes they were an "A" student (so they can study less); while an A student wishes they were a D student (so they could study less).
- 10% of the test questions are purposely hard or tricky to separate A and B scores.
- Build a strong academic base your first year. If you prove to yourself you can earn high grades you will more likely continue to strive for academic success. Once you get your first low grade, it's that much easier to allow yourself to get another one.
- Just by attending class each day, as simple as it seems, can profoundly improve your grade.
- A lot of additional knowledge and insight is gained through the process of learning and studying.
- Watch out for those classes that only have 100 points total for the semester—every test question you miss drops your final letter grade by 1%.
- Almost all honor societies require dues; be sure to find out what your money is going towards.
- Honestly, when it comes down to it, a 3.0 is going to get hired over a 2.0.
- It is almost as hard to get a 1.0 as it is to get a 4.0.
- Do the best you can.

CHAPTER 25

TEXT BOOKS
WHERE THE STORY BEGINS

"During the summer, you get to read the chapters YOU want to read."

You will find what books are required or recommended by your professor on the class syllabus. Your university will have a bookstore that will stock these books for you to purchase. You may want to wait until later in the first week to buy your books once you have all of your course syllabi to compile a complete list of books you will need. The lines at the bookstore can be very long at the beginning of the semester when everyone is buying their books. You will want to avoid multiple trips and these long lines. To help alleviate this situation, some colleges have a program where you can purchase your books ahead of time and then you only need to pick up a box of your books. Your campus may also have a competing bookstore with the university and you should compare prices at both stores for the lowest price. Another option is to buy your books online and you may be able to find a lower price, but you must also take into consideration shipping and handling costs as well as any time delay in receiving your books.

Should I buy new or used books?

The bookstore may allow you the option to buy textbooks that are brand new from the publisher or resell used books from students who sold their books back to the bookstore from previous semesters. The used books will sell at a lower price than a brand new book. However, there are some potential drawbacks of buying a used book which include poor overall condition and/or highlighted text. If you are going to buy a used book, you should thoroughly look through the stack of used books, because you might find a book that is more or less in new condition without any highlights or other markings. Be sure to save your receipt because you may need it if you are planning on selling your books back at the end of the semester.

Instead of purchasing your own books at some schools, you may have the option to rent your books for the semester. Typically, the school will charge you a flat fee (example: $200) for the books for the semester and the books will need to be returned at the end of the term or purchased for full value.

How expensive are books?

Books can range from $20 for an English literature class book to $100 to $200 for a hardcopy textbook. As a rough ball park figure you should expect to pay anywhere from $150 to $600 per semester for books and supplies. The costs will depend on your classes and your major. Some semesters you might not even have any required textbooks or will be able to use a textbook you already bought in a two part series course. You can save money by comparing prices between bookstores and online, buying used books and selling your books to friends or the bookstore at the end of the semester.

Choose a random page number that you will record your name in pencil in all of your textbooks. This serves as a way to identify your book in case it becomes missing, stolen or misplaced in a lecture hall or during a group study session. If you want to permanently identify your books, use a marker to write your last name across an edge of the book.

Don't forget the value of your book! It is important to take care of your books and protect them (i.e. you wouldn't leave $200 laying out on a common study table for two hours while you are gone). Someone could easily pick up your book and resell it.

Do you even need to buy books for your classes?

It depends on the class and on you. Some classes will only test you over lecture and class note material, and you could achieve a high grade without ever opening the textbook. Some classes will definitely have required readings that you will be expected to have completed for the test. You will soon discover if you are a "class listener" or a "book reader". Reading the book can help complete the picture or story behind the class lecture and clarify anything you missed or did not understand. Books can also supply you with additional information if you are interested in the topic. Go with which style works best for you.

Can I sell my books back at the end of the semester?

At the end of the semester your university bookstore might have a book buy-back program where you can sell your books back. Your book then becomes part of the "used" books for someone else to buy next semester. The bookstore will buy the books from you at a discounted rate from the price you originally paid. The price they offer you depends on the demand for the book. If the class you took will no longer be offered or if the publisher is printing a new edition, the bookstore will probably not buy your book. The demand and subsequent price paid for your book, can change within the week as other students sell back their books—that is, you may be offered more money for your book on Monday of finals week than on that Friday, if the bookstore no longer needs additional copies of your book as they have reached their "quota". Other books, such as lab manuals or workbooks, are generally not re-sellable. Selling your books all at once to the bookstore is a quick and easy way to make some fast cash as you are getting ready to leave for winter or summer break.

With a little extra effort, you can get more money for your books by selling them to friends or classmates who will be taking that course next semester. A fair price is somewhere between what the bookstore offers you to buy the book back for, but less than the price if your friend bought the book used at the bookstore. This way, you get more money for your book and your friend is able to buy a used copy for less money. It's a win-win situation for everyone! ...except for the bookstore.

If you are unable to sell your book and you do not want to keep it, consider donating it to a good cause. If this option does not exist at your college, then start a book drive to help a charity group or local library. This is an easy community service project that requires little set up consisting of a few collection sites and flyers. It's also a great way to help a less fortunate group of students and community.

Unlike high school books, you have purchased these books and own them. You can write or highlight in your books as you wish, but remember the sell-back value may not be as high if you are planning on selling your books at the end of the semester.

Should I sell my books back at the end of the semester?

There are different views on selling or keeping your textbooks. Some people like to keep all of their textbooks so that they will have a complete set of their college books when they graduate. This allows them to set up their own personal home library and use the books for reference. Other people like to keep the books that pertain to their major and then sell the "general education" books that everyone at the college is required to take. Other people sell as many of their books as possible to get some money back and so that they don't have to move them around. To sell or not to sell—that is the question. Just remember, over time books will lose their value as they become outdated; so if you don't see yourself using the book in the future, the best time is to sell it now, rather than moving around.

Should I bring my books with me to class?

In general, no, it is not necessary to bring your books with you to class, unless it is a lab manual or English literature book. Unlike high school, you are usually not provided a locker in college and can't switch out your books on campus in-between classes. Your books therefore generally reside in your room, unless you take them somewhere else such as the library for a study session. On the other hand, it can come in handy when you are in-between classes to have one of your textbooks with you so you can read a chapter.

 Make your own book covers for all your books and bring them to classes.

Final Thoughts

Don't be afraid to read your textbooks. Gaining knowledge is the reason you are in college--the more you can learn, the more you will advance in the classroom and your career.

Points to Ponder

- In some cases you may be able to receive the sales tax back from your state from the purchase of your books.
- Think of yourself as an information broker—the more information you can gain from reading your textbooks the more valuable you are to your colleagues whether it's for a group project or for a corporate team.
- Studying *is* cool. You're a loser if you don't know what's going on.

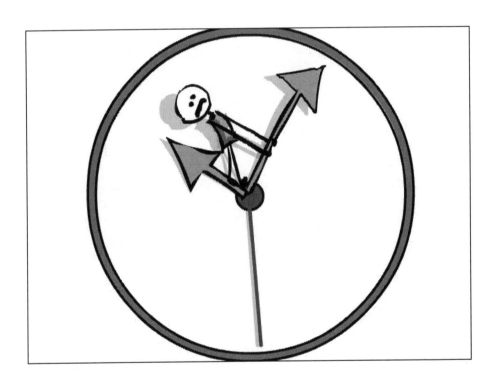

CHAPTER 26
TIME MANAGEMENT AND SCHEDULING
CLASSROOM CLOCK WATCHERS

"My to-do list just isn't large enough to be motivating"

College is full of demands: classes, homework, jobs, clubs, working-out, friends and daily necessities. There is no one strategy or secret for striking the perfect balance between studying and social time. Nonetheless, you need to develop your own personal system of organizing and remembering future events. Having a planner to keep track of all of your commitments is the first important step for most students in managing time effectively. Write on your calendar any upcoming events you know about whether it's your quiz in a week, your friend's party next month or your dentist appointment next year. Plot out your entire semester at once so that you can easily glance over any given month and determine your busiest weeks. You'll want to keep your calendar close at hand to keep you on track as well to constantly update changes. Your schedule should allow room for you to be flexible. When you first initialize projects you often encounter delays as you wait for an email response from a professor or realize you need another book from the library, etc. Create priority lists of what you need to accomplish daily and weekly. Once the semester begins, it doesn't slow down. Break large projects into more manageable daily pieces.

Early investment of your time, whether it's spending a couple of hours to create your semester calendar or completing class projects ahead of deadlines, will give you an extra cushion for any snags along the way and save you time and frustration in the end.

Procrastination may actually be beneficial for those who work well under pressure. Working on a project or studying "en bloc" can be helpful because you have a better sense of the big picture from the start to the end. However, it can be helpful to have some components ready or initial delays already worked out for really large projects that can't be finished in one sitting.

If you write something down on a list, you are more likely to complete it. If you set your goal to write out one essay question each day during the week you can free up more weekend time. Promise yourself something you really enjoy so that you are motivated to stay focused on your task. When you have completed your project you will be able to more thoroughly enjoy your reward or hang out with friends without having to worry about your schoolwork.

Don't forget to include time for miscellaneous errands or chores you need to complete on a periodic basis such as doing laundry, getting a haircut, health appointments, etc. Depending on your schedule you might want to block in an hour each day so that these things don't accumulate or to designate an afternoon each week that you will take care of any miscellaneous responsibilities.

When creating your semester schedule by compiling your class syllabi, you will notice a common pattern where tests and papers come within a week or two of each other followed by a few more weeks before the next "round" of projects and tests are due. During these bursts of tests your complete focus will need to be on studying: clear your schedule of anything else that will take away from your study time, including extracurricular activities, errands, and distracting friends.

Build "study hall" times into your schedule between your classes.

Use your semester breaks to work ahead on looming projects or papers. You can also use this time to get ahead of any miscellaneous to-do lists. Some colleges have a J-term (Joining-term) between semesters where you can complete a class; this can help free up time in your spring schedule.

Mike Story Box

With good time management skills you can make even the busiest schedule work. I completed several 25 or more credit semesters, while in veterinary school, while working as a Resident Assistant, while involved in campus organizations and several projects, while dating and still earning above a 3.5 GPA.

Kipp Story Box

When using   my planner, I keep an area where I can keep a running list of things that need to get done. That way when I have some extra time I can scratch one of those items off the list. It also serves as a great running "to do" list to add to when I randomly think of something I need to get done in the week.

To ensure you are not late, set your watch to official university time. Official university time could be the time on the campus tower clock, the campus bus route time or classroom clocks.

Final Thoughts:

At the start of each semester you promise yourself that this semester you are going to stay on top of things and not fall behind in your classes. Your plan works perfectly at first but ultimately it always fails. Why does this occur? The reason is test cycles. You want to do well on your first round of tests and so you devote most of your time studying for them instead of the regular reading and homework assignments. Some classes will move onto new material before the test and by the time all of your tests are over, you could be one or two weeks behind. The best strategy to escape the slipping slope of just studying from test to test is to try to as quickly as you can get back to your regular schedule following test rounds. It's hard though to break out of this cycle once you enter it.

If you find that you are constantly stressed out because you have no time to complete everything, let alone free-time, you probably need to take a step back and re-evaluate your schedule. Clearly state your top few priorities and redirect your time towards them. Determine if there is anything in your schedule that is using up your valuable time such as sleeping in too late. If you determine everything in your schedule is necessary, you may have loaded yourself with too many credits and outside commitments. It's ok to value your time and to withdraw from some of your outside activities. You should allow yourself some down time for yourself and for hanging out with friends; your friends will give you some of your favorite college memories.

Points to Ponder:

- Take 15 minutes every day just to update and organize your calendar.
- You're going to need to wear a watch.
- You're in charge of your schedule, no one else is.
- The week before fall or spring break will be busy.
- Keep track of email responses you are waiting on; follow up again if necessary.
- Whether it's waking up at 4am or studying on a Friday night, sometimes you just need to do what you need to do to get stuff done.
- Few things are more frustrating than not having enough time.
- Why are you giving the marching band two hours of practice a day, five days a week? Where are you and your flute going to be in four years from now?
- Figure out when your mind is the sharpest during the day and study during those times.
- Email, instant messenger, phone calls can all interrupt and consume your valuable study time; turn all of these things off for a few hours and reward yourself with a break once you have completed your studying by turning your computer and cell phone back on.
- When the slackers of the class start cramming for an upcoming exam, you *know* there must not be much time left, and you're in trouble if you haven't started studying yet.
- Attendance at home football games is a favorite freshmen activity but is also a huge time sink—you don't need to attend every hour of every game.
- Look ahead to see if there is any "prep" work you can get done before your first day of classes. Once the semester starts, there's no turning back.
- Help out your favorite class crush by writing them little reminders in their unattended planner such as "call (insert your name)"; "ask (insert your name) out for dinner".
- Consider the following 'time-sinks': social online networks, text messaging, checking your email, watching TV, playing video games.
- With all the inequalities in our world, there is one thing we all have in common, the number of minutes we each have in a day! How do YOU use this resource?

CHAPTER 27

STUDYING AND STUDY GROUPS
HANGING OUT WITH THE SMART KIDS

"There is no limit to studying."

Studying

The most successful college students are those who seek knowledge for life-long learning. Common characteristics of these students are strong motivation and self-directed studying. It is important to know what strategies work best for you. Some students learn best from classroom lectures while others would be lost without the textbook; some are more alert and focused by studying early in the morning while others are more productive by studying late into the night. You will learn a lot of *other* things in the process of studying as well (known as "the pains of studying") as you hone your studying skills, learn how to use resources and participate in study groups.

Use a note card as a bookmark and record words as you read you don't know to look up later. By continually building your vocabulary you will become a stronger reader and writer.

The best class notes to study from are those you took while in class; borrowing your friend's notes is not as valuable, because you may not understand their note taking system or they may have left out important concepts.

At some point in time you have probably come across a list from an academic department of "study tips" that were vague and unrealistic such as "study with a plant on your desk." Hopefully you will find the following list more insightful and useful to build your own base of studying tips:

Realistic Study Tips

- Look ahead to see what direction the course will be taking on lectures after your test to gain insight on the importance and relevance of the material you are studying now; it is likely the current material is the building material for later topics and emphasis will be placed on material that you will need to know for the next level of information.
- Keep a running list of stuff to look up and review for later off to the side so you can keep moving through your notes.
- Visualize a picture in your mind to help remember large amounts of information or difficult concepts; relate the concepts to things you are already familiar with.
- When you create a study outline, don't clutter it with information you already know—your flashcards should only be on those things that you keep forgetting or are difficult to learn.
- Find associations that connect the facts from various lecture topics—you will need to demonstrate your ability to make these connections on critical thinking tests (as compared to rote memorization tests).
- Read all class materials at least *twice* for better comprehension and understanding.
- Make your study outline one night and then study it the next night; dividing your time will allow you to focus on learning and memorizing the study material you outlined instead of trying to complete both tasks at once.
- Don't just recopy your class notes—reorganize them into a logical flow that makes sense to you.
- Just memorize the exceptions when you need to know a long list—then when you come across the information, if it's not on your "exception list", then you know it's part of the other data list.
- Make sure you know and complete any *unanswered* sample test questions or study guide questions—you will most likely be rewarded for your efforts on the real test.

- Don't pick and chose what you are going to study.
- Find out and know the correct test answers you missed and *why* your answer was wrong. This will give you more insight on what the teacher expects as well as prepare you for the final since some professors will repeat the exact questions from previous exams during the semester that a majority of students missed.
- If you don't understand something in your notes, don't just skip over it—every sentence was typed and printed for a reason. If it's confusing in the notes, it's going to be confusing on the test as well so it's best to clear it up beforehand.
- Watch out for *variations* on your exam as compared to any questions from old tests—professors know old exam copies are floating around and although a question may look like a question you saw on an old exam, the question may have been flipped so that the answer is a different letter choice or the question was slightly changed so that you need to identify the opposite answer than the question on the old exam.
- Ask your classmates questions about upcoming exams—you can gather a lot of little insights and "pearls of knowledge" from them.
- Test questions can be directly from your notes or can be material you should have learned during the studying process (connecting concepts, vocabulary, reading, etc.) that wasn't discussed in lecture.
- Know everything in your class notes—a minor section in your notes could turn out to be a major concept on the test.
- Keep a list of everything you don't understand from the notes—talk with your classmates and professor until you understand everything on your list.

If a teacher says, "You don't need to know this or write this down for the test." Write it down! There is some concept the teacher is demonstrating by using limited and valuable class time—it's not just some random, out of the blue class time "filler".

Kipp Story Box

If your textbook has any practice exams in the back or an online portion, be sure to check them out. I had a professor mention online practice tests that were part of the textbooks online package nonchalantly during class a couple times. One test was the exact same test. The few of us in the class that took the time to check it out online were very happy we did.

Split your large studying projects into smaller parts. For example, instead of trying to read five chapters the weekend before the test, divide the page numbers over a couple of weeks so you only need to read a handful of pages each day. This will allow you more time to thoroughly read each section with more time for understanding and less stress. Big projects aren't so bad once you get started...but that is the hardest part—just starting it! Constantly re-review the previous day's lecture notes before each class period—you want to expose yourself to the material as often as you can and iron out any questions you don't understand. By the time you need to study for the test, you are mostly just "refreshing" and not viewing and learning the material for the first time. You need to see the information at *least* twice before the exam to help you visualize your notes. This is the reason cramming doesn't work.

Studying Locations:

Some people like to study somewhere comfortable like a couch or bed with some background noise while others like to study at a desk with complete silence. Generally, the fewer distractions, the more likely you will be able to stay on task; but don't forget to give yourself mini breaks so the information has time to sink-in. Suggested study locations: your room, common space on your floor, designated study rooms, group study rooms, the library, unused classrooms at night, the Student Union (esp. unused food court area), a friend's room, and various buildings on campus or near campus (churches, study zones, etc.).

The less material for a test, the more detailed you have to know it; what makes a hard test is when you have to know the details of a large amount of information.

Mike Story Box

If a teacher gives you a mnemonic (that is, a memory aid to remember a list by associating the first letter of the list words into an easy to remember acronym or phrase), you should know it and the information it represents. Although sometimes teachers give you very non-helpful mnemonics such as my pharmacology teacher who gave my class the mnemonic CLLOODONENT to help memorize a list of drugs—how is that helpful and easy to know? It wasn't. No one knows what a CLLOODONENT is and I needed another mnemonic just to remember the first mnemonic.

Review sessions:

Review sessions are held before the exam, are usually optional and may be held outside of regular class time. During a review session the professor will either have a review lecture planned out or just open the time to answering any questions to clarify any questions on the class material. The message behind some review sessions will just be "know your notes" while at other review sessions you may gain insight into specific test questions. The amount of time a professor spends on a topic at a review session can also give you an indication to the importance of the material. Review sessions are also a good way to gage your level of understanding by listening to the questions asked by your classmates. Listen carefully to what they are asking, because they may be making an important connection in the notes you have not considered or are bringing up other "pearls" that will be helpful on the test.

Personality Line-Up:

A student: Already thought of that question and knows the answer
B student: Asking the question
C student: The answer to the question worries them that they really need to look at the class notes
D and F students: Not even at the review session; enjoying some quality video game time

Study Groups:

Studying with a group works well for several reasons. Teaching a concept to someone else is the best way to learn---to do so requires that you really understand what is going on. Plus, other people might bring up things that you forgot to study or didn't know about. Study groups are a good way to expose yourself to the information again and are an excellent way to quiz each other. By studying with others to prepare for an exam, you will also see if you have similar questions over the same confusing or difficult sections. Being in a study group is often fun and a great way to connect with another group of friends.

If you find yourself in a group situation and you can't remember someone's name that you probably should know by now, try one of these techniques to learn their name without having to directly ask:

- Announce to the group, "Does everyone know each other?" Then introduce yourself and then look to your right or left for the next person to follow your example.
- Ask the person to see their last quiz because you had a question about one of the answers; you can then easily see their name at the top of the paper.

Tutoring

You may consider a private or group tutor when you are struggling in a class. Tutors are typically upperclassmen or graduate students who have already successfully completed the course and often have the same major as the course they are tutoring. Tutors are more common in college and you are not a "failure" if you seek out a tutor—in fact, highly successful students often use tutors to gain the competitive edge in their hardest "weed-out" courses. If you do well in a course you may consider being a tutor for the class. Tutoring is a fun campus job where you work with other students and can review material related to your major. Teaching is the best way to learn and is also very rewarding.

Final Thoughts

In high school, cheating may have been rampant, but in college it's just not acceptable for several reasons: 1. You need to know this information as a professional. 2. The consequences far outweigh the benefits. 3. Your own reputation and integrity are on the line. When it comes to a job interview, it will be much easier to smooth over a C in one course than a blaring judicial record on academic dishonesty—which one of these would you rather have to discuss with potential employers? Be proud of a hard-earned C.

Points to Ponder

- Only you can learn this for yourself.
- Studying is an addicting drug you pay thousands of dollars for.
- Find your inner geek.
- If you love your major and are excited about the course material, then studying won't seem like a chore.
- You can't say a test was easy after you over-studied for it (over-studying is a good thing).
- Your study break is switching to a different subject to study.
- Two or three people in a study group usually works best.
- Naps in college are sometimes necessary; you won't be productive if you are fighting fatigue.
- Take mini breaks.
- Things that come in three or four make great multiple choice questions
- Collaborate, discuss and teach.
- You may be a tutor for one subject and a 'tutoree' in another.
- There is a "magic zone" right before a test where all of the material just seems to make sense and you are able to memorize vast amounts of information.
- Say to your first friend, "I'll do problems #1-5 if you do #6-10"; then go to friend #2 and say "I'll do 6-10 if you do #1-5". Homework complete!
- Release the inner study machine.
- Always go to the review session.
- You have to study to learn. Don't waste away your $50,000 or more education.
- Sometimes you have to wake up at 5am to get done what you need to get done.

CHAPTER 28
TESTS, PAPERS, AND PROJECTS
WHEN WAS THAT DUE?

"OMG! I don't know any of this!"

Tests

As a professional college student, your role is to learn, study and take tests. Test days are equivalent to athlete's game days--in the life of a full-time student, these are your moments to shine. Consider yourself part of the test-taking varsity team; go ahead, wear your tie on "game day".

 General rule of thumb: less information to study means a more detailed test, while more lectures to study means a test on broader concepts.

It is important to know the format of the test beforehand to determine your studying strategy. For example, a "recall" type test, such as short essay questions, will require more memorization time than a "recognition" type test, such as one with multiple-choice questions. This does not necessarily mean, however, that one type of test is harder than the other. Take-home tests are *always* more time-consuming than regular class tests, because the teacher assumes you have all of the information in front of you. Therefore, the focus of these tests is your ability to not only know but also integrate vast amounts of information. In classes with subjective grading (an English class as compared to a Math class), your classroom conduct can even affect your grade. The professor may be more likely to view your weak essay answers in a more positive light if you have presented yourself well in the classroom by coming prepared to class with quality homework answers completed, actively participating in discussions and asking questions. Even your personal appearance and where you sit in the classroom helps set the subconscious impression the teacher has of what type of student you are and how, subsequently, to grade your essay questions

For classes with a non-cumulative final, each individual unit test tends to be more difficult as compared to classes with cumulative finals.

Organization for test preparation can be overdone. With the time spent on recopying notes, entering information in a spreadsheet or making a stack of note cards, you could have already memorized the information. A good strategy when studying for a test is to summarize all of the important facts, ideas and equations onto a *single* piece of paper or note card. This will help you focus on the main, important concepts as you review your notes. By memorizing this streamlined outline of your notes with all of the key summaries, it's like having a "cheat-sheet" in your head.

Test Files:

Test files are collections of old exams given in previous years for particular courses. They may be kept on hand by the professor, the university library, an academic resource center, residence halls, fraternities, sororities or passed down from upperclassmen. Test files will not be available for all courses, professors or tests and may or may not be easy to locate. You may find the exact or similar questions you will be asked on old exams; however, never become dependent on just studying old exams! Test files are most valuable to gain a sense of the general format and type of questions you may be asked on a test. Study the class material first and use the test files as a way to quiz yourself and to identify any of your weak areas. Be sure to check that if these files are available, using them will not compromise your grade or get you into academic dishonesty issues.

Before an exam, brainstorm with your classmates as to what questions the professor may ask. Your combined guesses will often be correct.

If you are confident and have a strong grade, you can make a gutsy, yet calculated, move in those classes that allows you to drop your lowest test grade. Skip one of your tests. This strategy only works in those classes without cumulative finals and when you have already established high grades on your previous tests. If you already have an A in a class, whether you earn another A on the exam or a lower grade or receive a zero for not taking it (and then dropping it as your low score), it will not change your A grade for the class. Although skipping an exam probably goes against your natural intuition of keeping a high grade, consider it a "trick of the trade" of being an A student to help save precious studying time.

Mike Story Box

Although my classmates often questioned this strategy, I skipped several college exams and still earned an A for the class; this helped me free up study time where I could then focus my attention on more difficult classes. College often boils down to effective time management and this is one of those "secrets" of A students; it's risky though if you don't know what you're doing.

On the day of the test, sit up close to the front of the room; in large lecture rooms it can take 5-10 minutes just to pass out exams--that's ten more minutes you have gained through this simple location strategy that will give you more time to think about and review your answers. When you receive your test, zone out your surroundings so that it is just you and the test in the room. Near the end of the test is when you are probably going back to more difficult questions you did not answer earlier, and during this time, it is even more critical to fade out your surroundings to keep your full concentration and not be distracted by the commotion of other people turning in their tests.

ACADEMICS

Taking the Test:

- Make a habit to fill in your name on the bubble sheet as soon as you have it. This will ensure you won't forget it later but also saves you time by completing this part of the exam during the commotion of everyone receiving their test and/or the distraction of the teacher calling out instructions or announcements.

- College desk-seats tend to be small and so you don't have much room to spread out your papers--to save time, circle your answers on the test copy and then fill in your bubble sheet at the very end of the test. This also serves as a way to double-check your answers as you fill in the circles.

- The teacher probably did not give much thought to the fact that four questions in a row had letter B as the answer and you shouldn't either, so don't read into it or base your answers on the sequence pattern of the answer letters you fill in on the bubble sheet.

- Circle any hard questions and move on to come back to them later. You might obtain insights to the answer further into the test from other questions and their answers.

- Not filling in a circle on the bubble sheet when you have an answer is an easily preventable simple mistake. Meticulously check to make sure you have filled in an answer for every question so that you don't lose any points for forgetting to come back to a question you initially skipped or only partially completed.

- When completed, make a special point to check for any "simple errors" that will cost you points. Lost points from simple errors can make the difference between letter grades.

- If something doesn't seem right, make sense, or otherwise sit right, then something is probably not right. Check your conversion units on any math numbers that seem out of line.

- Teachers may not always write the best question and sometimes questions are thrown-out after the fact, so don't get hung up on one or two sketchy questions or you will waste valuable time and become frustrated. In these situations, determine which main point you think the teacher was trying to test over with the question; determine if this main point has or has not been covered in other questions; and then pick the better of the two wrong choices.

- Don't worry about those who finish early; some people are faster test takers, or they may not have accurately or completely finished the questions.

- Don't obsess over a test that is already turned in; it's done and there isn't anything you can do to change wrong answers. Start studying for your next exam.

Don't cheat on exams. If you haven't studied enough, swallow your pride and take the low grade. If you get caught cheating, the consequences could be much worse.

Kipp Story Box

Be wary of who you sit by. I had a student come talk to me as a RA, stressed out and crying, because she had been accused of cheating and had to go in front of a faculty board on charges of academic dishonesty. She was an excellent student. What happened? Someone else copied off her exam and their scores were similar. The professor had to first assume she was letting him copy.

Specific Test Types:

- For "all of the following except" questions, once you know you have identified the wrong answer, you then know the rest of the statements are correct—analyze all of the remaining choices, because they may contain insights or answers that will help you with other questions on the exam. Think of it as though you are still studying *while* taking the exam.
- If you are given a list of choices and you have to choose all statements that are correct, look to see how many points the question is worth. For example, if the question is worth two points, then most likely you need to find two correct statements; however this is not always the case and you may be rewarded one point for finding the correct statement and one point for not circling any of the remaining false answers.
- For "all of the following except" questions, you don't have to know whether all the answer choices are right, you just need to focus and find the one you know for sure is false.
- In a multiple choice question with instructions to "choose the correct statement" or "choose the false statement", if two statements are exactly opposite (for example, the same sentence is repeated but one sentence has the word "not" in it) then one of these choices is the answer.
- The overly long and detailed answer is probably the correct choice in a multiple choice question.
- Understand what is being asked in compare vs. contrast questions. Compare means to state similarities while contrast means to state differences.
- Always give as many examples or answers you can even if the question only asks for "3 out 5". The exam protractor will then have to decide what

answers to use when grading (hopefully the best and most complete answers you listed) and will have more material to use to award partial credit.

- When you aren't sure about a multiple choice answer, look for patterns in the choices and choose the choice that has different pattern from the rest of the answers.
- If something is unfamiliar (not talked about in class), it's probably not the answer.
- If all else fails, look for key-word associations covered in class; if you have never seen the word or concept, it's probably not the answer.

Mike Story Box

My biochemistry final was scheduled for the Friday of Finals Week. As most students wanted to leave before this time, the teacher agreed to offer an alternative final on Wednesday. The teacher informed the class he would post the answers to the Wednesday's final on the class website since the two finals would be different tests. I took the final on Wednesday and I missed the cutoff for an A in the class by two points (that is, if I had answered one more question right on the final I would have made the cutoff for an A). So I took the final again on Friday (I didn't have any advantages over my classmates since the Wednesday final with answers were posted on the web). With more studying, I scored two more correct answers this time around. The professor averaged my two final test scores, which give me the extra two points needed for the A. Some students would not have been willing to do what I did by staying until Friday to take a second final, but by thinking outside the box in this situation, I was able to improve my grade.

Papers and Projects

At some point, in any major, you will be required to complete a paper or project for your class. These assignments typically compose a significant component of your grade and will need to be worked on throughout the semester. Papers will often require journal article research and projects will often be completed in groups. Projects and papers are more manageable if you *start early* and break-up the assignment into smaller projects. Outline an action plan and stick with your timelines.

Plagiarizing

Plagiarizing is using someone else's thoughts and ideas in your work without properly giving credit. Students may do this knowingly or unknowingly. Either way, colleges take plagiarizing very seriously. If you are found to have plagiarized, consequences could range from a failing grade on the project all the way to dismissal from the university. It may seem obvious, but if you didn't do the work, you shouldn't turn it in. For example, if you are taking the same English class that your roommate took the previous semester, turning in their paper with your name on their old paper is not a wise thing to do. Also, buying a paper from an online source is very easily traceable.

A more innocent way this may occur is by simply not giving due credit where credit is due when working on a research paper. For example, if you were writing about the Great Depression and in one of your paragraphs you tell your readers about the thousands of people who died from famine. You may have read this in a textbook and remembered the exact number, but you still need to cite this textbook and where the information was found.

Bottom line, don't plagiarize and learn how to properly cite your sources. This is a skill which will be used throughout your college career, so learn it early and resist the temptation to take the easy way out.

Paper Insights:
- Ask the library reference desk for help locating journal articles—they are interested in helping students and can usually find what you are looking for quickly.
- Constantly save your documents as you work. And save them in multiple locations (on your computer, on a flash drive, as an email attachment, etc.) to save you the frustration of losing a nearly completed paper.
- Have as many people as you can look over and proofread your paper. Even ask your teacher to proofread it.

Look at the "works cited" part of articles you already have because this is an easy way to find other journal articles on the same topic.

> **Mike Story Box**
>
> My English Honors professor gave us the option to have our papers proofread before turning them in. English is not my strongest subject, so I made sure I had my papers completed a week or so before the deadline. She gave me feedback on the paper and I made the corrections--it was a simple strategy and it worked to earn an A in the class.

- Learn how to properly cite sources used in papers. If not done correctly, you could get accused of plagiarizing.
- When writing a rough draft for a paper, save some of your material back for the final copy. Part of your grade may include improvement since your first draft and professors will be looking for more than just the spelling and grammar corrections. You want to leave your teaching thinking, "Wow, look at this effort and improvement! Bravo, my young Hemingway, A+ for you!"

Project Insights:
- Your group members will influence your grade; be sure everyone is pulling their weight.
- Do a little more work than the other groups in your class. Projects are subjectively graded and the teacher is using other groups as the comparison.
- Learn how to use PowerPoint well.

 Take out a calculator for a non-math type test; look amazed that other people forget their calculator.

On the day of a test, ask people why the lecture notes weren't posted for today's lecture. When people tell you there is a test today, go into a panic, flipping through your notes, asking them to quickly tell you what you need to know; mumble, "Why didn't he tell us we had a test--he should tell us these things."

- Say "YES!" after every question as the teacher announces the correct answer--use appropriate hand-elbow motion as well. Look around smiling.
- Coordinate with classmates and "write in an extra credit test question" that the teacher did not give; however, if you get a large enough group of people to do this, it might confuse the TA grading the tests and they might award extra credit points.
- Remind people of time left before a test in panic voice, "People, we are at T minus 43 hours before our test". Your classmates will give you an annoyed look but be persistent in your reminders.
- For some tests, teachers may allow you to bring in "one note card of notes, equations, etc." On the front of your note card that you are showing other people right before the test it reads, "You just need to remember one thing for this test". On the back it reads, "You're awesome."
- When you see one of your classmates studying for a test, ask them what they are doing. When they tell you they are studying for the test that you both have tomorrow, respond by saying, "Oh really? A test tomorrow, huh? In what class?"
- If you didn't quite receive a 100% on your test remark to your classmates, "Well actually, if you read the latest Journal of Geology there are several published research articles that totally negate test questions 34 and 42. I suppose our professor was just busy and hasn't been keeping up with the professional journals." You know that you have never even seen such a journal, but you have forever left your classmates in awe of you.

Final Thoughts

It is typical that your first test score may be your lowest test score for the semester, even though as the semester progresses, course material will only become harder. This paradox occurs due to the initial adjustment of figuring out what the teacher expects (depth of material, what was emphasized in class, etc.) and the style and format of the actual test. Therefore, if your first test score is not what you expected, not all hope has been lost; use this score as your motivation for studying for the next test now that you know what to expect and what material to focus on.

Points to Ponder

- Use your "*ultra*-short" term memory for the equations, words or concepts you have a hard time remembering by looking at them the five minutes right before the test is handed out and then immediately writing them down on the back of the test or quickly finding the questions related to the information.
- Look for things in your notes that come in groups of three or four, since they naturally lead into material for multiple choice questions.
- Knowing what section in your notes information on a test has come from may help you determine the correct answer.
- You don't have to include all of the corrections suggested by your paper proofreaders, because some of their comments may be based on their own personal preferences and styles. Unless it's the teacher who is proofreading, then all of the corrections are relevant.
- In group work, let one person divide up the work to what they consider fair and then let other members choose their part.
- Keep your answers to essay questions focused on a couple of main concepts from class. If your teacher is a very busy person or has a large number of students, they will probably write test questions that are easy and quick to grade.
- Wake up early on test day and complete one last skim-through of your class notes to keep the main points and ideas at the forefront of your memory.
- If you have multiple tests in a short amount of time, determine which classes you need a higher grade in and focus your studying efforts on those tests.

Personality Line-Up:

- The nosebleed who finds an obvious typo on the test and points it out to the teacher who then interrupts class and your concentration. Usually it is something like, "class, class, can I get your attention. Nosebleed here found a typo on question #43. The answer choices read A B B D; that second B should be a C. Everyone, if I can have your attention for one more minute, please make that change now to question #43". Thanks nosebleed (not helpful).

- The annoying student at the end of your row is casually looking over the exam as they slowly pass the extra tests down.

- The person who can't find their ID when it's time to turn their tests in and verify who they are.

- The person in your group who can NEVER meet. They have four jobs, children, live 45 minutes from campus, etc. Trying to schedule a group meeting is like trying to find a unicorn...impossible!

CHAPTER 29
STRESS AND DEPRESSION
REMOVING THE WORRY WART

"I'm too busy to go to the doctor"

Stress

Everyone will experience some degree of stress while in college. It is normal and healthy and can keep you motivated when kept in check, but when you can no longer return to a relaxed state the stress becomes negative. Stress can affect every part of your life from your normal routine, health, happiness and relationships. The most difficult aspect of stress is when you no longer feel you have control of your time or decisions or when something unexpected happens that puts you into an emotional tailspin.

Some signs of stress include: being anxious; problems eating or sleeping; increased use of alcohol; inability to concentrate; general body aches; increased procrastination; depression.

Some ways to handle stress:
- Keep your expectations realistic and accept what you cannot change.
- Anticipate potentially stressful situations and prepare for them.
- Seek your own stress level and choose your own goals.
- Ask yourself whether it's worth being upset over the situation.
- List all of the things you think you need to do right away.
- Manage your time. Buy a calendar.
- Keep a "to do" list.
- Stick to a routine. Exercise, eat right and get plenty of sleep.
- Take mini breaks often.
- Ask for help and use a support system.

- Take time for yourself and take care of your health.

Stress creates more stress. Stressing about stress doesn't help. Sometimes the best way to alleviate stress is to quit worrying about it and do something.

The Domino effect
The time from your first day of class to your last semester final is a finite amount of time. Any time you fall behind due to a busy week, your projects and reading will carry over onto the next week. This cumulative domino effect of catch-up continually decreases the amount of time you have each week.

Depression

College is a major transition in your life: moving to an unfamiliar area, adapting to a new schedule and losing previous attachments. At times you may feel lonely and lost. Depression can decrease your motivation, cause you to loss interest in your hobbies and leave you with a persistent sad and empty feeling. You may also experience unexplained aches and pains, irritability and excessive crying. Depression affects many college students; it is not a sign of weakness or something you need to be embarrassed about. The good news is depression is very treatable with several treatment modalities including: counseling, interpersonal therapy and medication. Don't be afraid to seek out a counselor through student services; they have helped hundreds of college students throughout the years.

Many students may have suffered from various degrees of depression while in high school and thought coming to college would cure it because college is something new and exciting. Soon, they abandon any treatment they may have been receiving when they start college because their parents are not around to help regulate it. What happens? Things may be ok at first, but soon the stresses of college and the new environment pile up and they find themselves in a worse place than they were before; add alcohol to the equation and you're writing your own ticket out of college.

Being alone can be healthy. Alone time can give you time to reflect, be independent and be able to do things by yourself.

Final Thoughts

College is a time of many emotions one must learn to handle. It is a very exciting time, but it also is a time away from home, a time one must reflect on life and figure out what they want to do with it, and the time to do all of this can be limited with other responsibilities. Life moves very fast in college. Be sure to take time to reflect on all of this and seek council from trusted friends, family, or mentors.

Points to Ponder
- Don't do anything you'll have to lie about later.
- Simplify.
- Think positively.

CHAPTER 30
DEAD WEEK AND FINALS WEEK
SEASON FINALE

"Will this day ever end?!"

Finals week is the season finale to your semester. The last two weeks of the semester will test your academic strength and are crucial to your final class grades. This is what it all comes down to; this is why you have worked so hard all year--don't let yourself down in the end by not doing the best you can to prepare for finals.

Dead Week

Dead Week is the week before Finals Week. The purpose of dead week is to provide you with time for review and preparation for final examinations. "Dead Week" derives its name from the lack of campus activity during this time. During this week, student organizations will cancel their regular meetings and usually no major university events are held. Contrary to popular misconceptions, most of your classes will still meet at their regular times during the week. Some professors will cover new lecture material up until the final class period while others will hold review-sessions or question-and-answer sessions during lecture time, while a select few may cancel class completely. The university might help encourage you to study by extending library hours, enforcing 24/7 quiet hours in the residence halls, etc.

The weekend before finals will seem painfully slow as you nervously anticipate your first final. However, you cannot entirely devote this weekend to just studying for your first final, as once you start taking your finals, you will have minimal time in-between to study before you take your next final. Studying for multiple exams at once is difficult and is a test of your time management skills.

Mike Story Box

A student in my math class raised his hand during dead week and suggested to the professor that anyone with an A in the class shouldn't have to take the final. The professor said he would think about it and later in the week announced that anyone currently with an A grade would not be required to take the final—you never know, this could work for you too!

Finals Week

Regular lectures do not meet during finals week. Your instructor or course syllabus should inform you when (time and date) of your final examination, as well as the location. The date, time and location of your final exam may not be the same as where and when your class regularly meets. It will be helpful to ask your instructor about the format of the exam (i.e. multiple choice, short answer, etc.), and how much of the semester it will cover to help direct your studying efforts. That is, will the final be cumulative, covering material from the whole semester (or covering material since the midterm), or will it only cover the last unit, and thus be similar to a regular test. Some finals will have a combination of "new material" and cumulative material, but will emphasize the most recent class topics. Certain classes will not require a final or will replace the written final with a final paper or project.

It's impossible to study and memorize for all finals all at once. Your goal is to get through the material at least once, however, beforehand so that the night before you are refreshing, not learning and seeing it for 1st time ("re-learning curve").

Don't sleep in!! If you stay up late the night before, make sure you have a backup plan to wake up in the morning. Some instructors will not allow you to take the exam when you are late or if someone else has already completed the exam and left the room with a copy of the final. Give yourself the maximum time allowed to complete your exam.

Don't put off projects that are due during finals week; this will free up your time and reduce your stress. If you stay up on your reading and studying during the semester, finals will seem a lot easier and you can feel more relaxed while many others are stressing out.

Mike Story Box

My classmate and I studied for our freshmen chemistry final together by reviewing each chapter. We started at 8am the day before and finished our review at 1am—17 hours of straight studying with only the mandatory bathroom and meal breaks. In the end it paid off as we both earned A's for the class. Stay focused during finals week and prove to yourself you can achieve your goals by working hard; your relaxation over winter break will be that much more rewarding.

Finals Stress:

Finals week is stressful and stress can affect your health. There is a reason why you or the people around you become sick during finals week or soon after. When you are stressed, your body releases a stress hormone called cortisol to help you cope with the stress. Cortisol plays many important roles in your body, but it can suppress your immune system. A compromised immune system due to stress, combined with other factors such as lack of sleep, can tip the scales for you to become ill during or shortly after finals week. By being aware of the effect stress can have on your immune system, you can be vigilant to factors that can help you stay healthy through finals. Don't pull all-nighters, don't over indulge in junk food and wash your hands often. Finals week is not the time to decide to start the exercise program you have been meaning to start all semester. Don't plan extensive commitments with friends and families the first couple days of winter break--give yourself time to relax and recover after the week is over and catch up on your sleep.

Kipp Story Box

I can remember hearing students brag about taking a final while intoxicated. While amongst a small group of friends this may seem "cool," consider the down side. Will you brag to your parents when you fail the class and need to spend hundreds of dollars to retake that class?

Finals Thoughts

Know how much of the total grade the final is worth, as some finals may comprise a significant portion of your final grade (ex: 50%), while others will have a smaller impact on your final grade when combined with other points from attendance, homework, projects, papers and semester tests (ex: 100 point final out of a possible 1250 total points for the class). There is more strategy involved when studying for finals compared to studying for regular semester tests. You will want to focus your valuable studying time on the classes where the final is worth more of the final grade, where you have a weaker grade entering the final and those classes that are important to you to achieve a high grade; therefore the amount of time you spend studying for each final will not be equal depending on these factors.

You should determine the exact points you need for each examination to achieve your final grade goal. You may find, for example, that you could fail a final in one class and still earn enough points to make the cut-off for an A grade, while in another class you will need a high A on the final to make the cut-off for a B grade. Knowing the exact number of points you need to earn on each final will help you decide if achieving your final grade goal is feasible and then dividing your study time accordingly. As you will find, the more class points you can accumulate during the semester, the more room you will have to make errors on the final without it affecting your final grade.

Points to Ponder

- How will *your* season finale turn out?
- Knowing what material to study for a final, how much to study for a final and when to study for a final are the keys to a successful finals week.
- Your goal should be to score well enough on the final exam to at least retain your current letter grade you have before taking the exam. It is difficult (but not impossible) to improve your letter grade with a final exam as finals generally cover a lot of cumulative information and you have to divide your studying time between multiple exams.
- "Study breaks" are when you are *taking* a final exam.
- By the end of finals and the semester, you will be broke, sleep-deprived and desperate for social interaction.
- Every day for a week your schedule will either consist of studying for a final or taking a final. Minimize all other distractions and commitments.
- "Sleep" is for those who are ok with a C letter grade.
- The final exam is an important test. You may not need the whole allotted time to complete your final, but you owe it to yourself, the same person who has worked so hard all semester, to not rush and double check your answers.
- Bring extra pencils. You probably won't need them, but you can minimize the distractions caused by the nervous person next to you who will need one.
- Finals in the spring semester have the additional stressor of packing and moving out during the same week as your final exams.
- If you receive a care package from your parents, take the time to call them and let them know you appreciate their thoughtfulness.
- You could have a final scheduled for late Friday afternoon— arrange your travel plans accordingly. If you schedule your departure to occur as soon as your hand in your last exam, you may feel rushed to complete your exam and will have to take away valuable study time to pack before your exam---give yourself some breathing room and plan some time after your last exam to pack, run errands, clean, etc.
- If a final exam was difficult for everyone, the class grading scale may be curved. You might be surprised by a higher class grade than you expected on your grade report.

CHAPTER 31
4-YEAR PLAN
YOUR COLLEGE PLAN: LOOKING AHEAD

"Graduating in four years is like leaving the party at 10 pm".

Right now you have the most flexibility of the direction you will take over the next four years. By thinking ahead you can plan your path that will set you up for success on graduation day. Envision what you want your resume to look like when you are applying for jobs in four years and start laying the foundation to achieve that vision.

Writing out your four year plan will take many hours of thought and planning. This process will help you better understand and state your goals of college. The plan you write is not set in stone and will change over time, but it allows you guidance as you face future decisions to help you stay on track.

Academics

The first step in writing your plan is to determine how many years you want to be in college. Most traditional undergraduate programs take four years to complete; but some students, motivated to enter the "real world" and start a job, complete college in three or three and half years. Graduating one year early not only saves you a year of college expenses, but you will also be earning an income one year earlier. Depending on your program, you may or may not need to complete summer school courses to graduate early. Other students want to have more leisure time and elect to spread their class loads over five years or do so to pursue a double major, a minor, study abroad, or an internship, etc. Or you may be in college for six years if you want to pursue a graduate program to earn a masters degree or eight or more years if you want to pursue a professional program to earn your doctorate or PhD.

Map out exactly what classes you will take each semester for the next four years. This can be tricky because you need to make sure you take classes in the proper sequence (to fulfill any prerequisites) and some classes are only offered during certain times (for example, every other spring semester). Review the class requirements for your major (and any additional majors and minors) as well as the general university requirements. Don't depend on your academic advisor to catch all of these nuances; you need to take charge of planning your schedule with the big picture in mind. Having this plan in front of you will enable you to have an overview of what your semesters will look like. Are your semester credit loads realistic? Do you have a balance of easier classes mixed with your harder classes? Did you leave time in your senior year to prepare and go on job interviews?

Fill your first year schedule with general university requirements; this way if you switch your major later, you won't be as far behind, because you would have needed to take those classes anyway.

If you plan on entering a graduate or professional program, look at actual applications to determine what criteria are used for admissions.

If you plan on entering graduate or professional school, what entrance exam is required (i.e. GRE for graduate school, MCAT for medical school, LSAT for law school, etc.)? What can you do now to prepare for this exam? The MCAT, for example, concentrates mainly on organic chemistry, physics and biology so you may want to take this test shortly after you complete these courses in year two or three of college; which means you may to start preparing in year one.

Campus Involvement

Now is also a good time to plan what clubs will join and participate in. Remember, part of your goal is to build experience for your resume to help you during your job search upon graduation. During your first year you may be an active member in a club; then during your second year you serve on the executive board and by your third year you are president. There are many ways to gain experience beyond classes and clubs. Look for opportunities for volunteering or community service. Another excellent way to gain experience is to work in an internship or job related to your major. Plan what jobs you will seek over the remaining college summers and/or during the school year. Studying abroad may also offer you valuable experience.

 Staying involved on campus and demonstrating leadership will also make you a strong candidate for college scholarships and recognition awards.

Finances

Create a budget that calculates your college costs and your sources of income and financing for each year (see Chapter 14: Your College Budget). You may find that some years you have a shortage or excess in money; your budget might also help you see if you will have any cash flow problems.

Final Thoughts

Having a well-thought out outline of the direction you want to head during the next four years will led to success on graduation day. Build flexibility into your four year plan but remain focused on your main pillars. Create your own opportunities.

Points to Ponder
- Determine the exact courses you will take to fulfill your elective and general university credits.
- If today is day one of your work-out plan, think about how your overall health will benefit if you stick with regular exercise for the next four years.
- Dream the future.

You're now in the thick of it; classes are really starting to pick up pace as they dive deeper into the material and you probably have a second or third round of tests coming up. If your first tests do not go as well as you had wanted, you still have time to make a recovery, so don't give up hope! But now is the time you need to kick it into high gear and focus on studying—your new mantra is, "I'm a studying machine!"

At midterm, you may receive some "shocking" news from home such as, your family is moving to another state, grandma died, the cat died, your middle school is being demolished, etc. Actually these events may have been developing over the last couple months, but are shocking news to you because you are now in the college bubble, often isolated from the daily home-life conversations and community happenings. You may have been so busy lately that you don't really even know what's going on in the

news—quick, who's the president? Ok, good that you knew that one, but give college a few more years and we'll see...

At this point you probably have established a group of friends that you hang out with on a regular basis. These people who you meet your freshmen year will most likely continue to be your friends all throughout college and beyond—they will become your roommates next year, they'll be there when you graduate and will be in your wedding party when you get married; just like they are there now during late conversations and movies, when you need help because you glued your eyelid shut again and help you study for your next Calculus exam.

How's your relationship with your roommate? Now is the time to have an open and honest discussion about any problems—otherwise it could explode at the end of semester with the stresses of finals.

Now that you have adapted to your new college life for a few months, pretend you don't know something that everyone should know by now, such as the student union. Student what now? Where's that?

CHAPTER 32
A TYPICAL DAY
FROM DUSK 'TILL DAWN

"I hate my Mondays, Wednesdays, and Fridays!!!"

What does a typical day look like in college? If the same question were asked to a high school student, the answer would be pretty standard: wake up, go to school, do an after school activity, go home, and repeat the next day. College is much different as very few days will be exactly the same. There will be some things you have control over and some things you will not have control over.

The Parts of Your Days

While no two days may be alike, there are various things which can occur each day or every few days. Of the things listed below, one day may consist of all ten of these things while another day may only have three of them.

1. Classes

Isn't this why you go to college? On some days, you may have up to eight hours in class and on other days, you may not have a single class. They may start as early as 7:30 AM or as late as 7:30 PM. While there are some exceptions, typically you'll meet for one hour for a class that meets on Mondays, Wednesdays, and Fridays while Tuesday and Thursday classes will be about an hour and a half. Classes that have a lab section or recitation class usually only meet once a week, and that may be at a time unrelated to the regular section.

When creating your class schedule, try to schedule to your advantage. For example, if you can take two classes back-to-back, you will limit your trips to campus.

2. Work

For many, working is another very real part of their college day. Work can be a welcome break from studying and a great way to meet other people. Working on campus is a great way to work near where you live and work at a job that either can help you learn more in the area you are studying or allow you some time to study while working. Some students may not have class all day one day of the week and may try to schedule a lot of work hours that day. It's probably a good idea to not work more than 20 hours a week. Some will choose to work as little as five hours a week as a way to earn just a few extra dollars for weekend fun.

3. Exercise

Going back to the dessert area in the dining center doesn't count as exercise. Playing on an intramural team, a pick-up game of basketball, a fitness class at the recreation center, going for a job, lifting weights, or doing sit-ups and push-ups or yoga in your room are all forms of exercise which can take up time in your day. Depending on the activity, the travel time to exercising as well as getting cleaned up afterward can also take a lot of time. But it's important to make this an item that appears on your daily schedule more than a few times in a semester.

4. Meetings

Depending on how involved you become, meetings can become a significant part of your life. Typically clubs or organizations will meet once a week, but activities beyond the meetings may take up more time. Other meetings may include work meetings, meeting with your advisor and floor meetings within your residence hall.

Joining a lot of clubs at the beginning of the semester may seem fun, but they may add a lot of meetings to your given week.

5. Meals

Don't forget to eat. In college there are many times you have to think out when you'll eat because each day is different, especially if you are working around the dining center's meal schedule. If you are eating by yourself in the dining center or grabbing something on the run, meals can be as short as five minutes. Try not to get caught up in stopping by the student union for fast food, eating out of vending machines or missing meals all together.

Most meal plans from the dining centers offer some type of sack lunch/dinner option.

Watch out for the "Two Hour Dinner Trap." This occurs when you eat in the dining center and midway through your meal, other friends join your table group, extending the time you feel obligated to stay there. This may happen several times in one meal period and your manners may be screaming at you to be polite and not get up during the meal. See Chapter 10: Campus Food.

6. Study Time

Unlike high school, you will intentionally need to make studying a part of each day. This can come in many different forms. Reading a of couple chapters between classes, going to the library to study in a quiet area, meeting with others to study a subject together or sitting in your room reviewing your notes before bed (among many other forms of studying). It's wise to actually schedule study time as there are many distractions in college. Until your last final is over at the end of the semester, there is always *something* you can be studying.

A general rule of thumb is for every hour in class, you should plan on two hours of studying or homework outside of class. Is this always the case? No. But it's something to keep in mind and strive for.

7. Sleeping/Napping

While sleep may seem like something that naturally comes with each day, certain times during the semester may require you to actually schedule time to go to sleep to stay healthy. It would be ideal to get eight hours of sleep each day, but you'll find this is very difficult to do with all of the other things which come in a day.

There is always something going on at a college campus. Sleep is something you shouldn't neglect while in college. Resist the temptation to start a "movie marathon" at 1 AM with the people down the hall who don't have a class the next day (and even if you don't have class, that can really derail your sleep schedule). Even when keeping a good sleep schedule, you may find yourself reverting back to your preschool days and needing a nap sometime in the day. While this is ok to refresh, avoid making it a part of your everyday routine. If you keep a somewhat regular sleep schedule, you will be able to keep napping to a minimum.

College creates a unique environment where no matter what time or day it is, you can usually find someone still awake.

8. Opening/Closings of the Day

This is the time it takes each day to get rolling in the morning and doing the opposite at the end of the day. Waking up (and for many hitting the snooze button), taking a shower, getting ready, getting your materials ready for the day, and whatever else is part of your routine. These processes actually can take more time than you may realize and will be a part of most days.

9. Internet/Phone time

These times are not usually scheduled, but keep track on any given day how much time is spent on your phone and various internet activities and you may be shocked at how much time is spent. In fact, for many this may be the first time they have a high-speed internet connection and computer of their own and internet addiction is a very real problem for some college students. And while some of the time spent on these various devices is a useful and productive part of your day, much of it is time lost. Be especially careful of time spent using online messaging tools. A conversation which would normally take about ten minutes if spoken can take hours using one or two sentences at a time.

Some people will be intentional about setting boundaries for their technology use. They may check their email once in the morning and once in the afternoon or only having their cell phone turned on in the evening, etc.

10. Free time

When all of the above have been accounted for, you have your free time left. Again, some days you may have hours of free time, other days it may feel like you have only a few minutes of free time. Take advantage of it when you have it. This is where errands, hang out time with friends and various other forms of entertainment will fall. If you have too much of this, you may want to rethink your schedule as college students typically don't have a whole lot of free time.

It's very important to have some free time each day and week to keep a well-balanced life and to not be overwhelmed with stress. Some college students get so busy and involved they actually need to physically write free time into their schedule.

Mastering Your Days

Now that you've seen what typically can happen on any given day, it's important you take control of what's happening and make the most of every given day. Your days are unique to *you*! No two days will be exactly alike and even if you have the exact same schedule as a friend or classmate, your days will still be very different than theirs. Be sure to keep this in mind when comparing yourself to your peers. Some majors require a lot more time in class or studying, while others may require more projects that take up a lot of time. If you are an architect major and your friend hasn't chosen a major yet, you may not be able to go with them each night to listen to music at the performing arts center as your schedule is more time intensive. Be sure to consider the following when setting up your schedule or evaluating your schedule:

1. You may have to bite the bullet

Sometimes the class you need is only offered at 3:30 PM on Fridays or at 7:30 AM. Or you may want to have your Mondays and Fridays open to create four day weekends, but the lab section you need is only offered at 8 AM on Monday. What if a class is only offered in the evenings? Bite the bullet and make the most of the schedule you are able to create. As you progress through school, it will probably be easier to get classes at better times, but you also will run into some classes for your specific major which have fewer people, only offering one meeting time.

2. Utilize your down time

If you have 30 minutes while on campus between classes or while waiting for an appointment, use this time to read a chapter or review your notes. If you need to stop by the bank, for example, you could leave ten minutes earlier to class and swing by on your way, and thus saving a whole other trip some other time. Down time pops up all over if you're looking for it.

Another downtime many forget about is the morning time. Some feel if they don't have class until 11 AM, they should sleep until 10 AM. Why not get up and go to the rec center? Or maybe read a few chapters for class? You'd be amazed at how much you can get done in the morning.

3. Plan your days

By the end of a day, you'll be tired. The day before each day you should plan out how you want the next day to look. If you are going to be on campus over the lunch hour, will you pack a lunch? Will this require you to alter your morning routine? Do you need to buy supplies between classes? Be sure you have your money and list of what's needed. While some of these things may seem trivial, you'd be surprised at how quickly they will save you time and make your days more efficient.

4. Early is better?

Some people avoid early morning classes like the plague. Why not take an 8AM and 9AM class and be done for the day?

5. Evenings are very much a part of your day

Prior to college, after dinner usually meant free time and relaxing. Now, it is time to study, have class, work out, have meetings, or any of the other parts of a day. In fact, sometimes you won't really start your evening activities until after 10 PM.

Final Thoughts

As you've seen, there are no two days which will be exactly alike and days can become pretty jam packed with things to do. Be sure to take a breath once in awhile and don't get too overwhelmed. As the weeks go by, you'll begin to establish somewhat of a routine to follow.

As cliché as it may sound, the time really does fly by fast in college. Each person handles time management differently and requires more or less of each of the things listed for a typical day. Remember, you need to figure out what works best for you.

Points to Ponder

- No two days are alike.
- Plan ahead and maximize your days to your advantage.
- Don't forget the essentials...eating and sleeping!
- Be sure to leave time for fun.

CHAPTER 33
FRIENDS, FUN, AND WEEKENDS
COLLEGE MEMORIES

"College would be so much more fun without all the classes!"

You've got your classes in order, books bought and know where you live. What are you going to do with your free time? Who will you spend it with? What about Saturday and Sunday? While it seems like these things should come naturally, being in a new environment presents opportunities to get to know many more new people and form lifelong friendships. This may take some intentional efforts on your part and some will just happen without you realizing it. And what will you do with the extra time outside of class when you're not studying? Continue reading as we explore friendships, fun, and time not spent in class.

Everyone is anxious about making new friends. Some will hide it better than others. Every opportunity in college is an opportunity to strike up a new friendship.

Friendship 101

You can scan the course catalog, but this isn't actually offered at your school. Making friends is something that should happen naturally. It can be complex, however. As soon as you move into your residence hall, there are going to be 40-100 other people living a stone's throw away. What a great opportunity to get to know people right away. Each person will have their own unique story and journey which brought them to the floor. ASK THEM! We all have much more in common than we think. What does your space say about you? Don't be afraid to make your living space unique to you as a way to meet others on the floor. A well placed photo, poster, or other decoration will help others ask questions about your life.

An easy way to strike up a conversation with someone on your floor is to get into their room and look around. Ask about the trophy or picture on their shelf. Why do they have that poster up on the wall? If it's in their room, they put it up for a reason. So strike up a conversation with someone.

One thing you'll have in common with hundreds if not thousands of people? You're a brand new student on campus. Surely you'll be able to strike up a conversation about this!

Before we go much further, it must be acknowledged that college is not a popularity contest. In many high schools, there are definite cliques of people: the "band nerds," "jocks," "drama kids," "popular kids," and many others. Challenge yourself to get set aside stereotypes such as these as you get to college. It may seem cliché to say everyone changes in college, but it is true. If there is someone on your floor who is doing something that looks fun, join them! You may never have interacted with the "computer kids" in high school, but if you want to learn more about computers now is the time to strike up a conversation. If you are genuinely nice to all people from day one, you'll see how much you actually have in common with them. Be yourself and just be honest. You can always use more friends and different types of friends.

Pearl of Knowledge: College math and science classes are full of equations. While there is no official equation to making friends, we've come up with a simple one: **Proximity + Randomness = FRIENDS.** Relax, be yourself, and friendships will happen. As it's been said, half of life is just showing up.

One of the easiest things to do to help meet people is be open to do things. If someone random stops by and says a group of people from the floor is going to go have a cook out, go with them. Maybe they are going to the student union for an event, go with them. As said earlier, there are no equations to making friends. If invited to do something, take advantage of this time to get to know another group of people (even if the activity isn't something you normally enjoy). Many times at these functions or events the people you go with will introduce you to other people they know (and vice versa). If you decline invites too often, soon others will not invite you.

Be sure to reciprocate invitations. If you and your roommate are going to go grab a bite to eat or check something out on campus, invite someone else on the floor with you. This is a great way to be inclusive of others and get to know others. Inviting others is a great way to establish yourself as someone who likes doing things with others and will help your friendship circle grow quickly and create opportunities to get to know many people.

The People You'll Meet: That loud, obnoxious guy that is initially popular and everyone tries to tolerate. People will nervously laugh at/with him, but in the end people find their "right" group and move away from him. Don't be that person in an attempt to quickly get others to notice you.

High School Friends

In most cases, there are at least a couple of people you know from your hometown coming to your same school. These high school acquaintances may become very appealing the first few days because they are familiar and create a sense of security. When looking for someone to run to the store or go to dinner, your first thought will be to dial someone you know. There is nothing wrong with this, but it's a good idea to talk with your high school friends prior to getting to college about what the expectations will be of your friendship as you move to college. Do you want your college experience to be an extension of your high school or a brand new experience? Don't run and hide from your high school friends, but remember college is much different than high school. Your schedules will be different, you'll get involved in different areas of campus, and you'll all make new friends. All of this is normal and a great way to grow as you begin and continue through college. The more you and your high school friends do to gain your own individual experiences, the more fun stories you'll have to share with each other when you do see each other.

High School friends are a great way to find rides home for the weekend.

While it may seem very comfortable to preference the same residence hall as your friends, how are you going to meet people across campus? If you and your friends lived in different buildings, when you visit them you'll get to know their new neighbors and friends, and they'll do the same when they visit you. These types of encounters are the essence of getting to know many people with many different stories.

Kipp Story Box

Should my high school friend and I be roommates in the residence halls? From my experience working in a residence hall, I've seen it work great and I've seen it backfire. The key to any roommate situation is open communication prior to moving in and continuing the dialogue as the roommate relationship continues. I've even had roommates who were friends in high school come do a room switch, because they valued their friendship and didn't want it to get ruined by being roommates.

The First Weekend

Resist the temptation of going home...stick around the first weekend! Too many college students get all moved into the residence halls, start making connections with their new neighbors, and then leave the first weekend. It can be very tempting after a couple of nights of homesickness and that feeling you don't know anyone. Maybe your friends from high school are going home and ask you to come with or your mother is putting some pressure on you. This is all very normal and, as we'll say one more time, can be VERY tempting. There will be many college students who cannot go home, because they live too far away or have no means of getting home. Stick around and hang out with them and get to know them. Go explore the town with your new friends and neighbors. Many colleges will have welcome activities which are a great way to get to know the college and get to know people as well. You wanted to go to college, right? You don't want the memory of your first college weekend to be sitting on your parents' couch with your cat watching a movie on TV, do you? Will it be fun when you get back to your residence hall after the weekend is over and hear about all the fun everyone had who stuck around? Will they even think to invite you to dinner or other activities? Not if you're gone every weekend. Think about that. Ok, you can go home sometimes, but you get the point.

You are not a loser if you're not partying the first weekend or any weekend for that matter. There will be many students who've watched many movies on college who believe the only thing to do the first weekend at school is drink heavily and make poor decisions (See Alcohol Chapter). Will there be a temptation? Probably. For most, this is the first time they are officially away from their parents and truly on their own and there will be no one holding you back. Is this the group you really want to hang out with the first weekend? Or are you just giving into group mentality/peer pressure so you're not left sitting in your room by yourself? Be creative! There will be a lot of great things going on the first weekend at school. Be the person who is suggesting an activity you've seen on a flier posted somewhere. Pick a meeting time, gather some people, and go check something out. While you may not impress the "partier" on your floor, you will impress many others with your creativity and desire to have fun and get to know other people. And don't worry about the "partier," they usually don't last very long at college.

A lot of time you don't know your friends' last names in college. Always awkward when you are in a position to introduce them to someone else, but it'll happen.

Weekend Life

The weekend life on a college campus provides many opportunities to socialize, relax, study, run errands, go home, and do many other things. Just as each student's weekday schedules may vary greatly, how one uses their weekends are equally as diverse. Some students will sleep the weekend away, while others will use this time to get away from campus. Proper utilization of your weekends is one of the keys to having a successful college career.

For many, the weekend is a break from the busy week. Rest and relaxation are essential to a college student, and the weekend can provide a temporary break from the day to day rigors of college. However, be careful not to rest and relax TOO much. Sleeping in until noon on Saturday and Sunday may be relaxing, but a lot of precious day has been wasted. Try rewarding yourself after doing homework or a project. Maybe on Friday night after dinner you can get an assignment done before you go out with your friends? Or you'll get up Saturday morning and put a load of laundry in and while that's finishing up, read a chapter for a class (rewarding yourself with an afternoon nap for your early morning completion of various school projects). Some weekends you will have to utilize for studying or projects if the upcoming week of class is loaded with tests or projects are due. Even in these cases, if you spend the better part of the day studying, reward yourself with a Saturday evening break.

There are often many fun, free (or very reasonably priced) activities taking place on a college campus on the weekend. Concerts, movies, athletic events and cultural events are just a few of the things offered most weekends. Keep your eyes open for postings around your residence hall or around campus all week. These activities are great opportunities to gather a group of friends and have a fun evening. These types of events are also known for giving away free food or door prizes, so go check them out.

Many students feel going to parties is the best way to spend their weekends. While these can be good opportunities to get to know people, some people use this as their only way to get to know people. Some people also find they spend more time after the party recovering from lack of sleep and feeling ill, wasting away a lot of their weekend. An occasional party can be fun, but do you want these parties to be the only memories of your college experience?

Weekends also provide an excellent opportunity to get your various errands completed. Believe it or not, a small residence hall room can get pretty dirty in a short amount of time. Tidying up your room, getting your laundry done, and other small tasks in your room can really help you feel energized and get you prepared for your upcoming week. You may also have errands such as going to the store, getting a haircut or having your oil changed in your car. The weekend is an excellent time to get these done while you explore your college town as well. If you don't have a car, it's usually pretty easy to find someone else to tag along with as they do errands. And if you do have a car, inviting those without a vehicle is a great way to help them out.

If you have a job while in college, the weekend is a great time to get in a few extra hours. Students with jobs learn to appreciate their weekends pretty quickly if a lot of their extra time is taken up by work. Make sure if you have a job you are not getting burnt out with work and school or both could end up suffering.

Some of your best memories could come from your weekends at college. Be open to try new things. If a group of people from your floor is road-tripping for the weekend and invite you along, do it! Maybe some people are going to get together for a bonfire at a local park, offer to bring the hot dogs. And, believe it or not, some of the best weekend memories come from unplanned, random events such as a late night chat over a cheap pizza in your residence hall room or a game of capture the flag on central campus.

What Do College Students Do For Fun?

The unique thing about college students is just about *anything* has the opportunity of being fun. Having an open mind and willingness to try new things will provide you with many opportunities for fun in college. Here is a random list of things which could provide you with fun while in college, but in no means is all inclusive, just a way to help you brainstorm ideas:

- College sporting events-College clubs or organizations
- Tailgating-Cultural event on your campus
- Movie marathons-Go to eat at a local restaurant
- Hike at a local park-Host a theme party
- Shop in your college town-Organize a floor video game tournament
- Go to a local coffee shop-Invite a friend from home to visit
- Bowling-Take college friends to your hometown
- Go get ice cream with your friends-Visit local points of interest

Final Thoughts

Your college years are going to give you many great, lifelong memories. Take advantage of this great time in your life. You will meet many unique people while in college and form friendships which will be with you forever. All of this doesn't need to happen in the first year. People you meet your first year may show back up your second or third year of school, so don't burn any bridges and treat every encounter as a great opportunity. Making connections with people throughout your experience will help college really feel like home quickly.

Alcohol doesn't need to be the center of your social life. It may seem that way on television or in the movies, but the more open you are to various weekend activities, the more opportunities you'll have to diversify your memories and friendships.

Points to Ponder

- Give making friends time. You won't have a best friend who understands you by week two.
- If you see an advertisement for an upcoming event, jot down the time and location in your planner so you don't forget!

CHAPTER 34
LEADERSHIP AND INVOLVEMENT
LEARNING OUTSIDE THE CLASSROOM

"I joined the rock climbing club and I'm afraid of heights."

Coming out of high school, most students have had the opportunity to be involved in anything from sports to the chemistry club. And for many high school students, they were involved in every other activity in between because they had the time and energy. When a student steps onto a college campus, opportunities for leadership and involvement are around every corner. Balancing your involvements with your academics can be difficult, but if done correctly can be very rewarding.

Why get involved?

Your schedule will have about 15 hours of class and about that much time for studying a week. The other time is yours to use however you'd like. This outside involvement, whatever it may be, can really help you learn time management skills as well as other skills and talents which are not taught in the classroom. Most students coming to college were involved in their high schools, and it's natural to carry on leadership and outside involvements to maintain a healthy lifestyle. If done correctly, your leadership and involvement can be a tremendous asset to your education and overall college experience. These are the memories outside the classroom which will stick with you for a long time.

The Various Types of Activities Available

It's hard to categorize all the activities available to a college student. Depending on the size of your school, student clubs alone may be in excess of 500! There literally is something for everyone. Below are a few categories of activities and leadership opportunities available to most college students.

1. Intramural Athletic Activities

Intramural athletics are sports played against other students at your school. Typically students will form a team from members of their residence hall floor or Greek house. If a team is not available where you live, intramural offices usually help place individuals on already established teams. Divisions are usually formed based on skill level or living arrangement (residence hall floors vs. other residence hall floors).

These activities are a great way to get exercise and have fun with your new friends. Old stand bys like basketball and football are typical as well as sports such as ultimate Frisbee and inner tube basketball. Most sports will offer a co-ed team option as well. Winners of categories will typically win a small prize such as a t-shirt and the team may receive a trophy.

There usually are other intramural activities for singles play and sometimes the events are not even "athletic" such as a poker tournament or a quiz competition. Many of these are one-time events, allowing your participation to last only one evening, not a few weeks.

2. Residence Hall or Greek House

One of the easiest ways to get involved right away is doing so in your living environment. Typically a floor will have leadership positions available such as floor president and vice presidents, intramural chair, social chair, birthday char, and just about any other chair you can think of. These are an excellent way to get to know other residents on your floor and have a say as to what types of activities happen on your floor. Sometimes these types of positions can even add some perks like preferential parking. Similar positions are usually available within a Greek house as well.

Each residence hall usually will have some sort of government structure. Usually a floor president will go to a larger governing body which has a governing board structure (president, vice president, etc.). These groups usually have some sort of financial say for their areas activities and may also serve in a student judicial board role. Depending on the structure, there may be an even bigger government structure this group reports to such as a student senate or Residence Hall Association. Some of these positions are based on elections while others are by application. Freshmen are encouraged to get involved in these various levels.

Greek houses also have a structure similar to the above mentioned residence hall structure. Each house will have various positions, some of which will report to a larger governing body.

One great way to get involved after your first year in the residence halls is to apply to be a Resident Assistant. This is both a leadership position and an on campus job. This is an outstanding way to get to know lots of people and assume a huge leadership role which is respected by many future employers for the assumed responsibility and social skills that go with being a Resident Assistant.

3. Academic Clubs

Another great way to get involved is by joining clubs which are part of your individual college or major. These activities are a great way to connect with other students in your major in a more laid back setting and also to enhance your knowledge in various subject matters related to your college. Many times these clubs will do activities related to your academic program, but unable to be accomplished through classes. For example, the Food Science club may use their meetings to tour local food production facilities or the Physics club may sponsor a "catapult competition" for area high schools. These clubs also create opportunities to interact with faculty members in a more laid back and social environment. If you decide to take on more of a leadership role in one of these clubs, this allows faculty to see your leadership skills first hand. This can create connections with these faculty members, leading to a reference for you for an internship or job.

Honor societies are another form of an academic related organization. These groups usually have a minimum GPA requirement to be involved, and there usually is either a nomination or application process to join these activities. These organizations may be directly related to your field of study and sponsored within your college or they may be a broader organization open to students from any field of study. There may also be fees associated with joining these types of activities, so be sure to evaluate if this is a good investment of your money and your time. These groups may meet on a regular basis to do various forms of career development or they may base their activities around philanthropy.

4. Interest Clubs

Interested in water skiing? How about politics? Juggling? Bagpipes? Balloon Animals? Interest clubs are those which allow students with similar interests to gather. These are a great way to keep your hobbies active or learn about a new activity which you have little or no knowledge about. Some of these clubs may have over 100 members, while some may have as few as three people. Student activity centers at each college will usually maintain a list of all of the clubs available, and they will often host some type of activities fair at the beginning of the semester to learn more about these clubs.

Official clubs on a campus allow for the use of university facilities for meeting purposes and usually allow for financial benefits to help the club do activities. These clubs usually are required to have a governing body (president, treasurer, etc.) and some type of written by-laws. If you and your friends have an interest and there isn't already a club, starting one is often not difficult.

5. Student Government

For those who were involved with student council in high school or for those interested in government, there are plenty of opportunities on your college campus. Depending on the size of your school, student government may actually have a lot of say in regards to campus policies and how student fees are spent.

Usually student government positions are filled via some form of election. These elections are usually in the spring semester, unless positions went unfilled and need to be filled in the fall. Students who are elected will meet on a weekly or biweekly basis and will vote on various allocations of funds and on university policies and procedures. There usually are committee assignments as well for students to get more hands on experience. If a student chose to run for a judicial type of position, they will probably work closely with their advisors and may hear university level judicial cases.

6. University Leadership

Remember your first visit to your school when a college student gave you a tour of campus? Many students find giving tours, being an ambassador for their college, calling prospective students, or being an orientation leader a rewarding experience. Some of these positions are volunteer positions while others are paid opportunities. Either way, they are a great way to get to know your campus better and get others excited to come to your college. They are also a great way to learn and hone presentation skills.

 Becoming a tour guide or orientation leader will give you the opportunity to be trained to know all the services and traditions of your school.

7. Community Involvement

Activities such as volunteering with the Boys and Girls club, church involvement, community service, or other off campus opportunities allow students to get away from campus a bit and do other meaningful activities to supplement their education.

How to get involved and how much?

A college campus provides literately hundreds of opportunities to get involved beyond the classroom. These opportunities may present themselves as early as orientation prior to your official start of college. While the water skiing club may seem like a good option for you, be sure to evaluate how it will fit into your schedule and how meaningful will that experience be to your college career. Getting involved with a club is usually as simple as just showing up to a meeting. There is usually a listing either on a website or at an activities office with contact information for each official club if you need to find out when and where meetings occur.

It may be tempting as you begin your first semester to sign up for a lot of different activities. Before you commit to a group, realize there are usually weekly meetings associated with being in a club and a bunch of one hour meetings add up really quickly. Be sure to also evaluate why you are joining a club. Clubs are a great way to try and learn new things, and there is no better place than a college campus to provide these opportunities and resources. However, be sure to remember your first commitment should be your classes. Some clubs can serve a dual purpose and provide fun and supplement your academic program. Be sure to take involvement slow at first so as not to get in over your head.

Kipp Story Box

I had a friend who in her first week of college was persuaded to join the women's rugby club. She and her friend had never played and thought it would be fun to tell their friends they were on the rugby team. While they learned a new sport and met new friends, they didn't realize joining the team would bring daily practices lasting about two hours and many weekends taken up by road games.

There will usually be an activity fair at the start of your first semester to meet people already in clubs and organizations.

There are several things to consider when joining a club or organization:

How long will this commitment last?

One semester? Your entire college career? Beyond college? Make sure you understand the level of commitment prior to getting too involved.

Are there any fees associated with joining?

Some clubs have some small dues to join. Others may be significantly more expensive. For example, if you join the sky diving club, your discounted flights and jumps may still cost over $100 per jump. Some honor societies have membership fees of over $100. Outfitting yourself to join the paintball club could cost hundreds. Think of all of these costs when you join.

What do you want to get out of the experience?

Are you joining to just meet new people; if so, be sure the people in the club are the types you want to associate with for this social experience. Are you joining to learn a new skill? Be sure the meetings are conducive for this to happen.

How is the leadership in the group?

Some groups on campus are more active than others. Be sure you are getting involved in a group with solid leadership who make the most of the time allotted for meetings and events.

Making the most of the experience

There are several ways to really make the most of your involvement while at college.

1. Run for open leadership positions within a club or group.

This will allow you to help shape the direction of the group and provide great experiences which will carry over to your career. Providing leadership within a group shows future employers dedication, work ethic and leadership and organizational skills. Even positions which may not seem relevant can be, such as being the treasure or social chair of a group. If you are involved with the group for a couple of years, your commitment to taking on leadership could lead to you being in charge of the group.

2. Try something new.

Attend a meeting which seems interesting. You don't have to join, but you can say you tried something. College is the time to do these types of things, because after college, work, family and lack of resources may make it more difficult to be able to do the things available on a college campus.

3. Make Connections.

Being a part of a recognized group affords you opportunities to interact with advisors and other administrators in various roles at your school. Take advantage of these interactions. Volunteer to help out if needed, ask questions of them and show them you're willing to go above and beyond. These connections can be valuable when you are job searching or have other university business to take care of and need to run a question by a trusted faculty member.

> ### Kipp Story Box
>
> My freshman year I was in the office of an advisor for a campus group asking a few routine questions. He said he only had a few minutes to meet because he was off to a welcome party for the new Assistant Dean of Students. He invited me to come with him. I was the only student at this gathering and was introduced to many important people on my campus and they remembered me later when I interacted with them in other settings on campus. My first interaction with the Dean of Students was sharing a glass of punch and a piece of cake.

4. Start your own!

Sometimes you and your friends may have an interest that isn't yet an official campus group. It may be that you and some friends love playing board games or several of you have an interest in building robots. In either case, getting an officially registered group won't be that difficult. Starting your own campus group is usually as simple as filling out a couple forms, getting an advisor, and having a couple of other people sign up with you. There usually are various things a group needs to do throughout the year or to renew, but nothing too difficult if you start on the right foot.

The advantages of starting your own group is the ability to decide the direction of the group, access to campus resources to support your group and a great way to meet others with interest similar to yours. It is also a great way to show your leadership to future employers if the group starts small and grows bigger over time.

Final Thoughts

Your college will have many, many ways for you to get involved beyond the classroom. Take advantage of all the great opportunities, but do so in a way that is most beneficial to you. Keep your academics a focus, but use outside activities as a way to enhance your overall experience as a student.

Points to Ponder

- Leadership is a skill developed through experience, training and exposure to different people and ideas.
- A leader is someone who envisions a goal and is able to *inspire* and *guide* others to achieve that goal.
- A leader: leads by example; makes fair decisions; realizes the value of all team members; helps develop other's leadership potential; inspires others to succeed; acts in the times of crisis; provides complements; knows when to yield to the strengths of others and follow; often takes the least desirable position and does not use his/her position for privilege; is resourceful in utilizing the talents of others.
- The characteristics and traits of a leader are: dependability, professionalism, solution-orientated, creative, cheerful service, sense of humor and networker.
- Roles of a leader include: encourager and motivator, role model, entrepreneur and team player.

CHAPTER 35

COLLEGE TOWNS AND COMMUNITIES
TOWN AND GOWN

"My haircut was only $5 with this coupon!!!"

While your college campus itself may seem like a small or even a big city, the community surrounding your college also has a lot of things to offer for students. It's easy to get tunnel vision as most things you need will be right on campus, but venturing out into the community can offer many things for college students. Understanding the "town and gown" relationship will be another asset as you arrive and thrive at college.

More Town or Gown?

Your school probably falls into one of the following types of communities. For simplicity sake, three different types of relationships will be described and you can identify which area you think your school fits into.

1. The Campus IS the Town

In this situation, the school is the reason the community exists. The school you are attending may have 7,000 students and the size of the entire community is about 10,000. In these cases, there is usually a very close tie with the community as the members of the community probably play some part in the college and understand what the school brings to the community. The community is usually geared toward college students with more restaurants, shops, and other amenities which wouldn't be present in a town of similar size without a college.

2. The Campus and Community are Equals

When a college or university community is the same size of the community it is a part of many refer to this as a true "college town." For example, if the college has 30,000 students and the community has 35,000 (not including the college). In these situations, the college and community are closely tied as one couldn't survive without the other. Community pride for the university is usually present and many of the local residents probably have some type of connection with the college. These communities are usually used to what college students bring to a community and offer services for students. These communities may also have an area referred to as "campus town" where many restaurants, shops and other services are close to campus for one-stop shopping.

3. The Campus is a Small Part of a City

When a city has many more people than that of the college, they usually fall into this distinction. In these situations, the college is just a part of the city, but in no way the focal point. This can occur in bigger cities or in medium-sized cities with smaller colleges. There usually are areas around the college which are designed for college students, but nothing like the previous two examples. However, bigger cities often have a lot of other options for students that smaller communities don't have.

What a Deal!

One of the biggest advantages of being a college student is the fact businesses know your money may be tight, so they'll try their best to get your business. Keep your eyes open for deals geared toward you. Pizza places, for example, know their product is a favorite of college students even outside the regular hours and will usually have very good deals to try to out-do their competitors.

Keep your eye open for places offering discounts if you show your student identification card. You'd be surprised at how many places have some type of college discounts. Student newspapers will usually advertise some of these specials, but don't be afraid to ask a business. Some places will offer a "buy one, get one free" on certain nights if you have your student ID. So, find a friend and get to eating!

A good time to take advantage of these meal deals is on nights when your meal plan may not be in effect. Remember, you've already paid for your dining center meals, so you don't want to pay for a meal at a restaurant if you've also paid for your meal in the dining center. Going to a restaurant off campus is also a great way to get to know others. Round up people on your floor for a trip off campus to take advantage of the great deals.

If you bring a vehicle to school, there will usually be some good deals to get your oil changed or for some other routine maintenance. This is another great way take advantage of the deals offered for college students, but be cautious. If they change your oil for $15, they'll probably also tell you ten other things wrong with your vehicle and offer to fix it for an additional cost. If you have a trusted mechanic at home, you may want to use them if available.

Keep your eyes open at the beginning of the year for coupon books geared toward college students. There are usually some really big savings and even free things!

Talk to upperclassmen to learn all the "great deals" available in your community. Their experience finding deals is worth its weight in gold.

Where's THAT?

As you arrive to college, there will be so many new things on campus, in your residence hall, and in the area near where you live. The thought of venturing out into the community may seem scary and not necessary and it may not be necessary at first (unless you need to pick up some items after move in). Ask around if you're not sure where something is located. Resident Assistants or upperclassmen can usually point you in the right direction to find the store you are looking for.

Exploring the city or town can be a fun way to get to know the area. Venture out on your bike, on foot, in a car, or on the bus to just check out what is around you. Invite a new friend along on your adventure. You'd be surprised at how fun it can be to see what the town has to offer. By getting to know the community you live in, you'll be more likely to feel truly at home in your new surroundings.

Be intentional about suspending judgment about your new community. It most likely will be different than where you came from. Many students will unfairly compare their college town to where they came from, citing lack of certain stores or entertainment options. Have an open mind about your new town as it will be a part of your life for several years.

It takes some time to figure out the quickest way to certain areas of town. Often times, after the fact, you'll find you made a simple trip much longer than it needed to be. The more you explore the town, the quicker you'll know all the shortcuts and hot spots in town.

Campus Town Area

The area near campus with businesses geared toward the college crowd is sometimes referred to as the "campus town" area. These can vary greatly from school to school. Some areas are very well established and celebrated, while others may just be a few shops or restaurants. With a close proximity to campus, these areas are usually one of the first outside of the actual campus a student will navigate and learn.

The campus town area will often serve as an oasis for food outside of the on-campus dining facilities. The restaurants are typically geared about college student's appetites and pocketbooks. If your meal plan doesn't cover every meal for the week, trekking to the campus town area is a great way to gather friends and enjoy a meal in a different setting. These restaurants may become busier during the lunch hour as faculty and staff may walk from campus for their lunch hour. Another nice feature about a lot of these restaurants is their delivery services due to their close proximity to campus. Coffee shops are also usually found in this area offering students a place to study, socialize or enjoy a light meal.

If you are tired of seeing the many retail chain stores, the campus town area often offers unique shopping experiences with stores for college students. It's not uncommon to find music stores, gift shops and even book/supply stores geared toward you, the college student. Check these stores out early and see what types of items are available for you closer than the bigger stores located further from campus. You may also find it fun to bring your family and friends who visit you down to experience some of these unique shops and restaurants.

The campus town area also serves as a gathering spot for students to socialize. As mentioned before, coffee shops are a popular place to relax and share conversation with your friends. You will also likely find bars/dance clubs in this area. Laws vary from city to city as to what ages are permitted in these establishments. Many times these places do offer an 18+ night for students not old enough to drink alcohol. While it may be tempting to try to get into a bar with a fake ID, be aware that bars in college towns usually have high security standards as they risk losing a lot of business if they are cited for providing alcohol to minors.

Lastly, the campus town area may be the hub of the local or regional music scene. Look for posters and other advertisements promoting these shows. Many students enjoy hearing local bands perform and sometimes hearing more well-known bands come through town. You may have the opportunity to see the same local band several times in a year or over your years at school. Coffee shops are also known to feature some quieter, more low-key music on occasion. Keep your eyes open for when these music events take place, and if you're musically inclined, especially look for the "open mic night" posters and consider sharing your talents.

Wanting to go to a bar underage? Forget it! It may seem logical to borrow your older siblings ID, but if caught using someone else's ID or a fake ID you can face serious criminal charges.

Community Opportunities

More and more high school students have found ways to integrate themselves into their communities they grow up in. This may include volunteering, working in the community, church involvement and recreational activities among many other things. As you move into your new community while in college, keeping some of this involvement active is important for maintaining a well-rounded lifestyle. Opportunities should be available within the community to help satisfy some of these needs. Getting away from campus can be refreshing and meaningful for you as a student.

Volunteering and service learning is a great way to spend some of your extra time to help others. Often times these opportunities will surface if you keep your eyes open on campus or if you simply pick up a phone and call around to areas you'd like to help. Many residence hall floors or organizations will pick a project or organization and offer their time and efforts. Not only does this help others, it can be a great way to meet others interested in service and give back to the community. This volunteering can be as complex as helping to build a house or as simple as reading a book to a child at a daycare facility.

If you were unable to find a job on campus, keep your eyes open for "help wanted" signs around the community. There usually are opportunities to earn a few extra dollars somewhere in the community. Be sure to remember you'll probably have to drive to a job off campus and an off campus employer may not offer as forgiving of schedules that are needed for a college student.

Many students use their religion as a way to connect with their communities. Getting involved with a church can offer opportunities for fellowship with community members and opportunities for service as well. It usually isn't very difficult to find information about religious organizations in a community. For more information on this topic, see chapter 37 on religion.

Each area of the country offers various other activities for recreation. It may be hiking, shopping, fishing, running, sight-seeing, skiing, and about any other activity. Be adventurous and try activities you may never have experienced, especially if they are unique to the area. You may also do activities you've enjoyed in the past as a way to continue pursuing these hobbies and introduce them to your new college friends. For example, if you are an avid snow skier and none of your new friends have ever skied, offer to plan a Saturday outing. And if anyone else is planning something you've never done, consider giving it a try. Be open to try new things and explore the community you are now a part of.

Final Thoughts

For the most part, colleges and the surrounding communities usually have a pretty good relationship. But be mindful, sometimes a few bad eggs on a college campus do a few dumb things and community members develop ill-will toward college students. Be a good representative of your school by being a good citizen and offering your time when you have extra to help the community. The more you do to help the community, the more likely the community will be to support your school.

There will be many new things as you move to your new surroundings. Be patient figuring out your new community. It may be frustrating at times, but before you know it you'll be an old pro and know your way around your new town. And if you find yourself "stuck" on campus, take a time out and go out into the surrounding community to clear your head, find something new and cash in on some discounts geared toward college students.

You probably received some materials from the local chamber of commerce prior to arriving to campus via orientation or in the mail. Read through what your new community has to offer. Hop on the internet and do some research and find out what your community has to offer or stop by your local chamber of commerce. Many great college memories can be rooted in this community, and you'll cherish these memories for years after college.

Points to Ponder
- Explore the area surrounding your college.
- If you are not old enough to go into a bar, don't go into the bar.
- Find a unique restaurant in your community so when friends and family visit, you have a place to take them to eat.
- Keep your eyes open for great deals geared at you, the college student.

CHAPTER 36
PARENTS, HOME LIFE, AND HOMESICKNESS
LOVE AND SUPPORT FROM AFAR

"I miss my mom!"

You are all moved into college, the parents have left and you are now on your own. How will your relationship with your parents change now that you're at school? How will it stay the same? You were so excited to get away from your parents, but do you find yourself greatly missing their rules you hated so much a few months back? Do the frequent phone calls home help or hurt your situation? The changing relationship with your family is something you may not have thought about much before leaving for school, but as soon as you are gone you'll start having some of the above questions permeate your thoughts. And when you have a bad day, the familiarity of your home will be something you may miss greatly. We'll explore all of the above and give you some helpful hints to help this transition be as smooth as possible for you AND for your parents and family.

Everyone is going to be homesick. Some just cover it up better than others.

The Parents Point of View

Just as transitioning is tough for you as a student, it can be equally as hard for your parents to watch their child spread their wings and "leave the nest." Are you the first child going to school or has an older sibling already left the home? Your birth order can play a big part in your parents' transition. If they've watched a child or two leave the house already, they will probably be a bit more comfortable knowing what this experience will be like and may even be excited for you to leave. If you are the last to leave, they'll be old pros at sending children on their way, but could experience a bit of "empty nest" syndrome as they find themselves, for the first time, without children at home. If you are the first to leave home, they've never seen a child leave and may not know exactly how to act or may be very involved in the process as they want to be sure things are done right.

There are such a wide range of emotions your parents and family will take on as you leave. They will be proud of all you accomplished to get you to this point in your life. But, they also are faced with the sadness of seeing their "little baby" growing up and moving out. Some parents experience some guilt as they may feel they haven't spent as much time with their kids that last year in high school. And lastly, they may have anxiety about their own parenting during this time if they compare themselves to other parents going through the same thing. If they hear one of your friends' parents visited or sent a care package, they may feel they are failing as college parents.

Sometimes the above emotions can take on different looks. Parents may become unreasonable or demanding as they are trying to grasp onto their last bit of parenting as you leave. Or if they've been through it before, they may seem excited to get you out of the house as they know everything will be fine, and their eagerness to have you move out may make you feel unwanted. Just remember through all of this that your parents have done a lot for you over the last 18 years, and the more you can try to understand what they are feeling, the easier this transition can be for everyone involved.

Mike Story Box

I am the youngest of four brothers. When my oldest brother moved out to college, it was a family event, complete with the parents, three brothers and the family dog all loaded up in the vehicles. By the time my third oldest brother moved out of the house for college, he had to wake my mom up to let her know he was leaving.

Stolen Moments

Just like you like to receive real mail in your mailbox, so do your family members. A postcard from your school is a great way to show family members you're thinking of them.

Home Life

Life will continue without you at home. It may seem weird to hear that your high school's volleyball team is undefeated and they are doing that without your help. You may be surprised to hear your parents are letting your younger sibling drive the family car to school (they never let YOU do that). Or you may be surprised to hear about a new hobby your parents are partaking in on the weekends. All of this will happen as you begin a life away from home. It may seem weird to you at first as that was *your* home and that's not how it was done when *you* were there, but *you're* not there anymore.

Younger siblings will have a transition period as well after you've moved out. Show interest in how this is affecting them. They may not tell you this directly, but they will miss you. Keep them updated on your new college life, but also be sure to ask about their lives. Younger siblings grow up fast and your genuine interest in their lives can help develop much deeper relationships with them. Your phone may ring with them calling asking you for advice when situations come up in their lives.

Does your school have a family weekend? This is a great opportunity to have your family visit after you've learned the ropes of your new school.

Speed Dial: Mom and Dad

If you talk to someone who went to college 20 or 30 years ago, they'd probably tell you they talked to their parents about once a week on the phone (if even that often). Their primary form of communication would have come through a mailed letter. As you are well aware, things have changed a lot. Cell phones and email are used by most, and many college students (and parents) have the opportunity to have everyday contact with each other. In the past, if you had a bad day in college you figured it out on your own or talked to your roommate about it. Now you may have an issue come up and within minutes, your parents are aware. Your parents' first instinct will be finding a way to "fix" whatever is wrong. A simple disagreement with a roommate (which everyone will have) usually can work themselves out in a day or two, but if you get your parent involved they may start calling your Hall Director, the college's Dean of Students or the President (remember, some parents will really want things solved quickly...remember the emotions they are going though?).

As you are transitioning, there will be some rough days and your first thought may be to call home. Resist that temptation at first. There are a lot of others at school going through the same types of things and connecting with them can help you both adjust (without getting your parents worried or worked up). And when you do have legitimate issues come up, first try to solve them yourself. If there is a problem with your financial aid, walk to the financial aid office and ask questions and get answers rather than telling your parents and having them call. You're an adult now and a college will see you as an adult. If your parents call to try to solve some of these problems, it may not get very far as the college is not able to release information due to confidentiality. Learning how to do these types of things for yourself will help you grow and mature more than you probably realize.

Kipp Story Box

In my role running a residence hall, I am amazed at how often I get calls from parents saying their student's room is too hot or cold. Their student could have easily come down to the front desk to report this issue, but their first instinct was to call home and have their parent call me. That type of thinking actually delays the response time to fix issues such as these.

 Do you want your parents to have your passwords for various university websites? It may seem like a good idea during orientation, but do you want them seeing all your parking tickets on your university bill?

Help your parents understand your new life and new schedule as well. It may have been completely normal for you to be in bed by 10 PM when you still lived at home. In college, you may be at the library until midnight. If your parents call at 10 PM and you're not in your room, they may worry. They may also worry if you don't call them back right away, forgetting you will be very busy. The more you communicate with your parents about your schedule, the easier this kind of stuff will be for them. You may also want to set up a calling schedule. Maybe every Saturday afternoon you'll call home to just chat. This can help reassure your parents and provide something to look forward to each week.

 Most colleges have some type of Parent/Family Association as a way for families to be connected to your school.

Parent → Friend

One of the neatest things that usually happens during college is the magical transition where your parents become your friends. The timeline for this happening for each family varies and you may not even realize it is happening. As both your parents and you adjust to your new lives and get comfortable with them, conversations begin to change and you are able to relate more to adult types of issues.

I've seen this process work faster when students show their parents they are maturing by acting more responsible. Solving problems for yourself is a great way for parents to see you are capable of making decisions and help them gain more respect for you. A very simple way to do this is by, prior to asking your parents for advice, providing them with the options you've already come up with. They'll be impressed you've thought through the issue and will trust you can make a good decision. Remember, the more you let them parent, the more they will. And also remember, if you make poor choices in college, it will be harder for them to not try and parent you.

Like we've talked about, this process can be difficult for all involved at times. There will be times you'll want your parents to make a decision for you and times your parents will still want to "parent" you. If you call home and tell them you were issued a ticket for underage drinking, they'll probably go into "parent mode" on you. If you call and tell them you are seeking their advice on how to set up a personal budget, they will respect and appreciate your maturity. Your parents will be flattered if you include them in big decisions in your life, especially if you approach it in a way that shows them you respect what they have to say and want their advice to be part of your decision making process. Your parents will even start asking your opinion on things in their lives as they begin to see you mature through college.

If you are from a split family, be sure you are rationing out your phone calls, visits, and other communications.

Homesickness

As exciting as your new college life is, there will be times everyone gets homesick. Even the best dining center meal will not hold a candle to one of your favorites that mom would make for dinner. Even the coolest residence hall room isn't the same as the bedroom you slept in for many years. Having your laundry done and put away for you probably doesn't happen in college. All of these types of things can lead to homesickness. Many of the comforts of home are hard to replicate at first, but by building connections with other students and feeling a part of your new college community can really help create new comforts.

The People you'll meet:
Believe it or not, there will be someone on your floor who moves back home within the first week or two of school.

Resist the crying phone call home. As discussed in an earlier paragraph, a call like that will be especially hard on your parents, and they may find it hard not to come pick you up. Talk to your roommate or another friend on the floor. You will not be the only one feeling homesick. It is ok to call home at some point and tell your parents you miss them, but if done too early or with too many tears, it will be even harder on both of you. Sometimes homesickness will happen in the few days prior to class starting as your life hasn't gotten really busy yet, and you are thinking a lot about the life you left, rather than the new life you're starting. Usually as soon as classes start, you'll get very busy and not have as much time to miss home. Resist the urge to go home right away as that will make it hard to build connections at school and feeling at home there. A great way to help with this is pre-plan your first visit home. Maybe two weeks into school you'll plan on coming home? That way both you and your parents know a visit will happen. This can be more difficult if you live a significant distance from school, but in those cases you can plan on Thanksgiving being your first trip home. Either way, committing yourself to staying at school a certain amount of time will force you to tough it out and not tempt you to return home.

Final Thoughts

Leaving your family and joining your new college family is a wonderful opportunity to grow and mature as a person (and as a family), but everyone will have some sadness or rough times as you all go through this. Talking about these things prior to the big move to school is a great way to be proactive and get through it all without a lot of bickering or unneeded stress. Just as you are excited to be at school and your parents are to have you there, be excited for them on successfully raising you and entering a new stage in their own lives. And remember, missing home is normal and a good thing...and that home will always be there to welcome you.

Points to Ponder
- Some things have changed since your parents went to college, some things have not. They may not be able to understand some of the things you are going through, because they didn't have to go through them when they went to college.
- Be sure to exercise your own problem solving skills before calling home to have your mom or dad fix an issue.

- If you are a parent reading this, letting your student navigate some of their issues will be better for them in the long run.
- At winter break, you may be excited to return back to school because, that is starting to feel like your new home.

CHAPTER 37
RELIGION
YOUR OTHER ADVISOR?

"Well, I'm Methodist every Easter and Christmas."

For some of you reading this chapter, the whole religion thing has been something you're comfortable with and have been for many years. Memories may go as far back to the days of vacation bible school, confirmation, a youth group ski trip or your first communion. You and your family have had a routine and understanding as to what you believe in. While for others, you may be confused when people are mad that Santa Clause and the Easter bunny have become the icons for their respective holidays. No matter where you may fall on this continuum (or not on it at all), this chapter will help you understand the dynamics of religion in the college period of your life and help you understand and navigate it all.

What do you believe in?

While this question may be one you've been asked and thought about, many don't *really* think about their answer. For most, one's religious views and beliefs are those of what their family have held and passed on as they grew up. Church is something many just went to, without a whole lot of their own thought process. Knowing what is beyond one's own family is often unknown. And for some, they have beliefs but their family was not active in a church. Can trying something outside your family's own set of beliefs create some tension? Yes. Can it be managed? Yes.

There are so many changes and developmental moments which happen as one transitions to college. The movement away from home creates great opportunities to explore various areas of your life, including your spiritual life. If you feel you already have a good grasp on your spiritual life, college can be a time to solidify your beliefs and gain a greater understanding of them. With beliefs already in place, you can start pursuing the answer to the question, "*Why* do I believe in this?" If you are a "rookie" in terms of your spiritual life, there are lots of great resources and opportunities to explore this area of your life while at college.

The Benefits of Solidifying Your Spiritual Life in College

Your plate is already pretty full as a college student and, unless you are a religious studies major or at seminary, religion and spirituality is another thing to occupy your time. There are, however, several reasons why this is the time to explore this area of your life.

1. Abundance of resources

College campuses offer many great resources to help answer your questions. Some campuses have professional staff dedicated to the development of their students spiritual lives complete with an office full of resources. There are also usually several independent campus ministries on campus, depending on the size of the school, with several staff members and students' who are in place to help students.

2. Serves as a Grounding Point

Having an active spiritual life can help serve as a grounding point as the many stresses and pressures of college and life after college come flying at you. With various peer pressures, busy lifestyles and unforeseen life events all happening in college, many students find their spiritual tools as one of the best ways to help guide decisions and process the events of their lives.

3. See the "bigger picture" of life

After pulling an "all nighter" working on a project or having to miss a trip home to study for a big test, some students ask, "Is this as good as it gets?" Or while turning on the world news and seeing killings or other tragedies happening, one may ask what their time on earth is really worth or how going to college is going to solve anything. Having a solid spiritual life can help keep all things in perspective and help you understand your role in the game of life.

Someone's spiritual journey is very personal. Be careful not to compare your journey with others as each person is on their own timeline. Remember, it's not a competition.

4. You have the time

Wait, this may not seem the case. Doesn't it seem your schedule is already filled up? You *do* have the time now. College days tend to go from morning till late at night. You'll probably never again be around so many other people in your same situation. Late night talks with groups of people, events planned by your university, educated people offering lively debates on spiritual issues and organized religious groups offer great opportunities which fall into the normal college day.

5. Learn how you and others think

Through conversations with others and your own self reflection, you can begin to solidify how *you* think about various aspects of life. These conversations can be challenging sometimes, but in the end the internal conflict you may have internally working through these issues can really help solidify your own beliefs. Talking with others also helps gain a perspective different than your own (and your family's) and you may like what you hear or what is said may reassure you of your own beliefs. With such a diverse group of people on a college campus, these conversations and observations can really be eye opening. And be prepared, you may begin to realize how you are perceived by others which may either make you happy or make you rethink some things.

6. You can meet similar people

Getting involved in conversations and groups will soon help you meet people similar to yourself. While it's important to interact with many different types of people, forming relationships with people with similar thoughts, ideas, and beliefs can foster great friendships. These people will be fun to hang out with and will know where you are coming from and will be able to encourage you in various areas of your life. And for some, this is where they may meet that "special someone."

Things you may see

Religion and spirituality may take several different forms. Here is a list of various things you may hear of or see on a college campus. Seeing some for the first time may be confusing or scary if you're not prepared.

1. People Handing out Bibles

Once or twice a semester, you'll probably be greeted by people handing out small Bibles on the edge of campus. They are usually volunteers for their respective church and have good intentions. If you don't want a copy, just say, "No, thank you" and continue walking. If you stop to get one, they may try to engage you in conversation.

2. Free Speech Preaching

Sometimes a "buzz" is evident on campus when a radical, fundamentalist preacher finds their way to an open spot on your campus. They are usually very vocal and will be preaching to anyone who will listen (or no one at all) and could have signs with them as well. They may also verbally attack people walking by, posing questions such as, "Are you going to heaven?" or "Did you know you are going to hell?" There will inevitably be students who shout back or debate on the spot with these people. Usually these people know the law well and are doing this to create a scene. Your best bet is to keep walking or watch a bit to be entertained.

3. Bible Study

This is a group which gets together to study scripture and other religious types of material as a small group. They usually meet once a week for an hour or two. There are several ways to get involved with one. Churches will usually help set these up. Campus ministries are also a good place to go if you are interested in joining one. And lastly, many times individuals on a residence hall floor may start a group you could join. They are a great way to grow spiritually and connect with others also looking to enhance their knowledge.

4. Information Booths

Many college ministries will set up a booth in a high traffic area to chat with students the first couple of weeks of school. There may be some type of survey to fill out to receive a snack or a soda. If you take the time to stop at a booth, this is a great place to ask questions about their ministry and to evaluate if they could be helpful in your spiritual growth. Many times when you divulge contact information, someone from their group may wish to follow up with you personally. If you don't want someone to visit, be sure to let them know.

Kipp Story Box

My freshman year my roommate and I stopped by a booth by a campus ministry set up near our residence hall, because they were handing out free soda with a questionnaire. My roommate checked the box he'd be interested in learning more. For the next few weeks, there was someone calling our room or randomly stopping by our room to talk about their group. Be careful what you sign up for!

---

5. College Worship Services

Usually one evening a week, campus ministries will have a worship time with a message. These usually consist of contemporary music, prayer and some type of message by a speaker. Oftentimes students who attend these activities actively recruit others to go with to experience them. Don't feel pressured to attend, but if it seems like something you'd like to check out be sure to do just that. There are usually several different options, so be sure to shop around for what fits you, don't just go to the one "everyone" goes to.

Finding a Church or Other Place of Worship

Finding a place of worship is usually not that difficult in a community with a college or university. Church information can usually be found during orientation or in the first few weeks of school. Some students will look for a church similar to one they may have attended while at home. Other may choose to explore other churches. Many schools will also have some type of worship service on the campus. Finding a church shouldn't be that difficult.

Many churches in a college community offer study space or recreational activities for students attending their church

Churches in a college community will usually offer services conducive to college students such as a Saturday night service or later service on Sunday morning.

Mike Story Box

During the spring semester of my freshman year I went to a different church each weekend with a group of friends. It was a great way to explore the different atmospheres of the local churches, see various religious services and bond more closely with this group of friends.

Those NOT interested in Religion

As mentioned earlier, college is a great time for self-discovery and exploration with one's values and beliefs. Some students either have not been introduced to any sort of religious system or have chosen to not believe. **Agnostics** are individuals who believe it is impossible to know the truth about things such as God or issues of spiritual existence, but believe there is some type of higher power. **Atheists** do not believe in any type of higher power.

A college campus is about learning from each other and providing resources for all. Depending on the size of your campus, there usually are groups for agnostics, atheists, those practicing witchcraft and about any other group. It's important to remember each person has a right to believe in whatever they'd like to believe in. It's also a great time to learn more about what others believe in. This can help you better understand your set of beliefs and understand why others believe what they believe.

Personality Line Up

Below are a few of the various types of people you may see on your campus regarding spirituality and religion.

1. The Over Ambitious New Believer:

This person is REALLY excited about their new found religion. They may be seen knocking on the doors of everyone on their floor trying to get them to come to church or a worship service. They may take it upon themselves to tell people they are going to hell and point out other sins being committed. They may also go out of their way to incorporate their religion into every part of their lives, clothing, music, vehicle, room decorations, etc.

2. The "I'm Spiritual, but not religious" person

This person makes it a point to always tell people they believe in something, but don't believe in organized religion. This may be a way for them to avoid attending church services or a way to show individuality and not conform to what a group thinks.

3. The "Christmas/Easter" Christians

These folks identify with their religions when certain religious holidays come around, but not at any other part during the year.

4. The "Thankful to God" person

While many people are sure to thank God for things in their lives, these people thank God *all* the time for EVERYTHING. Maybe the ketchup just got refilled at the dining center? They thank God for keeping the condiments supplied so they can better enjoy their hot dogs. When anyone has any joy or sorrow in their life, they quickly will thank God for the opportunity to hear about these things.

5. The "Check Box" people

These people feel if they go to a church activity or service they can "check" that off for the week and proceed to do whatever they want. They may be sure to attend church on Saturday night so they can use the rest of the night to party hard and sleep in the next day.

6. The "against the status quo" people

These people are *very* anti-religion. They'll jump on any opportunity to tell you why your beliefs are wrong and why anyone who practices any religion is wrong. They'll go out of their way to wear clothing which is anti-semantic and will argue with anyone about issues of religion and faith. Sometimes these people grew up in a church going home and now use this as a backlash against the years their parents made them go to church, but many times they may just be against the status quo on many social issues.

Final Thoughts

Having a spiritual component to your life can really help motivate you, meet other people and find a greater meaning to your life. The spiritual journey is a very personal one and one that has a different timeline for each person. The college atmosphere is an excellent place to learn about what you believe and connect with others in the same stage of their spiritual journey.

Use the great resources available to you to ask questions and to learn about what you believe in and what those around you may believe in. Remember, religion is not a competition, and you'll see many different forms of it on a college campus.

Points to Ponder:

- Without your parents no one is going to stop you from sleeping in on Sunday mornings, but you may *want* to attend church service.
- Becoming active in a church group is another way to connect with a group of students and friends you may not have otherwise met.
- The 'free pizza' isn't free, be ready to be recruited at any church social.
- Explore your options—what do you know about other religions besides the one you were raised with?

CHAPTER 38
DIVERSITY
CULTURAL COMPETENCE

"I'm pretty diverse. I really like Chinese AND Mexican food."

Like it or not, we all have a long way to go when it comes to understanding and respecting the wide variety of different types of people in our world. Whether you are from a graduating class of 1,800 in a big city or a graduating class of 13 in a rural part of the country, there will always be groups of people you could learn more about. Rather than cringing when you hear the word "diversity," consider taking an honest look at yourself and approach the subject with an open mind and a humble heart, and you may come to realize differences can be fun, informative and eye opening.

What IS diversity?

What *isn't* it? Diversity means different things to different people. Some will look at diversity and think of skin color alone. Others may think of it as where someone comes from. We will look at diversity as any differences among people. This could be skin color or nation or origin by our definition, but it also may mean one's sexual preference, socioeconomic status, or city one is from. Ever been around someone from a farm and someone from a big city? They may look the same, but chances are their experiences may be very different.

The list of various differences is endless: religious views, nationality, male/female, social class, political views, parents divorced/still together, musical interests, age, ability/disability, hair length, tattoos, piercing and about ANYTHING else. As you can see, it's impossible to create an all inclusive list of all the differences among us.

What's the Big Deal?

The term diversity is a hot topic, especially at a college or university. Sometimes among all the hubbub of definitions and expectations, the true meaning of diversity is lost. Colleges are very intentional about creating an open and inviting environment for all students. Times have changed and not being sensitive to various groups of people can hurt a university and also can get individuals in trouble.

Keeping this in mind, it's important to remember when going to college you will encounter many different types of people who may have differing ideas of how the world works. While some may view this as scary and intimidating, one should look at this as a great learning opportunity. Everyone going through college is exposed to new things and new types of people. Some cover their intimidation with insensitive remarks towards a group of people. How would you react if you heard something insensitive? Would you laugh along or would you point out it's not appropriate?

Plain and simple, all individuals deserve to be treated with respect and treated fairly. Most universities have policies in place to make sure this happens. Be familiar with your school's policies and seek to understand why they are in place. It's important to understand these policies, because schools take them very seriously.

Kipp Story Box

What used to be deemed teasing is now deemed harassment or a hate crime. I had a resident who had words written on her dry erase board on her door that talked of her race. This was taken very seriously and campus police documented it as a hate crime. Think twice before doing or saying things...do you want "hate crime" on your official record?

While cracking an insensitive joke about a group of people may make some laugh, it really just makes you look ignorant.

What YOU can do...

Don't be scared! It may seem as if diversity is a scary thing or something to be weary of. But it isn't! The simplest thing to do is, prior to arriving to college, acknowledge you don't know everything, put assumptions aside, and be ready to learn about lots of different people.

Be prepared. Many times groups of people are magnified on a college campus. Many times groups of students will meet formally or informally as a group. This may be something you encounter the first few days of being at college as groups are usually trying to get to know new students. Understand that these students are all finding ways to be a part of the university and are committed to their groups. You too will be looking for ways to connect.

Remember everyone has a story to tell and comes from a different background. Get to know people different than you. If you grew up on a farm, ask that person on your floor from a big city what their high school experience was like. If you see a flyer for a step competition being sponsored by a black student organization, go check it out. Many students go into college with an attitude that they already know all they need to know. Challenge yourself to suspend these thoughts, be humble, and learn about those around you...and share your own story with others.

Kipp Story Box

My freshman year, there were two guys on my floor from England. It was so neat getting to know these guys. They were able to tell me about their country, tell me their observations about being here and showed my friends and me how to make a "proper cup of tea."

Uncomfortable...

By nature, things that are familiar to us are generally more comfortable and things that are different tend to make us uncomfortable. This is a totally natural reaction to being in situations or around people who are unfamiliar. There will be many things you'll encounter on your residence hall floor or somewhere else on campus that will be different than things you are used to. Some people will choose to ignore or avoid these situations and, sometimes, make comments that are inappropriate with no true experiential basis to comment on the situation. Others will endure the uncomfortable feeling and take this as a learning opportunity. For example, maybe there is an educational program about the healing power of meditation and incense. Many will see this or the people involved and say something like, "They're crazy. That would never work" without ever experiencing or hearing about how this works. Someone with a more open mind may check out the program and see why these people do this activity. After the activity, you can make a more accurate decision as to what you believe, AND you'll now have experienced something new. Maybe you will enjoy the activity and meet new friends? And remember, you too are probably part of a group that makes others uncomfortable. Don't you wish others would just ask you about those activities rather than judging from afar?

As mentioned many times in this book, there are many opportunities and things happening on a college campus. There is no way possible to experience EVERY one of them. Just be sure to remember whomever is involved with each, there is a unique reason why, and they should be respected for their involvement. You wouldn't like people teasing you for being a part of the Scuba Diving club would you?

Hitting Home

After some time at college, it is natural to become enlightened about diversity issues, feel more open to the world around you and forget about the bias beliefs and other stereotypes which may have been part of your upbringing. Fast forward to one of your first trips home. It may be at Thanksgiving dinner when one of your uncles makes an inappropriate comment about a group of people at the dinner table and everyone laughs. But you don't want to laugh because, little do they know, you have met and become friends with an individual in that group at college. What do you do? Do you call your uncle out in front of everyone?

This inevitably will happen whether it is a family member or one of your friends. Follow you gut instinct. Many times, if done correctly, you can help educate others about how their comments or thoughts really can hurt. If someone says something blatantly inappropriate, it's important to show them it's not appropriate by not laughing and having a conversation with them. Again, follow your heart and your gut with these. If your sibling says something, if confronted in a non-embarrassing manner this can be a great opportunity. Choosing to confront a group of college guys at a party may not be as good of an idea.

It Starts with YOU

Unfortunately, there still is hate, stereotypes, and bias thinking in the world we live in, and it may seem like an uphill battle. The easiest thing to do to work on this issue lies with you. Genuinely get to know those who are different than you. Be the person who seeks out opportunities to get to know others. Understand that if you are in the majority group, life is harder for those in the minority.

Final Thoughts

Diversity is a part of everyday life at a university. College brings together people from all over with different backgrounds. You will probably learn more about people and the diversity of the world through your everyday 'ordinary' activities such as eating at the dining hall, studying or working on a group project or hanging out with new friends than you will at a formal 'diversity conference' where more buzz words are used than real discussions. College is about personal growth, discovering who you are and figuring out how you see the world and how the world sees you.

Points to Ponder
- Be proactive in this process.
- Reach out to international students and learn about how they arrived on campus.

- Don't be afraid to educate your friends.
- Share your story with others.
- You're family visits you at college and one of your family members makes an inappropriate comment in front of your new college friends. What do you do?
- How many of your friends are of a different race? Are you friends with any international students?
- Have you ever accepted an award that was gender or race restrictive?
- Are there areas or tables in the dining hall that you would feel uncomfortable sitting at?
- If a homosexual lived on your floor, how would you feel using the community bathroom and showers?
- Have you ever pretended to be someone you're not to fit in with the group?
- If you live close to campus, think about students from far away. Ask them if they'd like to go to your home some weekend...maybe Thanksgiving?

Freshmen Moments
FALL AND WINTER BREAK

Fall break usually coincides with Thanksgiving so it typically occurs late in the semester. This will be a much anticipated break as it may be the first time you have had to return home and see your family and a much needed break after completing most of your first semester. It will also be your first taste of reentering home-life and you may realize how many freedoms you have been taking for granted at college doing your own thing on your own time. So are you going to tell your mom and dad about your new tattoo or tongue ring or hide it for now and cross that bridge over winter break? Fall break is also different from most other breaks, because it occurs so late in the semester. You typically will have final exams within a few weeks of returning to college; meaning you'll need to get some project work and studying completed during this time.

Winter break is a time to rejuvenate. Plan for some down time and playing it low-key the first couple of days you are back to recoup from your first semester—you will need sleep. Winter break, unlike most high schools, usually coincides with the completion of the semester, and so you won't have any homework or projects to complete. But you may want to get a head start on some other things over break and take care of any scholarship applications, work on your FAFSA form or get things ready for your spring classes. If you can, stick around for another night or two after finals—it can be fun to hang out with your college friends when you no longer have to study. It also gives you more time to pack, clean and get some things in order for when you come back in the spring. You might also want an afternoon in your college-town to pick up some holiday gifts for your family. Check the bulletin boards for any December "moving sales" from graduating seniors. You might find some great deals. Oh yeah, don't forget to check your grade report online!

CHAPTER 39
SPRING SEMESTER
INTRODUCTION
COLLEGE: TAKE TWO

"Hey, so how was your break?"

By the end of winter break, believe it or not, you may actually be excited to come back and start spring classes. Home-life isn't the same, sometimes feeling like a guest in your own home, other times frustrated at curfews and restricted freedoms you took for granted at college. You may have a new perspective on high school relationships as you find your friends have changed and grown over different experiences and you are no longer as close. You are excited to go back to college to be with your college friends and to be, well, at home.

Spring semester is a time to reflect on what went well and what didn't go well last semester. You now have that first semester of experiences under your belt. Reevaluate your priorities and what you want to change this semester. It's a new beginning for your classes. You are entering with a clean slate and essentially have "straight A's"—the goal is now to keep these grades by attending class, studying and scoring well on all class assignments and tests. How were your studying habits last semester? Do you need to find a new study location? What classes are you taking? Do you still feel your major is the right fit? Are you learning what you need to know for the next level of classes? How did finals go for you? Now is also the time to think ahead to finals—how will you prepare for finals differently?

The Reality of the Situation:

Daily review of your class notes from all your courses and reading ahead is the best preparation for finals. But, it's also almost impossible. A realistic strategy is to do well on tests and quizzes for the units you are currently covering so that you have a strong grade when you enter the final. This will help reduce stress during finals week because you have "more room" to miss points on the final exam.

Besides classes, the spring semester also provides a fresh start on relationships, campus involvement or any lingering issues like roommate conflicts. Are you planning to work this semester? Are you too involved in clubs or not enough? How will you meet new people? There are generally less "welcome-back" social activities when you come back in the spring as compared to the fall.

Some people in your major or on your floor may have boarded the struggle bus one last time and didn't return for the spring semester. They may have decided college wasn't for them at this time and dropped out, were academically dismissed, or transferred to another school because your college wasn't the right fit for them. The floor sure seems a lot quieter without John and his bass guitar, doesn't it?

You may also notice some new faces. Reach out to people transferring in to your college or switching rooms to your floor. You remember how it felt not knowing anyone, looking for a place to sit at dinner, not knowing how to read your class schedule. When you are new, little things mean a lot to that person. Being friendly and helping someone learn how to use the laundry system can lead into a great new friendship.

Get a jump start on summer plans in the spring:
- Will you take any summer courses?
  - Will you take those courses at your college or closer to home at a local community college? Are the community college credits transferable to your college? Have you registered?
- Will you work?
  - Will you find a job related to your college major for your resume or will you work the same job you had in high school to help build your savings?

- Where will you live?
  - Will you live at home or on college campus?
- Do you need a summer storage unit?
  - Can you move your entire stuff home, or do you need a storage unit for your large items like your loft, futon, couch, etc?

Storage units near college campuses fill up quickly—reserve yours early in the year.

- Where will you live in the fall?
  - Can you tour the place now? Do you need to fill out an application or make a deposit?
- Who will be your roommates for next fall?

See Chapter 41: Preparing for Summer and Chapter 42: Preparing for Fall, for a more in depth look at these things.

FAFSA

FAFSA (Free Application for Federal Student Aid) is the federal application to determine your eligibility for financial aid including college loans, federal grants, and work-study programs. The application can be found and completed online at www.fafsa.ed.gov. The FAFSA collects information about you and your background, your student status, your finances, your parents' finances, etc. After reviewing your application, the Department of Education will then send you and your school a Student Aid Report (SAR) which states which federal programs you qualify for and will serve as a guide for your school to determine your eligibility for university funding.

Things you should know about the FAFSA:

- If you are going to get any financial aid or scholarships, you need to fill out a FAFSA **every** year. You still need to fill out a new FAFSA even if you filled an application out last year. Find out the priority date set by your university to have your FAFSA completed; submit your FAFSA by this date to ensure maximum benefits and school funding.

- Even if you don't plan on using federal loans or think you don't qualify for federal grants, you should still fill out a FAFSA because your university will use the FAFSA to determine your eligibility to qualify for school funding such as scholarships.
- Your parents will need to complete or estimate their tax return in order to complete the parent finance section on your FAFSA form.
- Start working on your FAFSA early as it requires information from various sources. Apply for your personal identification number (PIN) first.
- Keep a folder of your financial records. This is a good practice and habit to develop and just like taxes, you may be "audited" to prove the information on your FAFSA. Oh yeah, don't lie on your FAFSA.
- Don't do drugs. This is a felony charge and you can lose your federal funding.
- Do you qualify for Work Study? Work study is a program where federal financial aid pays part of your on-campus job. You need to fill out the FAFSA to be eligible for this program.

 Along with filling out your FAFSA form, you should learn how to file your own taxes, too. Your financial portfolio probably isn't that complicated at this time and now is a good learning opportunity.

Final Thoughts

Spring semester also brings out student government election campaigns. Let's see, this year's number one issue: to increase communication between the student population, faculty and the student government; just like it was the year before and the year before that on every college campus and every year. What does that really mean anyway "to increase communication"? Oh, and the other "hot" topics for this year's election include student parking, rising tuition costs and campus lighting at night. And the last issue addressed by student politicians is student apathy in the student government....which definitely includes voting, including your vote in this election. Are you sensing the sarcasm? It is a good time to learn how your school's student government structure works and could be an area you choose to get involved with during your time at college.

What about your New Year's resolution? The student fitness center will be jammed-packed but should return to normal shortly after spring break.

Set yourself up for success by making your New Year's resolution months ahead on October 1ˢᵗ—then by the first of the year you will have already established a routine of eating right and exercising regularly, and will have missed holiday weight gain.

Points to Ponder

- You just *can't* find an apple at the dining center because everyone is trying to eat healthy. Here, have a cookie.
- Is that guy wearing dress socks at the fitness center? Clueless.
- Look at you using those grown-up words in the adult world: "1040 tax form", "FAFSA application", "subsidized Stanford loan".
- Without even realizing it, you're a pro now at college skills such as laundry, the bus system, time management, class registration, etc.
- Invite the new person to dinner with you and your friends.
- You missed your room, your college friends and you even missed the food.
- Go ahead; start rearranging your room at 2am.
- Seasonal Affective Disorder (SAD): suffer from depression during times of decreasing sunlight (late fall/early winter). People who suffer from SAD benefit from using and being exposed to bright lights to help improve their mood.
- Spring semester always seems to go faster than fall semester.

CHAPTER 40

SPRING BREAK
PSH, CANCUN? ...HELLO ICELAND!

"It's always an once-in-a-lifetime opportunity...well, until you do it again".

Spring Break: What it is and what it isn't

Spring Break is typically one week long in the middle of spring semester around the month of March. Most college students will use their spring break to catch up on schoolwork, to earn cash by working, to visit family and home or to travel. The weeks prior to and after Spring break are during the midterm "crunch-time" as it occurs right as tests, papers and projects are due as well as when other deadlines or events are looming, such as housing applications or summer job interviews. It is important to balance your week between accomplishing your schoolwork as well as relaxing and allowing yourself some "down-time". Spring Break plans do not have to be financially draining. Just remember you have four or maybe five Spring Breaks ahead of you. If you want to have the college experience of visiting a tropical island for spring break, maybe save that for your senior year. Research and explore all of your options (see below).

Options for Spring Break

Stay at your college
- Enjoy some downtime by relaxing with your college friends and exploring new parts of your university or surrounding community.

- Work on catching up or studying ahead for your classes, complete semester projects or papers, and finish homework assignments.
  - o This is also a good time to work on your resume for summer job applications.

Spring break can be different from other breaks in that you may have homework due or a test as soon as the break is over.

Where will you stay if you stick around campus? Make sure to check if your current place stays open over breaks.

- Work on completing those miscellaneous "to-do" lists you've been meaning to complete all semester.
  - o Use this time to research housing options for the summer or fall and to tour apartments.
  - o What classes will you take this summer/fall?
- Broaden your knowledge or satisfy an interest by completing a mini-course for credit or attending a seminar offered by your college or community (i.e. American Red Cross).
- Make some "breakthroughs" by logging extra hours if you are working on a research project

Go back home and spend time with family, friends and/or pets

- Schedule in your "yearly check-up appointments" in your hometown with your family physician, dentist, optometrist, gynecologist, etc.
- Invite one of your college friends or significant other to come home with you, check out your hometown and stay with your family; or accept an invitation if someone invites you to spend time with them in their home. Be sure you have your parents' approval before bringing your friend home with you.

Pack up stuff in your room that you haven't used all year and bring it home with you. Moving a couple boxes or large bulky or awkwardly shaped items now can make a big difference for move out.

The dates of your break may not coincide with your friends' spring breaks if they attend a different university; so, you could be at home when none of your high school friends are around.

Work

- Earn some additional cash by picking up extra hours if you have a part-time job on campus or can work a temporary job.

Contact your former employer in advance if you had a job while in high school and see if they could use you for additional support or special tasks during the week

Travel

- Pack up your car and your friends and check-out a nearby tourist attraction, state park, beach or random town. Be flexible in your planning as half of the adventure is the road trip.
- Check with your school's activity or recreation center for school-organized trips such as skiing, canoeing, backpacking, etc.
- Give back to others and feel good about yourself through community service by completing a mission-trip or a service-learning trip.
- Explore a popular U.S. city such as New York City, Las Vegas or San Francisco.
- Travel to the foreign country of choice. Europe and tropical island countries are popular destinations, but mix it up and choose a unique place such as Iceland or Madagascar.

If you have a 4-wheel drive vehicle and enjoy camping, consider a trip with *Badlands Off-Road Adventures, Inc.* On your adventure, you could relax in the hot springs in the Mojave Desert, visit a ghost town and hike a volcanic crater in Death Valley or stand inches away from a 3000 foot vertical drop in the north rim of the Grand Canyon. For more information on adventure descriptions with pictures, trip dates and costs, go to www.4X4training.com.

Know the Plan

If you aren't the primary person in charge of planning your trip, make sure you are well informed with as much information as possible including:

- Emergency numbers
  - how your family can contact you in case of an emergency back home; how to contact your friends' families in case of an emergency; how to contact local emergency services; how to contact the U.S. Embassy
- Maps and Itinerary
  - Even if you aren't the one driving, know the route to your destination; pass on your airplane flight number and itinerary to your family.
- Weather Forecast
  - What will the weather be like where you are going? Did you pack appropriate clothes for the weather?
- Costs
  - What costs will you have? How will costs be divided among friends? How will you carry your cash?
- Lodging, meals
  - Where are you staying? What is the plan for meals?
- Road Trips
  - Does the car need the oil changed, air for the tires or a general tune-up? Do you know how to repair a flat tire or get road-side assistance if the car breaks down? Do you need to help drive? Do you really want to be with your friends for over 1,000 miles in a car?

Costs

Major costs associated with traveling include:
- Transportation costs
    - Gasoline, airline tickets or public transportation (buses, subways, trains)
- Lodging costs
    - Hotels, camping sites
- Meals
    - Restaurants, groceries
        - It can be quite expensive to eat out every meal for one week.
- Miscellaneous and hidden costs
    - Passport application fees and photo fees (see below).
    - Currency exchange rates; Purchasing traveler's checks.
    - Required or recommended immunization vaccines prior to your departure. Plan ahead as some vaccines require boosters separated by several weeks.
    - Some countries may charge you an entrance fee upon entering their country.
    - Souvenirs; printing pictures
    - Toll roads
    - Others: car maintenance; tanning

Check with a travel agency to see if they offer any college student discounts or package or group travel discounts.

Even if you do not plan an extravagant trip to a foreign country, you may encounter other costs during spring break, such as providing your own meals if the dining center is closed or gasoline for driving back home.

Read the fine print. Many times flyers advertise for "Spring Break Packages" to great locations for $289. Ask lots of questions and be sure you're not getting scammed.

Passports

- If are traveling to a foreign country, you will need to obtain a U.S. Passport. Applications (government form DS-11) can be found online at http://travel.state.gov/passport and turned in to an Acceptance Facility such as the U.S. Post Office.
- You will need to provide proof of U.S. Citizenship (ex: certified birth certificate-better call your mom for this one) and provide proof of current identity (valid driver's license).
- In case your passport is lost or stolen while you are in a foreign country, it is a good idea to carry these other documents with you (proof of U.S. citizenship and proof of current identity). Make a copy of your passport and place it in your suitcase. Be sure you know how to contact the U.S. Embassy of the foreign country you are visiting.
- Applications fees to obtain a passport amount to no less than $100.
- You will need two, two inch by two inch passport photos showing your current appearance. Many professional photographers or copy centers offer this service.
- Processing time for U.S. passports can take up to six weeks or longer. You can expedite this process if you need your passport within two weeks but additional fees are required. If your spring break plans are in March, you should apply for a passport no later than January.
- As of January 2008 you need a passport to travel by car to Canada and Mexico.

Safety Tips

Rules

- Know the rules of the host country: at what age is drinking permitted? If you are on a school-sponsored trip, are you expected to follow the U.S. drinking age? Are you allowed to drive?

Culture

- Do you know a few key words if you aren't fluent in the language? Is the water safe to drink? Any unique customs you should be aware of?

Current Events

- Are there current events that may affect your travel plans or ability to leave the host country?
- As a citizen of the U.S., you represent the United States while visiting other countries. Be polite and friendly. You may be asked about policies on current events, customs or American history.

Money

- How much money will you bring with you? How will you carry and securely store your money? Is your ATM card valid where you are traveling to? Should you purchase traveler's checks?
- If you will be gone for an extended time over break, don't leave valuables in your room including cash, laptops, music players, DVDs, CDs, etc.

Cell Phone

- Will it work in the foreign country? Does it have the same technology? How much will it cost to use?

An inexpensive way to communicate with friends and family if you have an internet connection is to an internet-video (webcam) telephone program (example: *Skype*), which you can download for free.

Packing List

With You/In Pockets: see below

Carry-on: see below

Suit-Case:

The specifics of your destinations will determine what you will pack. Below is a list of some additional items you may consider taking with you:

- Suitcase identification
- Laptop and power cord
- Cell phone and charger
- Camera and computer cord
- MP3 player
- Belt
- Umbrella
- Swim suit
- Gloves/hat/coat/boots
- Extra shoes
- Voltage Converter (needed if using U.S. electrical plugs in some foreign countries) or just a plug converter

Preparing your Room Checklist

- Turn off your alarm clock
- Remove perishable items from your fridge
- Take out the trash
- Turn off your computer
- Remove valuables from your room
- Adjust your thermostat
  - If you are living in a northern climate, it is a good idea to leave your thermostat at a minimum heat level (see your Resident Assistant for exact setting) to help prevent water pipes from freezing, cracking and then subsequently flooding your room and ruining your stuff. This is especially important in older residence hall buildings.
- Turn off lights
- Have a plan for care of your plants, fish, pets, pet-rock, etc.
- Shut windows, close curtains and lock your door
- **Don't** write a message on your white board stating you will be gone all week—potential thieves will also see your message board.

Staying in your room Checklist

- Will dining services be open during break?
- Will mail still be delivered and sorted over break? When can you pick up packages?
- Will maintenance enter your room at anytime during break (ex: to replace a filter)? Are there any scheduled water shut-offs or fire alarm tests planned?
- Will the hall desk be open? How can you contact someone, like a Resident Assistant, if you have a problem over break?

Planes:

Your spring break plans may involve air travel. Even if you are a first-time passenger or a veteran, here are some insider tips to successful air travel:

- Sit right next to the ticket agent when you arrive at your gate. If your plane is overbooked, the airline may offer excellent incentives, such as free tickets, cash vouchers or hotel, phone and meal tickets, if you agree to take a later flight the same day or the next morning. As a college student on spring break, you are in an ideal situation to cash-in on this opportunity. Spring break is an adventure, turn life's "lemons" into fun.

- Request an exit row seat; not only does this provide you more leg room, but it also places you closer to the front of the plane. You will be able to exit sooner.
    - Otherwise, if you want a window seat, be sure to request one that isn't over the wingspan of the plane. If you think you will need to get up often for access to the bathroom or overhead storage, request an aisle seat.
    - Use the bathroom on the airplane—your belongings are safer while you are in the plane bathroom rather than carrying everything in with you in a ground terminal bathroom. Use it right before the seat belt light comes on before landing.

Kipp Story Box

While flying one time to visit a friend, I was placed in the exit row next to an older gentleman. The flight attendant came over and pointed to the instruction card for those sitting near an exit seat. She asked both of us, "Do you understand what it means to be sitting in the exit row?" and without missing a beat, the older gentlemen said, "Yeah, it means we're the first ones out if anything happens."

- Board the plane as soon as your row number is announced. If you are late to your section of the plane, you may find that you there is limited or no overhead storage left for your bag, and you may have to cram your bag into a small space. Plus you can then "people-watch" as others board the plane and struggle to make their bags fit.
- Wear comfortable, yet appropriate (ex: no shorts, flip-flops, etc) clothes and only carry essentials (ticket, identification/passport, cash, cell phone) in your pockets so that you can easily get through security check-points. If you can, leave at home or pack into your suitcase any metal objects (such as keys, loose coins and belts).
- Pack a light, small book bag to use as a carry-on. Items to include:
    - A change of clothes for the night and the next day in case your luggage is lost.
    - Essential toiletry items (toothbrush, toothpaste, deodorant, contact case, etc.) in case your luggage is lost. Check with your airline with what is allowable to bring onto the plane---you don't want to end up having to throw out an expensive bottle of perfume because you are bringing too many fluid ounces.
    - Snacks for the flight as well as a container, such as an empty water bottle, to fill up with water from the drinking fountain once you are past the security checkpoint (to save some money since bottled water at airports is quite expensive). Plane rides can

make you dehydrated. Swallowing or chewing gum can help equalize pressures of the high altitude with your inner ear.
- o   A book to read or other activity to work on during your flight.
- o   Any valuables or breakables that you don't want to pack in your suitcase such as a digital camera, laptop or souvenirs and gifts on the return flight.
- Prepare your luggage by placing your identification information (name, phone number, etc.) on both the outside *and* inside of your suitcase and carry-on. Remove any straps that can be caught in airport machines.
- Pack an empty compact bag in your suitcase to pack all those extras you bring back or if needed you can use it as a beach bag.

Final Thoughts

Cancun may sound like a lot of fun on paper but the reality of the situation is you don't need to spend a lot of money to travel just to change the scenery. There are a lot of other places to see and ways to make memories with your friends. If you want to tone-up your body for swimsuit attire, you will want to start months ahead of your trip, not weeks. If you are going to a sunny beach location, you can work on your tan by using sunscreen lotion while you are there; you don't have to use tanning salons before your trip.

If you really want to learn and immerse yourself in a new culture, skip the decadent tourist attractions (where you mostly see other Americans), and spend time with locals through programs like mission trips, service-learning trips or a course credit offered by your university.

Points to Ponder
- What you do for spring break says a lot about you.
- You're not a loser if you not lying out on a beach over spring break. Although, you might be a loser for other reasons.
- You don't have to travel for nine full days. Get your work done early by using the first weekend to complete your schoolwork or other projects so you can fully enjoy the rest of your break.
- Don't ever mention bombs or terrorism while you are at the airport or plane. Even if you were "just joking", you will make others uncomfortable and things can escalate quickly. You may find yourself in serious trouble.
- Don't forget to provide a care plan for any plants, fish or other pets you have at college while you are away on break.

- Don't forget to pack your cell phone charger.
- Stay out of trouble when visiting another country. Don't do stupid stuff just to act crazy. Foreign country law enforcement won't hesitate to arrest an obnoxious drunk American who is disrupting their community by disrespecting local ordinances.
- Whether you are applying for a passport or applying for work back home, the key to every spring break plan is early planning.
- Check your mailbox when you get back, it's probably full.
- Don't leave your residence hall keys behind when traveling back.
- Snow globes contain fluid and you cannot pack them in your carry-on.

CHAPTER 41

PREPARING FOR SUMMER
SPRING FEVER!

"Ah finally, summer...."

You may be feeling restless after a long winter as you anticipate the excitement of summer break. There are several things you will need to think about and take care of weeks to months before summer starts, including what needs to be completed for a painless move-out, where you will live and what you will do over the summer.

Move-Out

Whether you consciously realized it or not, you have accumulated more stuff throughout the past school-year than when you originally moved in. Evaluate how much "extra" stuff you now have--remember those storage shelf units you bought? Or the futon your friend helped carry up the staircase? And don't forget that heavy stack of college books on your desk from a year's worth of classes.

Depending on your summer plans (i.e. moving back home or staying on campus), you may consider these questions:
- Will all of your stuff still fit in the vehicle or vehicles used for move-in?
- Do you have the need for summer storage? (see below)
- Who is available (and willing!) to help you move-out?

 Keep an eye out for empty cardboard boxes you could use for moving. Start saving boxes early as they become a very valuable and scarce resource during the last two weeks of the semester when hundreds to thousands of students across campus are moving simultaneously. Check with the dining center, campus research labs or the local grocery store for free boxes.

 If your parents live close, every time you go home for a weekend or for breaks, bring a couple boxes of stuff you won't need or use for the rest of the semester with you to leave at home. This will help reduce your stress during move-out and free up more "car-space". Invite your parents up to see you too and before they leave, make sure they are carrying more of your stuff to take back home.

Watch for move-out instructions (mailbox letter, email, bulletin board, etc.) and talk to your Resident Assistant to learn more about the move-out process:

- What date **and time** do you need to be completely moved-out of your space? What are the penalties if you are late making this deadline?
- Do you need to sign-up for a check-out time for someone to inspect your space for damages and cleaning before you leave? Where and when can you sign-up for a time? Where do you turn in your keys?
- What are the cleaning expectations for vacating your space? Are there cleaning supplies available for you to use? What happens if the floor vacuum cleaner breaks down during move-out time, and you're not able to clean the floor?
- How will mail be forwarded to you over the summer—do you fill out a summer forwarding card with the hall desk or do you need to fill out a change of address form with the U.S. Post Office, or both?

Cleaning:

The Resident Assistant will hold the last person to check out of the room ultimately responsible for the cleaning. Be sure to talk to your roommate before the last week of school about when they plan to move-out and how to fairly divide the cleaning expectations, including common spaces (bathrooms, floors/walls, etc.) or poorly maintained areas that will need extra attention (trash can, windows, blinds, etc.).

Fines:

There are several areas to watch out for to avoid fines during move-out. An easy fine to avoid are cleaning fees, so be sure you understand what is expected of you before you check out. You can also easily avoid improper check-out fees by planning ahead and educating yourself about the move-out process to ensure you are checked-out on time and your keys are returned. Lastly you may be charged fines for any structural or furniture damage to your room. The condition of your room will be compared to the condition reported on your check-in card. Thus if something has broken in your room and is something that could be fixed by the residence hall maintenance department (i.e. a broken towel bar), it's in your best interest to have them fixed when it happens (or at least a few weeks before check-out), as they will be too busy to respond to your request during move-out time, and you may have to pay for the damage.

Mail-Forwarding:

Mail sorting may take less priority while the hall desk or mail center is processing move-outs (sorting keys, filing condition cards, updating mail forwarding cards, etc.) and preparing the halls for the summer. For this reason don't purchase or order anything online that will arrive the last week of school. Check your mail box one last time right before you check-out and leave town.

Change your address directly with places that send regular and timely mail such as bank or credit card statements, magazines or home newspapers. This will cut out the hall desk as the "middle-man" rerouting your mail and help ensure accurate and timely delivery of your mail. Remember, the hall desk will send all of your mail (except mail sent as "presorted standard", a.k.a. most "junk mail") to the address you listed on your mail forwarding card—will this be an awkward situation when June's Playboy® arrives at your home address or should you cancel that subscription now? Or, possibly better, can you change the subscription to arrive at your friend's parent's house? It is also a good idea to change your delivery address for your magazine subscriptions because the hall desk may only forward the first couple to you as a courtesy as this is second-class mail and takes less priority to first class mail such as letters (which also means your magazines could be delayed for weeks at a time).

What happens to the magazines that hall desks no longer forward or are not deliverable (i.e. missing mail forwarding card, etc.)? These magazines will usually accumulate at the desk before they are tossed into the garbage. If you are around during the summer, you might ask the desk worker if you could look through the magazine collection that is undeliverable and will be thrown away---you may enjoy five or more of your favorite popular college magazines for free over the summer!

Also check what the university has recorded as your interim or permanent address (usually your parents' address) to which university mailings will be sent, as it may not be on the same system as the residence hall mail forwarding system (i.e. you may need to fill out another form or change it online). This is also important if you decide to live on campus during the summer instead of returning home, as you will want your mail delivered to that address and not sent to your parents.

Remember, the move out process takes time. Your main concerns will be to pack-up your stuff, move your stuff out, and clean your space. Think back when you moved-in: you probably spent a day or two packing, a day just moving everything in and then another day or two unpacking and setting up your room. This is essentially the same process but now in reverse, with a lot more cleaning and right after you take your semester finals. If you have a 3 PM checkout time with your RA, don't think you can start packing up at Noon and be ready to go at 3PM.

Stolen Moments:
Don't forget to say goodbye to all of your friends! These are the people you lived with through the struggles and triumphs of your first college year experience. You will probably not see most of these people as much after this year (unless you are going to live with them again next year as roommates), but when you do run into someone "from your freshmen year" on campus, there will always be that special bond between you no matter how much time has passed. Time to start a lifetime networking list and keep track of peoples' names and emails.

Storage:

You may not be able to transport your heavy larger, bulky items, such as your loft, carpet or futon, home unless you make multiple trips or rent a truck. Another option is to rent a nearby storage unit for the summer months to store these items as you will most likely need these items again in the fall when you return. Before you rent a storage unit, consider:

- Does your residence hall offer storage space?
    - You will not be able to leave anything in your room (even if you are returning in the fall to the same room, as the room might be used for summer programs and conferences) but they might provide a space for certain items like lofts.
- If you need a storage unit because your futon won't fit into the trunk of your car, how do you plan to transport your futon from your room to the storage location?
- Is it economically justified to rent a storage unit?
    Example: if your rental unit costs $40/month ($120 for the summer), you will need to store more than just your $50 loft and $25 carpet. In this case, consider renting a storage unit with a friend and divide the costs.

Items to consider for storage:
- Loft wood and ladder
- Room carpet or area rug
- Futon or couch
- Chair
- Lamp

Items to not consider for storage:
- Refrigerator
- Most electronic equipment
- Food products
- Heat sensitive items
- Expensive items
- Irreplaceable items, such as photos
- Anything that would be difficult to clean, especially from dust

Storage Unit Questions:
- Is a deposit required? Is the deposit refundable?
- Will you be charged the full month's rent even if you vacate the unit early?
- What are the dimensions of the storage units available? What size do they recommend for your specific needs?
- Do you have 24/7 access to your storage unit? Are you the only one with keys to your unit?

- Evaluate the security precautions present (ex: exterior lights, fence and gated entrance, security guard on sight, strength of locks, etc.).
- Has the site ever experienced flooding or fire?
- What rodent or insect control measures are in place?
- What are the cleaning expectations when you move your items out of storage?

Storage Tips:

- Lay down wood pallets and store your items on top.
- Cover your items with sheets or plastic to help reduce the amount of dust covering your belongings.
- Do not store food products, heat-sensitive items or expensive/irreplaceable items
- Scatter rodent-control pellets on the ground. Be sure to sweep these pellets up afterwards as they are also hazardous to other animals, including dogs and cats.
- Check your parents' homeowners insurance and see if your belongings in storage are covered and if not, if short term coverage could be provided through an additional supplemental policy.

Don't wait until move-out week to call a storage place to inquire about available units as the more desirable places (i.e. clean, secure, close to campus, variety of unit sizes, good management, reasonable cost, etc) will have already been sold-out. Call the storage business at least two months before you need to move out; if necessary reserve your space by renting the unit a month before you need it.

If you go to any college campus during move-out week, you will see a lot of students who decided to neither store nor take home some of these larger items as evidenced by dumpsters full of lofts, carpets, chairs, couches, appliances, etc. And in many cases, it is probably good that grandma's 50 year old flower sofa doesn't see another year or the carpet with too many unexplained stains is destined for the dumpster instead of trying to make it work another year.

Dumpster Diving

You may try to sell your stuff when you are moving out to avoid having to move large bulky items and/or storage costs. The problem is everyone else is in the same situation (not to mention the dumpsters full of what you are trying to sell) and thus no market exists. However, if you are of the entrepreneur-type, consider not only storing your stuff over the summer, but also storing any salvable items (lofts, futons, couches, chairs, etc.) left for the dumpsters. Then in the fall, the market reverses and incoming students are in need of all of these items and now dumpsters are only full of empty boxes from moving-in. Since you did not pay anything for what you are selling, your only cost was the cost of summer storage, which you can quickly recover as you sell items in your "warehouse" for $25 to $75 or more a piece.

Mike Story Box

One fall I made over $400 just by selling loft ladders I had collected during move-out time.

Where will you live during the summer?

Most students will return home their first summer after college, usually to work for a previous employer, perhaps take a class or two at a local community college to "lighten" their fall class load and enjoy some time with family and friends.

If you decide to remain on campus during the summer to take summer courses and/or work for a campus employer, you will need to "sublease" a place if you aren't able to stay in your current space. As more students will leave during the summer months than stay, it's a buyer's market for sublease space, meaning you should be able to find a really good deal on summer rent since there are more people with apartment contracts who need sub-leasers than there are sub-leasers available to rent that space. In a sublease agreement, a deposit is usually not required, you may be responsible for all, some or none of the utilities and generally pay a flat fee (i.e. "$500 total for the summer"). If you wait until the very last possible moment to contact someone in need of a sub-leaser at the end of the semester, you will have even more negotiating power as the sub-leaser, because they may have already resolved they will need to eat the costs of an empty apartment for three months--and will be more than happy to listen to any reasonable offer you have that will help offset these costs. How long you wait, however, depends on your tolerance for risk and stress from the uncertainty of not knowing where you will be living.

Most sublease agreements are informal, so make sure you have a clear understanding of the expectations beforehand such as: Will you need to pay for some or all of the utilities? What are the apartment cleaning expectations, and are there any chores you are expected to complete, such as mowing? What are the rules associated with the apartment use, such as visiting friends, overnight guests, use of amenities? Will you have roommates? If you have roommates, will food costs be divided? When are payments due? When do you need to be out of the apartment? Is it ok with the landlord that you are subleasing the space?

If the subleasing is not approved by the landlord, you may find yourself in several sticky situations besides any contract violations (monetary fines or judicial judgments), such as: What will you do if the landlord gives notice of apartment entry for an inspection? How will you have something fixed if you aren't able to contact the landlord? How will mail be delivered to you if you can't add your name to the list of current residents on the mailbox? Will anyone know that you died in an apartment fire if the apartment was assumed to be empty?

What will you do?

Similar options as spring break plans exist for the summer, but in general most students will work or take classes. Here are some summer break options:

Summer School

- Maybe you want to graduate ahead of time, are working on more than one major or minor, want to reduce your fall credit load, you need to or want to repeat a course for a better grade or just want to take extra classes. The decision to take summer courses should not be considered lightly however as summer school is an intense experience as everything is accelerated due to the compressed time schedule. Weigh the pros and cons to completing courses at home at a community college or at your college:
    - The community college route
        - pros: no cost to live at home, credit costs usually lower, may offer small class sizes, see family and friends more often and perhaps continue work with previous high school employer
        - Cons: credits may not transfer back to main college and there may be a limit to the total number or credits you can transfer for your degree; avoiding taking a difficult course at your main college may be discouraged
    - Staying at your college route:
        - Pros: familiar with campus, strengthen college friendships, perhaps engage in work related to your major or career
        - Cons: usually higher costs (tuition and living expenses), being away from home, usually more difficult course work.

Work

- You need to determine first if your goal for summer work is to earn money or to gain experience related to your major (see Chapter 31: Your Four Year Plan). If you want to just earn money, consider working at home (no living costs) and contacting a previous high school employer for a summer job. If you want to gain practical experience related to your major, talk with a professor about opportunities, including summer research or a summer internship. For a different experience and an opportunity to live while working in another location, consider supervising kids as a camp counselor while teaching an activity you love or want to gain more experience with such as horseback riding, or lake water-crafts. Also consider volunteering to gain work experience.

Campus Opportunities

- There may be other opportunities for you on campus to help with including freshmen orientation, campus tours or summer conferences. Some of these options may also provide housing and/or meals. These jobs may provide other non-monetary rewards such as learning about available campus resources, or networking and establishing contacts with influential campus individuals.

Study Aboard

- As a student, now is the time to visit a foreign country and study aboard. By studying aboard, you will hopefully be more than just a tourist and really immerse yourself in learning about another culture. For shorter stays, consider completing a mission trip or service-learning trip.

Vacation

- Allow yourself some "down-time" during the summer to relax such as the annual family vacation, weekend time spent at your friend's lake house, a mini-trip planned to meet up with college friends for the Fourth of July or just time to do absolutely nothing.

Reality of situation:

Ask your friend if he would like to go "backpacking in Europe". Your friend will probably say that would be awesome. Then ask your friend how much experience he has backpacking and what he knows about camping. Ask them what he knows about Europe and where specifically he would like to go backpacking. If the answers to these questions are "none" and "I don't know" respectively, suggest to your friend that you start by "backpacking in America" by hiking a trail in town and see how quickly interest is lost.

Career Fair

Your college may organize a "Career Fair", typically a day where employers (from several to hundreds) come to visit your campus and set up booths at a centralized location such as a conference center building. Then students are welcome to visit with prospective employers about their companies and opportunities for employment after college or internships. Career Fairs are typically for juniors or seniors, but there may be some employers who are willing to hire freshmen students for a summer position.

If you head over to the career fair, know that you probably won't walk away with a high power internship with NASA, but you may have the opportunity to talk with someone from NASA and see what they look for in interns, so you can be a viable candidate in a year or two. Be sure to talk with an upper class student before you go to know what appropriate attire for the career is fair. Sometimes they are a more casual setting, other times more formal with most people wearing business attire.

You will not always succeed at everything you apply too, whether it is a job application or scholarship. The key is to keep applying yourself. Use failure as motivation to improve yourself. Always ask for feedback. **If you aren't failing at least three times for every success you have, you aren't taking enough risks.**

Mike Story Box

I was not hired after the formal application and interviewing process to be a Resident Assistant. I asked for constructive feedback following the notification. They reviewed my file and stated I was a strong candidate, but there were not enough positions available. A week later a position opened as somebody had turned down their RA offer for another job. By asking for feedback and showing an interest in the job, my name and file came to mind for this available position. I continued to work in college housing for seven years, gaining invaluable experience, reducing my debt load in half and gained experience to co-author this book.

Mike Story Box

Always follow-up an interview with a thank-you note. I interviewed for a veterinary technician job and the next day sent a thank-you note to the hospital for the opportunity to interview and for them taking the time to give me a tour. The office manager later told me that part of the decision to hire me was this simple act of writing a thank-you note, because it showed my genuine interest in the position, my attention to detail and my follow-through.

Moving Home

Many students choose to pack up their things and go back to their home. This is a great way to save money and to spend time with your family after a busy year at school. Be sure to talk with your parents well in advance to discuss what types of expectations will be in place. Will you need to work around the house? Will you have a curfew? Where will you stay (has your room become the new office)? What will you do with your time?

Moving back home is a great option many students and parents enjoy after a year at college. From your perspective, things will be different. Your same group of friends may not all be back, your relationship with your parents will be different, and you'll start to notice how you've changed while away at school. It may take some adjusting to be back in a place that most likely has fewer freedoms than your months at college. Be respectful of your parents; remember, having you move back in will take some adjusting on their part as well.

Final Thoughts

As you prepare to leave for the summer, think back to the day when you were first moved in and how new everything seemed. A lot of events and experiences have happened between then and now---hard to believe that wasn't even quite a year ago. What do you think of your college freshmen experience? Is it what you thought it would be or told it would be? Probably not, but one thing for sure has changed: you.

Points to Ponder
- There are few things quite like the feeling of turning in your last final, walking outside with the sun warming your face, and knowing it's summer break.
- You won't always have three months off a year, so soak it all in. Give yourself a break and be intentional about rest during summer.
- No food products in your stuff in storage, not even a box of leftover hot cocoa packets. Mice will find it, tear it apart, then poop all over your stuff. Trust us.
- Establish a regular habit of keeping a list of "address change notices".
- A laundry basket is useful for moving awkwardly shaped or breakable items
- This is just move two of many more moves of your college career; your stuff inevitably will gain scratches and other minor damage through all of the yearly moves, but as long as it remains functional, it's fine.
- Carry around a ten-pound sack of potatoes in your backpack for a week everywhere you go so you can get a good feel of what "backpacking in Europe" might feel like. Just ignore the constant questions of "Hey weirdo! Why are you always carrying around that sack of potatoes?" Those people obviously lack your sophisticated taste of culture.
- You're no longer a freshman.
- And that was just year one. Three more experiences to look forward to.

CHAPTER 42:
PREPARING FOR FALL
PRE-SOPHOMORE YEAR

"Already?! That went by way too fast..."

Although it may seem early to plan several months ahead, spring semester is the time to initiate and solidify your plans for the fall. Now that you "know the ropes" around college, use what you have learned from your first year experience to make the most of your living arrangements, classes and finances.

Living Arrangements

Where you will live and who you will live with, are the two main questions to consider when planning your fall living arrangements.

Housing:

Where will you live?

Perhaps you have decided, for a variety of reasons (see Chapter 7: Campus Housing), you would like to move out of the residence halls and try living "on-your-own" in an off-campus apartment. Or you may decide to live in the Greek Community (sororities and fraternities) for additional living experiences including social, campus and community activities. Another option is to stay in the residence halls for another year because of the convenience, proximity to campus and closeness to friends. Listed below are questions to consider for each of these three main housing options:

Off-Campus:

How far away from campus is the apartment (i.e. how much earlier do you need to start your morning routine to account for the extra time needed to reach campus?) and how will you travel to campus (walk, drive, bike, public transport, etc.)? Will inclement weather affect how you arrive to class? Will the distance from campus prohibit you from returning to your apartment multiple times during the day in-between classes or for lunch (i.e. do you need to plan to stay on campus and study until your last class of the day)?

What, if any, utilities (such as water, electricity and gas) are provided with the rent? Will you need to set-up other utilities on your own (such as cable, internet and phone)? Where do you deliver your monthly rent payment, and what are the consequences if you are late paying the bill (such as finance charges, bad credit or eviction)? Are deposits required, and are they refundable? When is the deposit due?

Do you need to sign a 12 month "calendar contract" or is there a nine month "school-year contract" available? Are you allowed to "sublease" your space if you do not plan to live there during the summer months? When do you need to sign the contract to ensure a space for the fall? When can you move in? Does the move-in date coincide with your current living arrangement, or will you be paying for rent for two places during the same month and/or do you need to move your stuff to another location while you're in-between places?

Keep the move-out date in mind as well, you don't want to be left in a situation where you need to move out of your current apartment on the 30th or 31st of a month, but can't move in to your next place until the 1st of the month---where will you keep all of your stuff overnight?

What happens if you violate a policy in the renters' agreement (such as noise, pets, structural damage, etc.)? Who can enter your apartment and for what reasons? What is the process to request having something repaired in the apartment? How quickly will the landlord resolve the issue? What actions will be taken if you file a complaint about your neighbors? How quickly will the landlord resolve the issue?

How old is the apartment? Is furniture provided? What appliances are provided? Where can you do laundry? What are the cleaning expectations when you move-out (such as, who pays to have the carpets professionally cleaned)?

Be sure to actually *read* the contract agreement you are signing. Have your parents and realtor look it over as well. Ask questions about any fine print needing further clarification. Don't be pressured into signing a contract prematurely based on the "landlord's deadline"; there are plenty of other great apartment finds, and the landlord will probably grant you an "extension" if you are a serious renter and need more time.

Pets

You may have the option to obtain a pet while living off-campus. However, this is generally not a good idea, because pets require a lot of things that college students don't have:

1. **Time** (do you have time to let a dog out three times a day? Do you have an extra hour a day to play with your cat?)
2. **Money** (Was an expensive emergency veterinarian bill in your college budget plan?)
3. **Commitment** (Will you always live in campus housing that allows pets? What happens when you graduate and move to a new town— will it be easy to move your pet with you? Will it be easy to find pet-friendly housing in this new location?).

Even fish aren't a good idea (tank cleaning is often neglected, a continual source of cash is need for food and new filters, difficult to provide care over semester breaks and tanks and fish are difficult to move). Sadly most fish obtained by a college student will not still be with the person within one year.

Greek Community:

Are there extra fees in addition to the basic rent fees such as initiation fees, local and national membership fees, etc.?

What extra time commitments are required such as household or yard chores, required campus involvement, community service requirements or mandatory study times?

How many people will share a room with you? Is furniture provided? Will you sleep in the same room where your stuff is located, or is there a common sleep corridor where everyone sleeps (a.k.a. "cold rooms")? How many people share one bathroom?

Is there anyone in the house that you really dislike? Are you ok living with 20 or more people of the same-sex? What are house-guest visitation rules? How much privacy will you have?

Are you expected to help with cooking and clean-up? What types of meals are provided, and what happens if you miss meal time?

What role does alcohol play in the house and social activities? Is the whole house loud on the weekends, or can you retreat to a quiet place?

Residence Halls:
As a sophomore, can you return to the same residence hall building? Can you request your current room? Are there other residence halls that better suit you (proximity to campus buildings you regularly use, higher percentage of upperclassmen, etc.)?

How and by when do you need to sign a housing agreement to ensure placement for next fall? How much will rates increase for next year?

How many of your current friends will be living in the residence halls again? Is there opportunity for you to take on leadership positions such as an elected house government position or working for the Department of Residence as a Resident Assistant?

Are there some early move-in options available to you as an upperclassman such as a Move-In Crew or New Student Day Leader to help orient new incoming freshmen students? Not only is there usually a direct benefit to you (such as moving in early or monetary stipend), but you also have the opportunity to meet incoming students and share your knowledge, advice and experiences with them.

Roommates

Who will you live with?

Deciding on where you want to live will help determine how many roommates you will have, and if you are moving off-campus this typically ranges from 1-3 roommates (2, 3 or 4 bedroom apartments). Decide if you would like to continue living with your current roommate and/or which of your friends you would like to live with.

Planning your fall roommates can cause a significant stress as this issue can define, as well as split, friendships. This can be a tricky subject to broach with your group of friends as there may be interpersonal conflicts between individuals to take into consideration as well as personality factors (i.e. a great friend may not make the best roommate choice if he/she is loud, messy, dramatic, etc.).

The timing of this discussion is also something to consider as you do not want to be left excluded from plans, but you also do not want to create hard feelings with your current roommate or group of friends. Be willing to compromise and be sensitive to the feelings of everyone involved to work towards an agreeable outcome. If you are approached by a friend or groups of friends and the arrangement is not agreeable to what you want, don't feel obligated to join their living situation.

If you are living off-campus, chances are you can cohabit with the opposite sex. Seeking the approval of your parents on cohabitation may be another issue.

Stolen Moment:
Amazing how the people who were randomly assigned to live near you are now the same people you are choosing to live with next year; and probably the year after that and the year after that...

Classes

You will probably register for your fall classes in the spring before you leave for the summer. Depending on your experience from this last year, you may want to either increase or decrease your credit load. When planning your fall schedule, take into consideration the time of day the class is held, the amount of time between your classes, the location of your classes and which professors are teaching the course section. These factors will affect how you manage your time in the fall.

Keep in mind, more time will be required for each class as you advance to higher levels of classes.

Now is also the time to re-evaluate your major. Are you enjoying your classes? Is this what you envisioned your major to be like? Are you already struggling with the first level of classes in your major? Do you associate and relate well to others in your major? Switching your major after your first year, when you have completed mostly general university education requirements, is more ideal than waiting to switch your major your junior or senior year, and most often you will still be able to graduate in four years.

Jobs

You may find you have some additional free time as your experience has allowed you to manage your time more efficiently, and you may consider applying for a job. The main reasons for working while in college are to earn additional money and obtain job experience related to your major or both.

Now is a good time to create a budget for the Fall to determine if you will fall short of your current lifestyle, taking into consideration inflation and yearly increases in college fees, new purchases and expenses (i.e. you are no longer living with your roommate who supplied most of the room furniture) and decreased funding and support (i.e. some of your scholarships were one-time, one-year scholarships no longer available to you).

Budget

Income:
Scholarships, Savings (summer job), Parents (and other relatives), Working (part-time during school year), Loans (and grants)

Expenses:
College (tuition, books, lab fees, computer fees, health fees, activity fees, etc.)

Living (rent, utilities, water, electricity, gas, cable, internet, cell phone and land line), groceries, laundry, haircuts, healthcare (doctor, dentist, optometrist)

Transportation (travel back home for breaks, campus bus ticket, car-monthly payment, insurance, gasoline, parking, ticket fines, maintenance)
Furniture (if living off campus, a new expense)
Miscellaneous (entertainment, gifts, clothes, new purchases, fines)

Final Thoughts

Congratulations! You are now almost one-fourth of the way done with college. Can you believe it? The year probably went by faster than you thought it would. You'll be back in the fall though and by thinking ahead of fall plans now, you have set yourself up for success.

Are there new opportunities you can take advantage of as a sophomore? Consider:

- Working more closely with a favorite professor on a research or independent project
- Taking a more active role in a campus organization and running for an executive board position
- Gaining experience and networking in an internship related to your career
- Taking on more credits through additional non-required classes or pursuing a minor

Points to Ponder

- Never rent a place without seeing it firsthand. Don't be afraid to inspect the apartment closely by opening closet doors, turning on water, looking in the fridge and stove, etc. How clean is it? Can you see yourself living there?
- When talking with your friends about living together and roommate selection, the best approach is to be honest.
- Living off-campus involves becoming more independent and requires more responsibility. For example, if your neighbors are being loud, *you* need to take the initiative to talk to them about the issue and confront the behavior.
- Living with a good girl or guy friend: good idea.
- Living with a current boyfriend or girlfriend: never a good idea.
- Living with your friend and their significant other: even worse idea.
- The more roommates you have, the more conflicts likely to arise, the more times the bathroom will be in use, the more times the phone or TV will be use, etc.
- Although that gorgeous weather outside is calling, it'll be there all summer long: Keep studying for your finals.
- Weigh the pros and cons of your decisions, and then just make the decision.

Freshmen Moments
END OF THE YEAR

Do you remember that first day when you were moving in your boxes? Man this year went by fast! Ah, the memories...the memories!! You may not feel you are a different person than when you first entered, but you have changed. You've learned a lot, about college, life and how to calculate the derivative of a line tangent to a curve. You've also matured. A lot. Just think about how much you have grown personally as an individual. Here is some final advice as you graduate from your freshmen year of college:

Mike's Final Advice:

1. Things will happen for a reason; you are forming connections now that will later boggle your mind as to how they play out.
2. Soak up as much knowledge as you can.
3. Be happy with yourself. Be confident.
4. Do what you need to do to reach your goals.
5. Keep a spare key to your vehicle in your billfold or purse.
6. Life isn't perfect. It won't always make sense. And, it's not always fair. But, it will move on.
7. Find more excuses to fit exercise into your schedule than not to, from day one. At the end of your four years, you will not regret establishing a work-out routine and staying healthy.
8. Take time to help others.
9. Be open to new opportunities, even if it's different from your original plan. You have no idea where your life is going to take you.
10. Keep looking forward; start today what you wished you began months ago.

Kipp's Final Advice:

1. Congrats! One year done. Take time to evaluate what worked, what didn't, and make the most of your next three years (or four....or five?)
2. The college experience is unique to each person. Make yours unique with involvement in activities and classes you enjoy--not what all of your friends enjoy.
3. Don't succumb to the "mainstream" thinking of many college students. Meaning, you don't *have* to drink and party to be cool and successful. In fact, it's probably a great way to not be successful.
4. Be a person of self respect and someone others respect. Appreciate those around you, practice good manners, don't swear, hold the door for others, etc. Those are the things future employers and others appreciate.
5. Take pride in your school and your experience.

6. Be sure to learn outside the classroom. There are so many resources on a college campus.
7. Be prepared for change. It's going to happen. Some of it you have control of, some you don't.
8. Connect with at least one university official. This could be your hall director, advisor, a professor, etc. These people are great mentors who care about your success.
9. Be positive, not negative.
10. Help others be successful at college. It's not a competition.

Made in the USA
San Bernardino, CA
07 August 2018